Harnessing and Guiding
Social Capital for
Rural Development

Harnessing and Guiding Social Capital for Rural Development

by

Shahrukh Rafi Khan,
Zeb Rifaqat,
and Sajid Kazmi

palgrave
macmillan

First published in 2007 by
PALGRAVE MACMILLAN™
175 Fifth Avenue, New York, N.Y. 10010 and
Houndmills, Basingstoke, Hampshire, England RG21 6XS
Companies and representatives throughout the world.

PALGRAVE MACMILLAN is the global academic imprint of the Palgrave Macmillan division of St. Martin's Press, LLC and of Palgrave Macmillan Ltd. Macmillan® is a registered trademark in the United States, United Kingdom and other countries. Palgrave is a registered trademark in the European Union and other countries.

ISBN-13: 978–1–4039–8196–7
ISBN-10: 1–4039–8196–5

Library of Congress Cataloging-in-Publication Data

Khan, Shahrukh Rafi.
    Harnessing and guiding social capital for rural development / by Shahrukh Rafi Khan, Zeb Rifaqat, and Sajid Kazmi.
        p. cm.
    Includes bibliographical references and index.
    ISBN 1–4039–8196–5 (alk. paper)
        1. Social capital (Sociology) 2. Rural development. 3. Social capital (Sociology)—Pakistan. 4. Rural development—Pakistan. I. Khan, Sharukh Rafi. II. Rifaqat, Zeb. III. Kazmi, Sajid. IV. Title.

HM708.K52 2007
307.1'412095491—dc22   2007007588

First edition: December 2007

10 9 8 7 6 5 4 3 2 1

Printed in the United States of America.

This book is dedicated to
Khalid Iqbal and Faiqa Sheikh,
Farzana Kazmi, Seema, and Rifaqat Zaman Khan
for all their support

Contents

Part III   Harnessing Social Capital:
Manual for the Field Researcher

List of Annexures

List of Tables

Preface

The Human Development Foundation North America (HDFNA) founded the Human Development Foundation (HDF) as a Pakistani development NGO to execute its Pakistan Project in rural Pakistan in 1998 and contracted the authors as research members of a Pakistani think tank based in Islamabad, Pakistan, to document the process of program implementation. The exciting part of this research was the complete freedom to design it and also to study the work of a rural development NGO from the very inception of the project.

Collective action via participatory development was the logical conceptual framework for the research. However, we felt that this really did not go to the heart of why collective action takes place and what rural development NGOs contribute to this process? The rapidly growing literature on social capital provided a possible answer to this question. Rural development NGOs claim to create social capital in the form of village organizations (VOs) or community organizations (COs) that subsequently catalyze the collective action. Based on our understanding of the literature, we hypothesized that social capital in this context is a feature of the community in terms of their norms, mutual trust, reciprocal obligations, and networks so that, if successful, development organizations (DOs) can harness the social capital and embody it in VOs or COs and guide these organizations to participate and engage in collective action for poverty alleviation and community welfare. Of course, other factors could also result in successful collective action, and although collective action could be induced, it could also occur independent of the DOs. We explore this issue using an in-depth case study. We think the documentation we engaged in is valuable, particularly because of the varied research method we employed, including placing an anthropologist in the field for a year, utilizing control villages for comparison, and adding two field-based updates. We also discovered and documented the importance of understanding history and culture for the process of harnessing social capital. We turn again to the inception of this book and return to research issues later in the preface.

The HDFNA was registered in 1997 in the United States as a charitable foundation to launch, as the project document states, "an apolitical movement for positive social change and community empowerment through mass literacy, enhanced quality of education, primary health care and grassroots economic development." The initial financial contributions came from the Noor Foundation, the Society for International Health, Education and Literacy Programs (HELP), and the Association of Pakistani Physicians of North America (APPNA). Subsequent contributions came from founding members who contributed $10,000 each. HDFNA has a 21-member board, drawn from all over North America.

Thus the HDFNA Pakistan project was an initiative of a community of North American Pakistanis who desired to do something for the cause of human development and empowerment among the poor in their country of origin. In this regard, the HDFNA Pakistan project is extending the work earlier begun by its supporting organizations. APPNA had been running preventive health interventions in rural Pakistan since 1989. The Society for International HELP had been supporting education interventions via the Tameer-i-Milliat Foundation (TMF) since 1992. Noor Foundation had its own charitable initiatives.

While the health interventions managed to reduce the infant mortality rate, there was little impact of such interventions on the maternal mortality rates. HDFNA analyzed the cause of this lag to be poverty, and a preventive health initiative, on its own, was therefore not enough to improve the overall human development indicators.[1] To address this issue, HDFNA commissioned a country strategy report for its future human development interventions via HDFNA Pakistan Project.[2] The report made several suggestions, three of which stood out.

First, it recommended a multisector intervention that would ensure an overall increase in the human development indicators. Recommending this approach now has solid foundations in Pakistan, one of which is the work of the Aga Khan Rural Support Program (AKRSP) that initiated the work of other Rural Support Programs and other development support organizations.[3]

Second, to build on the sector work already initiated by the supporting organizations of HDFNA, it suggested a multipartner initiative. In addition to APPNA[4] and Tameer-i-Millat (TMF), it suggested others including the National Rural Support Program

(NRSP) and Aurat (Women) Foundation as implementing NGOs. NRSP would be responsible for the social mobilization to harness and formalize the community social capital in the form of COs needed to pull together and further the sector interventions. In addition, the income generation and microcredit projects run by NRSP would provide the glue for the COs and enhance the standard of living of the poor. The Aurat Foundation was viewed as a potential partner for women's empowerment. Finally, it recommended two research organizations, the Human Development Centre (HDC) and the Sustainable Development Policy Institute (SDPI) as partners to do the research.[5]

Third, the report recommended that research partners develop a research method that relied on building the capacity of the local DOs and communities to do self-analysis of their needs.[6] The SDPI was entrusted with the task of evolving a research method and a communications strategy that would engage both the local communities and the partner organizations.[7] The HDC was to work with the communities to develop village-level human development indicators (HDI) in order to help them track their own human development. This would be the first attempt at estimating the HDI at such a high level of disaggregation.

Just as APPNA, Society for International HELP, and Noor Foundation collaborated as constituent parts of HDFNA in North America, the APPNA and TMF initiatives were to collaborate via the HDF in Pakistan when working in the same localities. In addition to the health and education initiatives, HDF also included training, microcredit, enterprise development, and establishing linkages with government and civil society organizations as part of its mandate. Ghani Marwat was selected as the first country representative to oversee the opening of a field office in Mardan of the North West Frontier Province (NWFP) of Pakistan in 1998. His past experience with Aga Khan Rural Support Program no doubt helped in his selection. Prominent board members of HDFNA who got this initiative off the ground included Dr. Naseem Ashraf, Dr. Musaddiq Malik, and Dr. Khalid Riaz.

After negotiations with NRSP, it was mutually agreed that they would provide training for the social mobilization to HDF staff rather than be part of the partnership. Aurat Foundation and HDC also did not join the partnership. SDPI initiated the field research in the summer of 1999 and placed an anthropologist in the field for one year and the research team made several field visits. The fieldwork came to a close in the summer of 2000. The completion of this manuscript was delayed for various reasons but we have taken advantage of that by making two additional field-visits, in the fall of 2001 and the summer of 2006. These are included as chapter 9 and 10 of this book.

In a nutshell, this book is about the harnessing and formalization of social capital in the form of VOs or COs to guide and facilitate collective action for poverty alleviation in particular and for community welfare in general. It mainly investigates the success of the HDF in these two endeavors in the early years of its existence. In this regard, it should be viewed as a benchmark, as DOs require more time to get established. However, in terms of problems and obstacles confronted in its attempt to harness social capital, the timing is perfect because, as far as policy is concerned, most can be learnt from the initial years. Also, starting the research with the inception of the project was important for documenting the process of social mobilization for harnessing social capital and embodying it in COs.

This book has three parts. In the first chapter of Part I, we review the conceptual literature and locate our own conceptualization within it. In chapter 2, we review the empirical literature with a particular focus on poverty alleviation and rural development. In chapter 3, we review the attempts at harnessing social capital in Pakistan by rural support programs of the kind HDF is modeled on.

Part II contains seven chapters that together present a detailed case study of the HDF. In chapter 4, we locate HDF in the context of the local Pukhtun history and culture.[8] In chapter 5, we evaluate the nature and success of the multisectoral interventions HDF instituted in saving, microcredit, training, and linkages. Social mobilization is the method adopted by development NGOs to harness social capital into grassroots organizations for collective action and participatory development and hence is the most critical part of their work. In chapter 6, we document the process of social mobilization at project inception and indicate how local Pukhtun history and culture impacted this process.

In chapter 7, we evaluate the success of APPNA's health intervention and in chapter 8 that of TMF's education intervention. A dedicated chapter on these cases was deemed necessary to provide more details about the project partners but mainly because it was possible to assess the impact of these two interventions by comparing project with control villages. In chapters 9 and 10, we present the project field evaluation updates based on field trips one and six years (respectively) after the initial data collection. We demonstrate the dynamics of iterative project learning by a development NGO. Chapter 11 concludes

Part II by drawing on the evaluation of interventions, project updates, and project expansion to make an overall project assessment.

By the time the fieldwork was completed, we realized that while our in-depth case study method was valuable for documenting and describing a process, it was not ideally suited for rigorously testing two related hypotheses thrown up by our fieldwork: first, the impact of the prior presence of social capital on the success in constructing COs and on the survival of these organizations; second, the impact of these constructed COs in inducing collective action for rural development.

Funding was secured for follow-up research to test these related hypotheses, and the largest development NGO (not HDF) in Pakistan agreed to the research because it was hoped that, apart from the academic value of the research, considerable project learning could also result for it. Eventually, the research was terminate literally a day before it was scheduled to start. The research design was approved, the instruments developed after a series of preliminary and formal pretests, the field team trained, and the field strategy finalized. The sticking point was the development NGO's insistence that their social organizers (SOs) should accompany the research team during the fieldwork and that the principle investigator should be present in the field for the duration of the field research. The latter demand could be considered reasonable, but no academic would accept the former.[9]

This might have been a blessing because, once the alternative research design was fully fleshed out and the numerous nuances and complexities followed up on, the output was likely to be of book length report. In Part III, we have carefully documented our planned study in the form of a manual for the field researcher, alongside we give relevant instruments and associated documents. We hope other researchers can execute this research study if we do not.

Acknowledgments

We would particularly like to thank Dr. Naseem Ashraf, Dr. Khalid Riaz, Dr. Shahnaz Khan, and Dr. Musaddiq Malik for being supportive and for their patience in our documenting field-research findings in a form that can be more widely disseminated. We would like to thank Ghani Marwat for being completely open and very generous with his time. Similarly, the new Mardan regional project manager Dr. Manzoor Ahmed (regional program manager), after Ghani Marwat established the head office in Rawalpindi (Islamabad's twin city) in June 1999, was equally welcoming and forthcoming during our first follow-up visit. Acknowledgments are due to Dr. Moazzam Khalil, country director, APPNA SEHAT, Dr. Shakirullah, regional director, APPNA SEHAT, Mardan region, Mr. Khalid Khan, regional supervisor, APPNA SEHAT, Dr. Zaheer Ahmed, chairman (Tameer-i-Milliat Foundation), Mr. Nadir Shah, program coordinator (education, Tameer-i-Milliat Foundation, Mardan region), Mr. Sultan Khan, program manager (operations), Mr. Nasim Ejaz, the third regional project manager in Mardan, Muhammad Ishaq, social organizer (SO), Mr. Waseem Moazzam (SO), Ms. Fehmeeda (SO), Ms. Fakhra, credit officer, Ms. Ravida, program manager (monitoring and evaluation). Thanks are also due to Mr. M. Iqbal, Mr. M. Jameel, Mr. M. Shahnawaz, Mr. S. Ataul Haq, Ms. Jasarat and Mr. S. Murtaza Bacha, teachers in Tameer-i-Milliat Foundation and government schools.

For our 2006 project update, we would like to thank Muhammad Ishaq who had been promoted to the position of regional program manager at the Mardan office and Azhar Saleem, the chief executive officer. Both were highly cooperative and generous with their time. We would also like to thank Mount Holyoke College and Dean Don O'Shea in particular for assisting us with the modest support needed for the follow-up fieldwork.

We owe thanks to Dr. Ismat Aziz, who was the research project consultant in public health, for her report, part of which was incorporated into chapter 7. We would like to thank Mahjabeen Hussain and Irshad Tabassum for their efficient and patient word processing assistance for the first draft. Finally, many thanks are due to our Palgrave Macmillan editor, Anthony Wahl, for his responsiveness and for helpfully and wisely setting the parameters of the manuscript revisions based on reviewer feedback. We acknowledge the many valuable comments of two anonymous reviewers that contributed to the improvement of the manuscript, and we claim responsibility for remaining errors. Palgrave Macmillan has developed an ingenious conveyor-belt mechanism that works smoothly and efficiently with very helpful persons at each stage. In this regard, we would like to thank Kate Ankofski, the editorial assistant, Katie Fahie, the production assistant, and the NewGen text-editing team.

List of Abbreviations

AKRSP	Aga Khan Rural Support Program
APPNA	Association of Pakistani Physicians of North America
CBO	community-based organization
CCB	citizen's community board
CHC	community health center
CO	community organization
DO	development organization
FGD	focus group discussions
FSO	female social organizer
HA	health assistant
HC	health committees
HDF	Human Development Foundation
HDFNA	Human Development Foundation North America
LHV	lady health visitor
MSO	male social organizer
NRSP	National Rural Support Program
NWFP	North West Frontier Province
PPAF	Pakistan Poverty Alleviation Fund
PTA	Parent teacher association
RPM	regional program manager
RSP	Rural Support Program
RSPN	Rural Support Program Network
SDPI	Sustainable Development Policy Institute
SHA	senior health assistant
SO	social organizer
TBA	traditional birth attendant
TMF	Tameer-i-Milliat Foundation
VDO	village development organization
VO	village organization

Glossary

Hujra	space for male congregation
Jirga	council of elders
Kissani	peasant movement for land acquisition in Mardan
Mashar	village elders
Mullahs	clerics
Nang	honor
Pukhtunwali	Pukhtun code of honor
Purdah	female seclusion including veiling
Qalang	tax or rents
Tanzeem	organization (local word for DO)

Part I

Background: Harnessing and Guiding Social Capital

Conceptual Issues: Harnessing and Guiding Social Capital[1]

1.1 Defining Social Capital

There is a vast and exponentially growing literature on social capital, and scholars from many traditional disciplines including history, sociology, psychology, education, political science, anthropology, demography, geography, management, business, and economics are now contributing to it. It is currently one of the main multi and inter-disciplinary topics enabling much cross-fertilization of ideas and some convergence of views.[2] Given this vast literature, we draw on the broader definitions and conceptualizations of social capital but focus on economic applications in low-income countries, particularly to rural development.[3]

Various scholars have characterized social capital as the glue that holds society together.[4] Some of the most common definitions include viewing it as "trust" within and across social organizations and institutions.[5] Building a good "reputation" in business is thus an investment in social capital that pays dividends by reducing transaction costs for others.[6] On another level, it is viewed as the willingness and capacity to cooperate and engage in collective action for mutual benefit and for reducing free riding.[7] At a minimum, this requires norms (including sanctions), rules, and procedures for organization and networks, which embody social capital. Woolcock's (2002, p. 22) definition of social capital as norms and networks that facilitate collective action is most suitable for our research on participatory rural development.[8] Implicit in this definition is trust and social interactions that make the norms and networks work for a positive cause.[9]

As with the definitions, there are many different conceptualizations of social capital. One overarching framework in economics is the household production model whereby with the input of time, resources, and social capital, the household derives utility from the consumption of produced or acquired goods and services.[10] An alternative would be to focus more on the collective action facilitated by social capital that produces, improves, or maintains collective goods.[11]

Woolcock (2002, p. 23) draws on sociological literature to conceptualize social capital in terms of bonding (between close family members, friends, and neighbors) and bridging (between more distant associates and colleagues or between communities). These represent horizontal associations in contrast to vertical linkages to people, associations, and organizations beyond the community with influence or in power. Thus, in this conceptualization, social capital can be bonding, bridging, or linking.[12] Streeten (2002) defines five aspects of social capital by using the metaphor of various kinds of commodities from consumer goods to durable goods to explain that social capital takes time to build and hence represents an investment for future returns, such as forging relationships or membership in associations, but differs from other investments in that the process itself can provide satisfaction.

Krishna and Uphoff (2002, pp. 86–88) make a distinction between structural and cognitive forms of social capital. Structural forms of social capital are, for example, associational and facilitate mutually beneficial collective action. Cognitive social capital includes shared norms, values, attitudes, and beliefs that predispose people toward mutually beneficial collective action. Structural social capital is external and more visible and pertains to rules, procedures, precedents, networks, and organizations, whereas cognitive social capital is internal and pertains to how people think. Cognitive social capital inclines individuals toward collective action and structural social capital facilitates this. They also make a distinction between mutually reinforcing primary mechanisms of social capital like trust, solidarity, cooperation, generosity, and honesty and secondary forms such as honesty, egalitarianism, fairness, and participation.[13] Based on these conceptual distinctions, they develop a social capital index for their empirical work.

Krisha and Uphoff also raise the relevant question, frequently discussed in the social capital literature, of where social capital resides. While they measure social capital at the household level, our study of collective action focuses on social interactions. At the cognitive level, it is trust and feelings of solidarity based on the shared norms, culture, experiences, and reciprocations, and at the social level, it is the mechanisms such as reciprocal obligations and local networks and institutions that give expression to this trust and solidarity and reinforce it.

Ashman, Brown, and Zwick (1998) work with the distinction between strong and weak ties where the strong ties are the economic bonds of friendship, intimacy, and reciprocity and the weak ties are the more removed instrumental associations. They argue in the context of nonprofit organizational survival that both kinds of ties need to be cultivated and that while strong ties help with social cohesion, weak ties often provide valuable resources in the form of the availability of funding and information.

Lyon (2000) seeks to clarify the concepts of trust, norms, and networks and how they become operational via a qualitative empirical study of tomato farmers, agricultural input suppliers, and traders in rural Ghana. He cites Woolcook (1998) to make a distinction between networks and the underlying trust and asks what makes the difference. In our view, trust creates social cohesion and gives meaning to and sustains the network.[14]

Social capital, as defined above, is about trust, reciprocal obligations, community responsibility, and civic sense. Countries can be simultaneously strong on some aspects of social capital and weak on others. Consider the case of Pakistan. Pakistan is in many ways very rich in terms of the population growing up with a sense of community. There is a deep cultural tradition of relying on neighbors, and even on complete strangers for help. Visitors often note this tradition of hospitality, goodwill, and being good Samaritans as strong points of the country and its culture. Ironically, on other aspects of social capital, such as civic consciousness, Pakistan is weak. Part of the problem is that individuals respond well to the needs of other individuals, families, and the poor, but not to abstract concepts that enhance civic consciousness. Thus, for example, while households meticulously sweep and clean their own living quarters, they throw garbage in the streets and other common areas. To overcome such problems and to build civic consciousness would require both mass education and effective communications campaigns and strategies.[15] Building social capital in the form of community organizations that build on a culture of trust and hospitality can also be part of a broader strategy in building civic consciousness.[16]

Putnam's research (section 1.3) seems to suggest that a rich tradition of civic life via a network of civic associations is positively associated with economic growth.[17] These lead to a virtuous cycle as the rich countries can provide better quality education and richer individuals or states have resources to build and support civic organizations that contribute to the general well-being and also, incidentally, enhance economic growth.[18] By the same token, poor countries are caught in a vicious cycle. This suggests an exploration of two issues. First, while a positive association of social capital, defined in various ways, and economic prosperity seems to have been established in the literature,[19] exploration of what gave birth to the social capital in the first place is lacking. Second, there seems to be evidence (as will be discussed below) that social capital can be harnessed, guided, and sustained.

In view of the definitions and conceptualizations above, we emphasize two points. First, that the concept can be defined very broadly.[20] Thus, social capital could include the government engaging private initiative, local associations (CBOs—community-based organizations), networks, or social associations. At a broader level still, one could argue that it represents the "ethic" resulting in well-functioning government institutions such as the police, administrative, and legal systems.[21] If these exist and work well, they can diminish the importance of informal mechanisms based on reciprocal trust and social relations that come into play when the state does not function well.[22]

Second, the concept of building social capital has been gaining ground.[23] This can include social organizations such as credit groups, water-user associations, and various kinds of community or development organizations. Consistent with the definition we have adopted, we view this concept of social capital as most useful from an operational and policy perspective for rural development, and hence this is the concept we work with in this book.

To summarize, the definitions above suggest that social capital, among other ways, has been conceived of at an individual level in terms of what the individual can tap into to improve personal or household welfare, at the meso or community level in terms of what can facilitate collective action to achieve collective goals, and at the macro level in terms of what can enhance service delivery and promote economic growth (such as institutions for good governance).

In the rest of this chapter, we review conceptualizations that are supportive of social capital and then review some critical literature. We then explore the concept of "harnessing" and "guiding" social capital to promote collective action for rural development. In chapter 2, we review some of the broader economics or related applications of social capital to growth and poverty alleviation in low-income countries and then devote a separate section to empirical research on the "harnessing" and "guiding" of social capital for rural development in low-income countries.

1.2   Supportive Conceptualizations[24]

Social capital has acquired interdisciplinary status and has been conceptualized by many scholars across the disciplines in many different ways as indicated in section 1.1. There seems to be a consensus that Bourdieu (sociologist), Coleman (sociologist), and Putnam (political scientist) are responsible for the current attention the concept is getting.[25]

Baron, Field, and Schuller (2000, pp. 3–5) point out that Bourdieu's focus was on the use of contacts by elite groups to reproduce their privileges. However, these authors essentially consider Bourdieu's views as underdeveloped.[26] Coleman (1989) defined social capital as obligations and expectations, informal channels and social norms. He showed that the presence of social capital within the family (parent-child relations and mentoring) and community (norms and social relations) resulted in the enhancement of human capital, that is, the combination could keep children from dropping out from school.

Putnam's (1993) operational definition of social capital, based on networking and social relations, was membership in voluntary associations. His empirical study showed that one of the main reasons northern Italy was more advanced and continued to grow more than southern Italy was a more heightened civic community, as indicated by his measure of social capital. The discouraging aspect of his finding was that the evolution of social capital was a slow process and that there was a great deal of path dependency in its development. Also, it is not entirely clear what accounted for the origin of the more heightened civic community in the north in the first place.[27]

As the concept gained acceptance across the social sciences, a deliberate attempt was made, as suggested by Coleman, to view social capital as an alternative form of capital, much as human capital gained currency when put at par with physical and natural capital. It was argued that social capital is a stock, much like other forms of capital, and gives rise to a flow of future benefits.[28]

Although some economists, both orthodox and heterodox (section 1.4), are skeptical of this suggested equivalence of social and physical capital, many others have joined the research program. Collier (1998, 2002) grappled with the concept and defined social interaction as the flow that generates a stock of social capital such as trust, knowledge, and norms that enter into the production process.[29] The "social" part of social capital is viewed to be social interaction, and this can generate various kinds of externalities such as knowledge, overcoming the free-riding problem, and encouraging collective action.[30] Based on Collier's work, Haddad and Maluccio (2003) develop a typology to indicate the types of externalities generated (collective action or information) and the form of social interaction that facilitates this. Durlauf and Fafchamps (2004) provide an exhaustive survey from an economic perspective of definitions, conceptual issues, and the empirical literature.[31]

On the consumption side, Glaeser, Laibson, and Sacerdote (2002) reduce social capital to the conventional economic modeling of utility-maximizing behavior of the rational individual. They quite openly state that this is so because "economists find it difficult to think of communities as decision makers."[32] Individual social capital includes both intrinsic abilities and results of social capital investments via networking that enable the realization of market and nonmarket returns. The model developed is a conventional optimizing model of specifying a utility function subject to a constraint, including time, and of arriving at comparative static predictions and then testing them empirically. The main conclusion is that individuals will accumulate social capital in response to private incentives.

The individual or households possess social capital in this model and contacts and networks resulting from belonging to local associations are mined for enhancing utility.[33] This is very different from viewing social capital as trust, networks, and reciprocal obligations that exists in a dynamic context in a wider entity such as a village or neighborhood.

On the production side, the neoclassical formulation is the aggregate production function. Here social capital is viewed as entering the production function as another factor of production much as natural, physical, or human capital are. They concede that aggregating from individual social capital to society social capital is complex as is true for other variable aggregation in economics in general.

It is quite clear from the various ways in which the stock of human capital is defined, including the definitions used by the pioneers above that it is extremely difficult to get a good proxy measurement in some cases and that in other cases it is impossible.[34] At a macro level, since there are no prices as such, aggregation would seem to be impossible. At a micro level, quality differences would again make comparisons problematic.[35] Most economists would probably agree with this critique, but given the pace at which the literature is mushrooming, many probably accept Dasgupta's (1999) contention that social capital is nonetheless a useful concept. We turn to some critical perspectives in the next section.

1.3   Critical Perspectives

Some of the literature reflects skepticism and even rejection of the concept. Arrow (1999) pointed out that capital can be extended over time, can be sacrificed now for future gains, and can be alienated. To this list we add that it depreciates with use.[36] While the extension property holds, social capital is not run down now for the sake of more later, is likely to grow with use, and is embodied in individuals, communities, and society and thus can certainly not be alienated.[37] Uphoff and Wijayaratna (2000) point out that while other forms of capital normally lead to individual or household benefit, social capital can also simultaneously result in broader community benefits.

Solow (1999) added to this critique by questioning the nature of flow that emanates from the stock of social capital, as is claimed to happen by the proponents of social capital.[38] He also argued that one ought to be able to measure the stock and flow in order to be able to calculate a rate of return to the stock. This would be necessary to justify allocating resources to building the stock of social capital relative to other economic activities.[39]

Silvey and Elmkirst (2002) contribute to the social capital literature by first pointing out that it is oblivious to gender. Based on their own fieldwork and various related streams of the literature on Indonesian development, they explore the use of social networks as coping strategies in Indonesia during the 1997–99 economic crisis and use this to reconceptualize the concept of social capital to one that is gendered and hence more sensitive to equity and inclusion.[40]

Rankin (2002, p. 10) suggests that the concept of social capital as promoted by the World Bank focuses on the poor as agents of their own survival and the framework obscures the structural sources of inequality produced by the current political economic system. She argues that the concept also provides a justification for reducing the state's role in the provision of basic social protections. Speaking of microfinance, she points out that the focus is more on the health of the financial system than on the welfare of credit recipients. The allusion to the concepts of empowerment is misplaced since the collective action or peer-group pressure deals with repayments and not with opposition to repressive social structures or social transformation.

Cleaver (2005) examines factors that critically inhibit the poorest from constructing and benefiting from social capital. These factors include ill health, unstable households, and suppression of their voice. Participation in associations or collective action can have a monetary or time cost, and since they live on the margin of subsistence, these costs are in relative terms unbearable. Thus, the focus should be on the lack of material assets and sociocultural constraints rather than on the dubious benefits from social capital, participation, and collective action.

Mayer and Rankin (2002, p. 807) argue that social capital in groups is made operational to "manage the social costs of neoliberalism and extend the reach of the market to areas hard to reach by the other agents of global capital." While the concepts such as "solidarity" have been borrowed from progressive movements critical of the social order, these groups are accommodated by and accepting of the existing social order (state and markets) so that there is no questioning of what resulted in the marginalization of the groups in the first place.

Baron, Field, and Schuller (2000) have edited a volume titled *Social Capital: Critical Perspectives*. The volume contains not only critical pieces including the one by Fine and Green reviewed below but also some that are supportive. The editors adopt an open-minded position and concede that the concept has heuristic value. Harriss and Renzio (1997) raise an interesting point from the perspective of the sociology of knowledge. The sharp critiques of Putnam's work reviewed in this paper may have been viewed as weighty enough to stop the social capital bandwagon, but judging from the mushrooming literature, these critiques appear to have hardly got any attention. It appears that the time for the concept was ripe and the need for it great. This point is alluded to in the progressive critiques of social capital.

Fine (1999, p. 10) argues that the concept lacks conceptual depth and rigor as it moves from one meaning to another. He alludes to the Marxist view that capital is in any case a social relation and that adding it back in the case of social capital requires an illegitimate prior exclusion.[41] Fine (2001, p. 137) argues that social capital has been used as "an all-embracing umbrella concept under which to gather anything that might be developmental other than physical and personal resources." For example, it has been argued above that social capital is a useful umbrella concept for collective action via participatory development. Fine argues (p. 138) that the value of this umbrella concept in a nutshell is that it "fills out everything that is not already taken care of in terms of standard economic analysis." Thus social capital is viewed as a convenient way of dealing with the troubling issues of imperfect information and transactions costs.

Perhaps, Fine and Green's (2000, pp. 82–85) greatest objection is directed at the attempt by economists to apply the "reductionist" approach of neoclassical methodological individualism to derive the social from individual utility-maximizing behavior.[42] Beyond this, Fine (2001, pp. 141–143) also points to a host of problems in the empirical research pertaining to specification, multicollinearity, omitted variables, multiple equilibria, and the use of cross-section to represent time series.[43]

To avoid the problems of standard empirical work we use a detailed case-study approach. However, we were not chastened enough to heed the advice in Fine's (2001, p. 151) conclusion that "Independent economists and noneconomists need not enter the highly loaded analytical terrain being established around social capital in the context of the post-Washington consensus. To do so would be to consolidate and legitimize the knowledge bank of the World Bank, whether as hired mercenaries or unpaid foot soldiers in other people's battles."

We proceed with caution for several reasons. First, while the more meaningful concepts of class and power are the most relevant and valid for sound social analysis, they unfortunately yield little in terms of the well-being of the poor in the short run. This is no doubt because of existing power configurations in low-income countries, but, while endorsing sound analysis, pragmatic alternatives that might make a significant difference to the well-being of the poor can still be explored. Second, more critical perspectives in this ever-growing debate should be welcomed.[44] Third, while we are hopeful about the value of social capital as an umbrella concept in which to embed collective action via participatory development as indicated in the conceptualization below, we view this as a testable hypothesis.

1.4 Harnessing and Guiding Social Capital

Conceptually, the argument is that the construction of social organizations is likely to be as successful as the prior reciprocal trust and positive interaction and networking within communities.[45] When that is the case, external intervention is really "harnessing" and "guiding" or "channeling" the existing social capital to work toward a particular goal, such as collective action for the provision of community infrastructure, rather than building or constructing social capital. Harnessing and guiding social capital may require the building of social organizations.[46]

Building social organizations via social mobilization is slow and painstaking work and, if they survive, it may be because trust, norms, rules, procedures, and productive social relations—that is, community social capital—are at the core of such social organizations. Thus we view created social organizations or indigenous associations as the shells that can be imbued with the spirit that represents the social capital. In this regard, we agree with Fukuyama (2001) and Portes and Mooney (2003) that social capital is determined by unique historical processes and culture and may be difficult to create via outside intervention.

In fact, we are agnostic on the issue of whether public policy or development NGO interventions actually create social capital. It would seem that inducing collective action should reinforce trust, ties, and networks.[47] However, we think that the social capital, which has taken generations in developing, can induce positive collective action and is present in varying degrees in communities. To the extent that external intervention is needed to improve upon autonomous collective action, the focus should be on harnessing and guiding social capital by building on the trust, social ties, and solidarity already present in communities in various degrees.

The distinction between social capital and harnessed and guided social capital is important. Thus, our hypothesis is that social capital already needs to be present in a village for it to be successfully harnessed and guided. The activation and direction we refer to is the forming of formal village or community organizations and guiding and assisting them to engage in collective action to enhance the welfare of the village and the community, with a particular focus on the poor.

Is there a way of testing this hypothesis against competing alternatives? In fact, there are several examples in the literature of such tests, most prominently the work of Krishna and Uphoff (2001, 2002). Collective action can succeed for several reasons, some of which are community need; good community leadership; economic, political, and caste homogeneity; literacy; modernization; quality of village organization; and the quality of the staff engaged in the social mobilization. If a social capital index explains success holding other factors constant, one cannot reject that the success of the collective action is premised on what is being referred to as social capital that is embodied in communities.

Endorsing the harnessing and guiding of social capital is for us associated with our normative view of what development is about. For us, development is about making the poor stronger in protecting their rights, extending their choices, and enhancing their well-being, both within and across generations: in poor countries, these, what the poor should be able to claim as citizen's rights, are particularly important because the state has been unable to deliver, due to a lack of resources or poor management. Thus, organizations that enable the poor to engage in collective action to protect their rights and also enable them to maintain and enhance services delivered to them are vital to development in the short to medium term until the political process can be used to make the state deliver. Thus, the hope is that such organizations would be less important when in the long term[48] the state can play its rightful role of providing and maintaining basic infrastructure and providing essential social services that constitute basic human needs.[49]

Our main focus in this book, as indicated earlier, is on the strengthening of local voluntary associations or the building of community or village organizations by development NGOs to harness and guide social capital. This process started with the promotion of participatory development for collective action, which grew in popularity in the 1980s.[50] In this regard, social capital, a broader concept, has subsumed participatory development via collective action.

Bebbington and Carroll (2000) discuss the "building" of social capital, but while they focus on federations of organizations for the poor, our concern is with created or supported community organizations that embody social capital and engage in collective action.[51] However, we share their view on the potential that development NGOs have in building community organizations. We also share with them the view, as elaborated on in chapter 4, that knowledge of local history and culture is critical in successfully building community organization. Further, our concern is with systematically exploring this process to see if it amounts to harnessing and guiding social capital.

Thus our approach to social capital and assessing its impact in this book differs in two ways from the conceptualizations in section 1.2. First, we consider the construction of social organizations, as explained in detail in chapter 3, as the agency that may be harnessing and guiding social capital. Second, for our work, these organizations represent inputs rather than outcomes or impact.[52] It is often very difficult to be able to assess qualitative differences in the nature of say participation or interactions and the complex motivations that bring them about. Thus our focus is on the outcomes of collective action resulting from harnessed and guided social capital.

We share Sorensen's (2000) concern with the role of social capital in rural development. The discussion of issues in this citation deals with "created" organizations, such as water-user associations, community forestry associations, farmers associations, or community organizations, and their interaction with the development NGOs that we are concerned with in this book. Concepts central to our analysis are reviewed including the internal and external strength of created organizations, that is, their ability to manage and to negotiate with external actors as well as with horizontal (other community organizations) and vertical linkages (with government and other organizations). One important difference in the created organizations we focus on is that they are multipurpose.[53] Thus, the mandate of development NGOs include natural resource management, microcredit, human resource development, extension service, enterprise development, physical infrastructure development, and other interventions depending on the expressed needs of the created community organizations.

Most, if not all, efforts for harnessing and guiding social capital by development organizations are generally funded by foreign donors and to some extent by national governments. Thus, there is serious concern about both the justification and sustainability of such initiatives. The justification is based on the externality argument as explained by Grootaert (1998). If it can be demonstrated that collective action results in the production of public goods that would otherwise be underproduced, a case can be made for inducing such collective action.[54] Thus the group, and often others outside a defined community, can benefit from such collective action. Further, in so far as "development" takes place and there is more prosperity, a market is created that benefits others. Finally, created village or community organizations of the type we study provide a platform for multisectoral public and private sector interventions such as those in agricultural extension service, education, health, and natural resource management.[55]

While an argument can be made for using local or foreign taxpayers funds for harnessing and guiding social capital as a poverty alleviation initiative, those funds are unlikely to be available indefinitely and so there are reasons to be concerned about the sustainability of both the development organizations engaged in harnessing and guiding social capital, often with high overheads, and the village or community organizations that depend on them. Our view is that if the social mobilization is of high quality, good community organizations can be created and they will survive and engage in collective action if the social and private incentive to do so exists. Also, once the target populations go beyond a defined threshold level of poverty, the need for the development organizations, or the created village organizations, as an approach to harnessing and guiding social capital for poverty alleviation may no longer be needed, at least in their original form.[56]

The critical literature (section 1.4) points out that the concept of social capital is attractive to the neoliberal right that is skeptical about the role of the state.[57] Presumably this is because social capital enables civil society to provide what the state fails to. Thus, in this context, the answer to "government failure" is not reforming government but bypassing it and paring down its role. In our view of harnessing and guiding social capital, the government remains involved in two ways. First, government resources are involved in funding the development NGOs and, second, one of the key outcomes of the collective action that results from the social mobilization is the solicitation and procurement of state resources by the poor that would not otherwise be made available.

We turn in the next chapter to some broader economic and related empirical applications of the concept of social capital and then to some empirical applications relevant to the concept of harnessing and guiding social capital for collective action for rural development.

Summary

Social capital is a rapidly expanding area of inter and multidisciplinary research. In this chapter, we review various definitions and conceptualizations in the literature and then focus on the concept of "harnessing" and "guiding" social capital by constructed community organizations to facilitate collective action. This is a reference to organizations created by development NGOs through a process of social mobilization. Our hypothesis is that the mobilization process draws on existing social capital and gives it organizational form for collective action via participatory development. We refer to this process as harnessing and guiding social capital. We also explore the issue of state and social capital and argue that, contrary to concern expressed in the literature, the state need not be displaced by harnessed social capital but rather its resources could be tapped more effectively as part of the process of tapping social capital.

Empirical Applications of Social Capital to Growth, Poverty Alleviation, and Rural Development

2.1   Introduction

Just as the theoretical and conceptual literature on social capital is vast, so too is the empirical literature now. This chapter limits the review by first focusing on broad applications relating social capital to economic growth and poverty alleviation, following which there is the more specific focus on rural development. Attempts to make the concept of social capital operational for empirical work have been criticized, as have the empirical findings reviewed below.[1] Most of them have utilized different conceptual frameworks and defined social capital in different ways, but the commonalities are evident. The selection below is not exhaustive.

2.2   Applications to Economic Growth and Poverty Alleviation

One set of empirical exercises explore whether or not some measure of social capital explains economic growth at a macroeconomic level. Using indicators of trust and civic norms drawn from the World Values Survey, Knack and Keefer (1997), in their study of 29 market economies, showed that social capital was positively associated with measurable economic performance. This was particularly true for low-income economies where enforcement of contracts is less reliable. Furthermore, they found that institutional rules restrain arbitrary authority and less income inequality were positively associated with the development of norms and trust.

Whiteley (2000) argued that social capital and the associated trust should reduce transaction costs (including the monitoring, security, and policing costs) and facilitate collective action and hence enhance economic growth. Once again, the World Values Survey was used to construct a social capital index and to show, using various specifications of an endogenous growth model, that social capital was a positive and significant predictor in a cross-country sample of 34 countries. In the same vein, based on a survey of several studies, Knack (2002) concluded that lower social trust resulted in lower economic growth.[2]

Morris (1998) pointed out that very limited research on the impact of social capital on poverty at a macro level had been done for poor countries and found that associational social capital (memberships), election turnouts, newspaper circulation were positively associated with mean consumption and inversely with poverty across the Indian states. Temple (1998) estimated a growth model to estimate the impact of initial conditions on economic growth and found that low social capability (proxy for social capital in the base period) was associated with low investment and growth and bad policy outcomes. The impact of some measure of social capital has been associated with income inequality as the dependent variable and Narayan (2002, pp. 63–71) presented a summary of this literature.

Poverty assessment studies of the World Bank include an account of social capital and its impact on poverty. The Panama Poverty Assessment of the World Bank (2000, pp. 22–23) concluded that social capital was likely to be higher among indigenous rural communities and that communities with high social capital were four times more likely to receive government assistance and two times more likely to receive NGO assistance than those with low social capital.

Grootaert and van Bastelaer (2002, pp. 61–63) showed that a 10 percent rise in social capital was associated with a 1.2 percent rise in per capita household expenditure.[3] Gray-Molina et al. (2001) concluded that social capital (membership in networks) increases the probability of escaping from poverty, although they conceded that the causality could be reversed. Carter and Maluccio (2003) in a study of stunting among poor communities in South Africa demonstrated that poor households with more access to social capital are better able to cope with idiosyncratic economic shocks. Grant (2001) used case studies of two poor urban communities in Guatemala City to show that social capital facilitated neighborhood development but that secure rights to land may be a prerequisite for this.

Narayan and Pritchett (1999) showed the positive impact of memberships in local associations on household expenditure in Tanzania. There were three follow-up studies using similar measurement tools and empirical methods based on the World Bank Local Level Institutions Survey in Indonesia, Burkina Faso, and Bolivia. Grootaert (nd.) and Grootaert and Narayan (2004) showed similar findings for Indonesia and Bolivia respectively. Social capital facilitated collective action, increased household welfare, reduced poverty, mattered more for the poor, and its impact on household welfare exceeded or was equivalent to that from education. Haddad and Muluccio (2003) reviewed the literature on trust and group membership and household welfare. Their own research showed that membership in financial and nonfinancial groups led to higher well-being. Gomez and Santor (2001) showed that social capital had a positive association with self-employment earnings.

Aguilera and Massey (2003) demonstrated that social capital facilitated migration from Mexico and had a positive impact on successful job search and wages in the United States, particularly in the nonformal sector. Ma (2002) showed that return migrants from rural China to urban areas acquired human capital that they used to acquire social capital on their return and this led to higher earnings in entrepreneurial activity. Information and credit were the manifestations of social capital that they drew on via informal networks.

Research has also explored the association of social capital with the better capacity for dispute resolution and with greater effectiveness in implementing development projects and overcoming poverty.[4] Colletta and Cullen (2002) explored how social capital interacted with violent conflict. McIlwaine and Moser (2001) studied the impact of violence on social capital in Colombia and Guatemala. They identified "fear" as part of cognitive social capital and "perverse" organizations as part of structural social capital and suggested mechanisms for converting fear into trust and perverse into productive organizations. Richards, Bah, and James (2004) reviewed the role of social capital for community-driven participatory development in the postconflict situation in Sierra Leone. They discussed how war destroys social capital and made recommendations for reconstruction.

Grootaert, Oh, and Swamy (2002), in a study of Burkina Faso schools, found that children were more likely to attend school if their parents were more active in parent teacher associations (PTA).

Gugerty and Kremer (2000) were also concerned with building social capital and the role of development assistance in this process using a control group methodology.[5] Their research studied the impact of assistance on the functioning of existing social groups such as women's community groups or PTAs. For the women's groups, social capital was defined to include participation indicators, use of fines or sanctions (organization strategies), time devoted to group activities, level of project assets, strength of external ties, and the mobilization of savings. For the school groups, social capital was defined as parental and community support for schools, teacher motivation, and school interaction with local government or educational administration officials.

Many of the contributions in Baron, Field, and Schuller's 2000 volume explored the association of human capital (education and health) with social capital. Brune et al. (2005) not only focus on the building of social capital via leadership and development training, but also demonstrate that higher levels of social capital are positively associated with general health behavior and civic participation in rural Nicaragua.

Daniere, Takahashi, and NaRanong (2002a) explored the possible impact of forms of social capital on urban environmental problems across various Bangkok slum communities. In another study (2002b), also based on urban Bangkok communities, they concluded that social capital could facilitate environment project effectiveness. They also argued that a critical level of social capital may be needed to achieve this positive effect and that poor communities, given their preoccupation with survival, may be less responsive to efforts to build social capital.

Pargal, Gilligan, and Haq (2002) showed that solid waste collection alternatives to municipal services were more likely in Dhaka, Bangladesh, in neighborhoods with a higher level of social capital. Beall (1997), also exploring solid waste management—using Bangalore (India) and Faisalabad (Pakistan) as case studies—argued that the issue is not necessarily straightforward and that the focus on social capital can divert attention from the power structures that could mediate the outcomes.

Katz (2000) used the case of Guatemala to show how social capital could substitute for well-defined legal property rights and facilitate natural resource conservation. Adger (2003) reviewed case studies in the coastal areas of Vietnam and Tobago to demonstrate the potential of social capital to induce collective action to cope with the negative impacts of climate change on the poor.[6] State civil society synergies and tensions in this regard varied by context.

2.3   Social Capital and Rural Development in Low-Income Countries

There are numerous examples from around the world claiming that social capital construction has facilitated rural development. Pretty and Smith (2004, p. 634) pointed out that during the 1990s close to half a million groups with a total involvement of 8 to 14 million households were created around the world to work on various activities such as watershed management, joint forest management, drinking water supply, integrated pest management, wildlife management, fisheries, and farm and resource management.[7] They indicated that the spread of new ideas was facilitated by social capital leading to positive biodiversity and resource management outcomes.

Westermann, Ashby, and Pretty (2005) analyze 46 randomly selected groups with at least three years working experience of a mixed composition (8 were exclusively women's groups, 6 men's, and 32 mixed), across 33 rural programs in 20 countries in Latin America, Africa, and Asia. They found that "women only" or mixed groups ranked higher on various dimensions of social capital such as solidarity, collaboration, and conflict resolution, and that these groups demonstrated a higher capacity for self-sustaining collective action.

Gebremedhin, Pender, and Tesfay (2004) used the presence of local organizations in the village as a measure of social capital and showed that it had a positive and significant impact on collective action for grazing land management in the highlands of northern Ethiopia. Mubangizi (2003) described how in rural South Africa, members actually paid a fee to join production groups to engage in various production activities such as poultry farming (for broilers or egg production), pig rearing, or vegetable growing. The groups were run democratically and members shared the dividends of the enterprise based on rules and norms set out in the formation constitutions.

De Hann (2001) similarly mentioned the more effective transfer of information within groups in the context of a Heifer Project International initiative among the marginalized in rural Tanzania. The project was based on working with groups built on existing social networks to provide, in this case, more milk productive goats, the offsprings of which were to be passed on to others in the community. The groups constructed their own rules and benefited from their own learning. Social capital was instrumental in helping every group acquire a goat each.[8] Lyon (2000) empirically explored the role of trust, norms, and informal networks among farmers in Ghana that enabled them to realize market opportunities and increase incomes.

Bebbington and Perreault (2003) described a three-layered process of social capital formation for rural development in the Guamote Canton in Ecuador. The lowest layer represented the creation and consolidation of community-level organizations. The second layer was the consolidation of these organizations into federations, and larger-scale organizations have drawn on these federations to acquire national outreach.

These organizations replaced the *hicienda* as the dominant mechanism for rural governance; the church, as a proponent of liberation theology, was instrumental in the social mobilization that brought about this transformation via land reforms and land buyouts. The state in turn required the formation of community organizations to mediate the delivery of services and the church facilitated the process. Literacy programs built the organizational and human capacity to link communities to the state. The building of Canton-wide federations of community organizations followed this grassroots activity.[9] These federations negotiated successfully with the state, via national development NGOs, for resources and development investments.[10]

Healy (2002) reviewed the impact that the replacement of the *hicienda* by indigenous grassroots organizations and federations had on Bolivia's rural development. Molinas (1998) found a positive relationship between associational social capital and the cooperative performance of peasant committees.[11] Rodriguez and Pascual (2004) showed that one proxy of social capital (membership in formal associations)—but not the others (participation rate in committees)—positively and significantly influenced the habilitation of scrubland for the production of cochineal (for natural dyes) in Ayacucho, Peru. Smale and Ruttan (1997) gave an account of *groupements naam* that were a part of transnational federation of farmers' groups that spanned the Sahel including the Yatenga in Burkina Faso. Exploring the latter region, they found that these groups had successfully undertaken costly public works in water retention infrastructure.

Sirivardana (2004) documented the case study of collective action by a federation of farmer's organizations in the Raana region of Sri Lanka. The Participatory Institute of Development Alternatives initiated the process in 1983 via a series of social mobilizations, each more intensive than the last, taking the collective action to a higher plane. Small neighborhood groups formed the village farmer organizations and these came together across 26 villages to form a district farmer's organization. The federation took control of the town market center to facilitate selling their products and proceeded to buy their own lorry (after negotiating a bank loan) to transport their produce to the city, where it could be sold at higher prices. They also cut costs by labor sharing and buying agricultural machinery.[12]

The villages had earlier been ignored by the state, but as the federation acquired more influence, the state interfaced with the farmer's organization to deliver social and physical infrastructure including a reservoir, drinking water, lift irrigation, a network of gravel roads, electricity, and social services. The organization successfully fielded candidates for local government elections to influence local level politics and took over the social mobilization task. As the fame of the federation spread, farmers from other regions replicated the collective action via their own federations. By 1992, the federation registered as a development NGO and negotiated independently with donors and the government.

Krishna and Uphoff (2002) developed a social capital index and found that it was consistently positively correlated with superior development outcomes in both watershed conservation and cooperative development activities. They ruled out other hypothesis such as need, relative power, quality of government extension staff support, modernization or the lack there off, literacy, and community heterogeneity that have been hypothesized in the literature as influencing collective action. In earlier research [Krishna and Uphoff (2001)] they found that villages that had stronger predispositions and capacities for collective action, captured by the social capital index, performed better in land use management. Krishna (2001) showed, using a similar social capital index to measure the stock of social capital, that agency in the form of informed leadership capable of linking the villages with local government and market opportunities was necessary for this stock to yield a flow of development benefits.

Cramb (2005) discussed the formation of community groups in the Philippines to facilitate the diffusion of knowledge and the practice concerning land conservation. He quantitatively showed that participation in groups significantly increased the probability by a factor of 2.7 of adoption of such practice. His qualitative analysis indicated that group formation reflected the initial stock of social capital and reinforced the pre-exiting bonds. In addition, land care groups were most easily formed and most sustainable in communities where bonding social capital was high.

Winters, Davis, and Corral (2002) used a neoclassical economics framework and factor analysis to develop three social capital factors including cooperation, formal production arrangements, and *ejido* (small farmer) organizations. These were then used in regression analysis and the findings were that *ejido* organizations were important determinants of participation in crop and livestock production, non-agricultural wage employment, and remittance income. Also, the lack of formal production arrangements hindered self-employment and agricultural and livestock income generation.

In her study, Ostrum (1997) attributed the success of Nepal's water users associations to their being built on existing social networks. The engineering was based on local knowledge and farmers were allowed to prioritize improvements. Mutual farmer exchange visits enabled learning from successful governance mechanisms. Some farmers even charged a fee to train others.

Kähkönen (2002) reviewed the role of community management in the success of irrigation management, rural drinking water, and urban sanitation. She noted the importance of exploring factors other than social capital in explaining the success of community management.

Reid and Salmen (2002) used the term social cohesion for social capital and in a qualitative study showed that the most important factor determining the success of external interventions in rural Mali, such as agricultural extension, was the degree of social cohesion existing in the community prior to the intervention. They suggested various indicators of social cohesion such as common maintenance of public buildings (e.g., school or a mosque), Friday prayer attendance, village cleanliness, associational activity and accepted leadership.

Isham (2002) explored the impact of social capital on fertilizer adoption in rural Tanzania by drawing on and extending a neoclassical model to incorporate characteristics of the social structure and then estimating it. Instead of a composite social capital index, distinct forms of social capital were separately included in the estimating equation to allow different mechanisms via which social capital characteristics such as group homogeneity, participatory norms, and leadership heterogeneity might influence adoption. The main findings were that households with ethnically based and participatory social affiliations were more likely to diffuse information about new technologies and facilitate adoption.

Uquillas and Nieuwkoop (2003) reviewed the Latin American Indigenous People's Development Initiative of the World Bank for rural development. The method adopted was that of building formal organizations onto the informal community networks of reciprocity to facilitate collective action based on participatory planning and self-management. The relationship of the individual organizations with the project was defined by their capacity-building needs. While the achievements of the project were not reviewed, the authors pointed out that strengthening existing organizations and forging alliances between them was a very difficult task.

Mondal (2000) referred to the work of the most prominent rural development NGOs in Bangladesh, the Bangladesh Rural Advancement Committee (BRAC) and Proshika, as social capital formation. Based on a field survey of 500 members of groups created by these organizations, beneficial and harmful effects of collective actions for rural development (the former overwhelming the latter by a ratio of about 140:1) were documented. The poor and women were shown to have derived much greater benefits from such collective action (ratio of about 4:1 and 2.5:1 respectively).

Bangladesh is also credited with inventing a widely replicated model of microfinance, referred to as "banking on social capital." Conventional banks avoid giving loans to the rural poor because of high transaction costs resulting from limited infrastructure, the lack of information, and the small size of loans. The lack of collateral and enforcement problems are additional deterrents. The Grameen Bank model overcame these obstacles via peer-group lending, where peer groups provide support and social pressure for repayments.[13]

The social mobilization process in building peer group organizations is very similar to that of constructing community or village organizations; for many development NGOs, microcredit is one aspect of a composite package used to engage, train, and attain community participation and development. The social relations and networks in poor rural communities are what many nongovernment programs bank on as social collateral to make loans without conventional collateral and to ensure timely repayment, hence the reference to banking on social capital.

The scaling up of microfinance has been successful in Bangladesh by most accounts and the big four—Grameen, Proshika, Association for Social Advancement (ASA), and BRAC—collectively served 13.7 million members and disbursed $7.46 billion as of June 2004.

The Grameen Bank put the basic microfinance model on the map, one of the indicators of its success is 233 replications in 55 countries by 2002.[14] Given this widespread replication of microfinance as a key poverty alleviation tool, more attention is devoted to it here.

Zaman (2004) reviewed the evidence and concluded that the literature "supports the conclusion that microcredit contributes to poverty reduction, but the evidence is not entirely clear cut."[15] While most of the literature is positive, microcredit has critics, particularly from a gender perspective. Perhaps the sharpest criticisms are about female empowerment. For example, Goetz and Sengupta (1996) argued that the control of the loan was mostly with men, but the burden of repayment was with women. This suited the programs because men were harder to locate and could turn violent when confronted. However, this could result in household tension, even violence against women, as women pressured the men for repayment. If women drew on domestic savings for repayment, this could be at the expense of expenditure on better nutrition, health, and education. The authors argued that there was no fundamental transformation in gender roles and that men in fact now control women's labor and capital. The programs (such as Grameen Banks sixteen points) focused on changing only female behavior.

Parmar (2003) claimed that the Grameen Bank training actually reinforced gender hierarchies. She argued that women were in fact doubly oppressed[16]: first, within the household by the males who pressured women to join the program and even beat them if they did not qualify for larger loans, second, by the institutions that passed monitoring costs on to women to keep their own transactions costs low. Microcredit is supposed to build group solidarity, but it actually created tensions resulting from peer group pressure and mutual interference even in consumption patterns.

Summary

Among other ways, social capital has been conceived of at an individual level to improve personal or household welfare: to achieve collective goals at the meso or community level, or to promote economic growth at the macro level. The focus on social capital in this chapter and the rest of the book is at the meso level.

"Harnessing" and "guiding" social capital by constructed community organizations to facilitate collective action was proposed in chapter 1 as a relevant conceptualization for rural development. This is a reference to organizations created by development NGOs through a process of social mobilization. Thus, in our view, the social mobilization process engaged in by development NGOs draws on existing social capital (defined as trust, social cohesion, or social solidarity manifested in norms, networks, reciprocal obligations, and local institutions) and gives it the organizational form of community organizations. The objective of the development NGOs—and by proxy of community organizations—is to induce collective action via participatory development.

In this chapter, we reviewed the broader empirical literature relating social capital to economic growth and poverty alleviation and then focused specifically on the literature pertaining to the role of social capital in rural development via collective action. While we view the concept of harnessing and guiding social capital as potentially useful, we are aware that one could argue that directly focusing on collective action via participatory development may be adequate. The challenge for us is to explain how collective action is successfully induced using this concept of harnessing and guiding social capital. In the next chapter, we review the model of rural development that has, with its interventions, made this approach operational in Pakistan. In Part II of the book we explore an application of this model via an in-depth case study of a rural development organization in Pakistan.

Harnessing and Guiding Social Capital in Pakistan[1]

3.1 Introduction

Various approaches have been adopted in Pakistan for harnessing and guiding social capital for rural development. Community-based organizations (CBOs), for example, represent a spontaneous civil society initiative and several apex government or foreign-funded NGOs have sought to harness this latent social capital by working with CBOs to enhance their capacity and effectiveness. Apex development NGOs such as Strengthening Participatory Organizations (SPO) and Nongovernmental Organization Resource Center (NGORC) have also often built on spontaneous indigenous efforts. Trust for Voluntary Organizations (TVO), set up by the government with an endowment fund, has financed the larger NGOs for capacity building and social sector interventions.[2]

One of the oldest and most successful models in Pakistan for harnessing and guiding social capital with the approval of the government is the Aga Khan Rural Support Program (AKRSP). Sungi, another development NGO in Pakistan, innovated by working with existing grassroots groups or CBOs to strengthen them via capacity building and training. Sungi does not rule out forming community organizations (COs) if CBOs do not exist in a particular location. Another difference is its focus on rights-based advocacy even as it does integrated rural development work. There are now several development organizations functioning in the country that have innovated with the basic AKRSP approach.

We start with only a brief account of the AKRSP model, as this approach has been extensively documented and reviewed. We follow this with a section on the extension of this model outside Pakistan (AKRSP, India) and within the country (Rural Support Program Network, RSPN). The largest member of the RSPN is the National Rural Support Program (NRSP), and we briefly indicate the scale of its operations.[3] Pakistan has been fortunate that the government has owned and tried to facilitate the harnessing and guiding of social capital in several ways, most prominently by attempting to take the Rural Support Program (RSP) approach to scale. We review these and other social capital initiatives and then end with a summary and conclusion.

3.2   The Aga Khan Rural Support Program

In 1982, in the northern areas of Pakistan bordering Afghanistan and China, the AKRSP, part of the Aga Khan Development Network (ADN), initiated social capital harnessing and guidance via the use of social mobilization for the formation of village organizations (VOs) or COs.[4]

AKRSP's outreach in the target areas extended in 2005 to 98 percent of the villages. Thus most villages in the target area solicited interventions or responded to invitations. Its mission changed over time and currently includes building the capacity of communities to sustain and improve the quality of life of its members. Their program areas include women's development, national resource management, enterprise promotion, credit and services, and building infrastructure.

AKRSP's approach is based on identifying village social activists and engaging them in intensive social mobilization via a process of dialogues with villagers. Once the community accepts the contract to engage in self-help or collective action, forms the VO, engages in regular meetings and regular savings, an infrastructure project, identified as a priority need by the community, is approved. This first infrastructure project, referred to as productive physical infrastructure (PPI), is viewed as a means of strengthening social capital and the community is expected to engage in other development work by tapping their social capital and financial collateral via the VO and collective saving.

Training and capacity building are part of the ongoing interaction of the project with the VO after the initial infrastructure interventions. Other interventions, say in the social sector, become possible depending on the level of participation of the community. Natural resource management, livestock, forestry, microcredit, and small enterprise development are also part of the program package depending on expressed community needs. Finally, there is the concept of partnership or linkage with government line or service delivery departments.[5] The idea here is that mobilized communities, with social capital embodied in VOs and with the development NGO often as an influential intermediary, are more effective in soliciting services such as livestock vaccinations than the communities on their own. Overall, AKRSP has been very effective in working with government and in tapping into, leveraging, and extending government resources for community benefit.[6]

One institutional innovation is cluster level organizations, supraorganizations of VOs.[7] These have been mobilized to run schools and health centers and to provide a model for social sector interventions. In addition, the community school program (CSP) brokered a partnership between the Directorate of Education (DOE) and Village Education Committees (VECs) to set up community schools. By 2000, about 500 schools were set up, with AKRSP playing the mobilization and monitoring role as part of their regular field management and unit operations. Similarly, in partnership with the Department of Health (DOH), a large number of village health committees (VHC) were set up to institutionalize the role of communities in managing health service provision in their respective villages

The AKRSP model is widely accepted as a successful method of harnessing and guiding social capital and creating sustainable livelihoods.[8] Shoaib Sultan Khan, the first general manager, referred to "social capital construction" as early as 1993, when synthesizing the lessons of the organization in a public lecture. As of May 31, 2004, AKRSP had formed 4,238 VOs (1,709 for women and 2,529 for men) with a membership of 155,440 households, catalyzed a total saving of half a billion rupees (Rs. 500.29 million), and had disbursed Rs. 1.81 billion.[9] The original goal was for AKRSP to create sustainable VOs and phase out after 10 years. The retirement of the first dynamic general manager after 10 years provided an opportunity for strategic rethinking by the AKRSP board. Although the staff could have been consulted more in this process, a new vision of a support organization is now well set and includes the concepts of technical assistance for communities and of building partnership.[10]

The World Bank, a partial donor, has evaluated the AKRSP three times, with the most recent report published in 2002.[11] This report concluded that between 1991 and 1997, farm incomes had more than doubled in all except the most remote and challenging Astore area and attributed about one-third of this increase to the AKRSP.[12] Overall, the project was assessed to been have been a remarkable success, with the efficacy of its programs either fully or highly satisfactory. The operations/overhead ratio, however, was 50 percent compared to 5 percent for the government in the same region.

The estimated low-end economic rate of return (without including the many positive externalities due to the program) was 16 percent, a rate that compared favorably with the opportunity cost of capital of 12 percent for that period.[13] Earnings in project villages were again estimated to be about one-third higher than nonproject villages.[14] Many of the VOs are active and thriving even 18 years after their creation, though there are other VOs that do not need to be there and are dormant.[15] The World Bank (2002) also concluded that the efficacy of the microfinance program had been high, the natural resource management (NRM) had a significant beneficial impact and the PPIs had provided substantial benefits.

Another way to assess the success of the model is premised on its widespread adoption outside and inside the country. The model has been exported to India, Kenya, Mozambique, and Tajikistan via the Aga Khan Foundation (AKF).[16] Here we briefly review AKRSP, India, and then the internal adoption of the model.

3.3   Aga Khan Rural Support Program, India[17]

AKRSP (I) was set up in 1983 in western Gujarat, as a development NGO with a focus on natural resource management. It has had a remarkably similar trajectory to AKRSP (P) and, like the latter, counts among India's largest and most successful development NGOs. Its board had very influential members of the government, the industry, and several NGOs. Once again, its first CEO was a senior (retired) government official holding a top rural development post. The operating philosophy of working with the government is the same as that of AKRSP (P) with whom it also shared its mission statement of empowering rural communities and groups, particularly the underprivileged. The program areas of agricultural extension, water resource management, soil and water conservation, saving and credit, alternative energy, and forestry are also common to both AKRSPs.

The software/hardware approach to rural development is also nearly the same. Thus an intensive dialogue process is engaged in to mobilize communities to build VOs as the software.[18] These VOs help build, operate and maintain the "hardware" offered by the project as a sweetener during the social mobilization. Thus an infrastructure project, such as a check-dam, is identified by the community and built via a self-help process with community labor and project financial and technical assistance.

There are some minor differences in that the rate of expansion for AKRSP (I) has been impressive but not as rapid as AKRSP (P). Thus, by the end of 2000, it had 507 VOs and almost 28,000 members.[19] Unlike AKRSP (P), it was set up with an endowment fund and so has a slower and perhaps more sustainable rate of expansion. AKRSP (P) started with and has remained dependent on soft money that has been forthcoming so far on the "success breeding success" principle. However, at the turn of the century, it turned its attention to building an endowment fund.

3.4   Internal Adoption: RSPN

Belying the skepticism that the AKRSP approach is unique to the relatively equitable social structures of the mountain areas of northern Pakistan, the model spread rapidly through out the country.[20] Initially, a small group of professionals within the NRSP informally did the backstopping for the new programs. Subsequently, the RSPN, which now has 10 RSP members, was established in 2000 with the support of the Department of Foreign International Assistance (DFID), UK, as a capacity building organization to provide program quality guidance, strategic support, and strategic planning assistance.[21]

It also has a mandate to disseminate key lessons and best practice of the RSPs internally and to other organizations, via internal and contracted research, and to institutionalize the interaction of the RSPs with other civil society organizations. Support is also provided to RSPs in their initial phases in matters such as expansion and portfolio management.[22]

As of March 31, 2006, the 10 members of the network collectively operated in 93 of Pakistan's 137 districts, formed 73,908 COs, and had a total membership of over one million (1,445,601).[23] About 683,625 community members have been trained, Rs. 1.33 billion has been saved by the communities, and Rs. 14.3 billion disbursed to about 1.65 million beneficiaries. On average, in the union councils where the RSPs are present,[24] they have organized 17 percent of the total rural households. Thus, the RSPs have collectively managed to go to scale.

Rasmussen et al. (2004) point out that the method of replication and scaling up of the "RSP movement" has been based on founding new organizations to extend provincial outreach rather than on expanding an existing one. They point out that this has several advantages including the development of a broader leadership, local ownership, adaptation to local needs, and proliferation of diverse experience.[25] This mechanism of scaling up has also been nonthreatening to governments compared to say the scaling up of Bangladesh Rural Advancement Committee (BRAC) in Bangladesh.[26]

A significant factor contributing to the strength of the RSPN constituent organizations is the organizational culture. This is characterized by a "do it now if it needs to be done" approach of senior management. Other strong points are the efficiency, self-confidence, and mutual respect of the professional staff, the helpful and efficient service of the administrative staff, and the dedication and commitment of the field staff. The pride among the staff of these organizations in being part of a dedicated, motivated, and competent group committed to a good cause is very evident to a social observer.

Talent is attracted by salary scales that are higher than other civil society or government organizations and by the many opportunities for training and broad exposure. The nonhierarchical management approach where the senior management earns respect by their hard work and demonstrated competence and encourages an atmosphere of open exchange is also striking. The credit for establishing such a culture goes to Akhtar Hameed Khan and Shoaib Sultan Khan—the founders of this participatory development movement in Pakistan.

Shoaib Sultan Khan is the moving force behind the scaling up of the RSPs and has been pursuing this objective with a quiet determination. He has allowed results to speak for themselves and used his acquired prestige, contacts, and access to high places to do the rest. He attributes the success of the movement to the cadre of over 40,000 social activists at the grassroots level whom he refers to as "the diamonds."[27] They are the pool from which the presidents and managers of the village or COs are drawn. He considers the social capital to be embedded in them and that they are made more effective by the training received from the RSPs. He views these individuals to be selfless and points out that there is an important distinction between being selfless and self-sacrificing; the latter trait is not called for in such grassroots work. He continues to guide this movement both from behind the scenes and in serving as the president of independent boards on the large RSPs such as the Punjab Rural Support Program (PRSP) and the NRSP.

3.5   The National Rural Support Program[28]

The NRSP is among the larger RSPs. It was established in 1991 as a nonprofit public company and it formally started field operations in 1993. The then finance minister, Sartjaz Aziz, who had a background in rural development as a senior official of United Nation's International Fund for Rural Development (IFAD), impressed with AKRSPs achievements, persuaded the government that replicating this approach throughout the country would be a cost-effective pro-poor initiative.

In 1992, the government pledged Rs. 1 billion a year for 5 years. On receiving the first installment of Rs. 500 million, the board shrewdly decided to convert that into an endowment fund (investing in high-yielding securities) and to have NRSP manage operations based on the recurrent income. This was sensible given their perception that change in government made it unlikely that the new government would abide by earlier commitments (and they were proved right). In any case, the absorption capacity of NRSP at that stage was limited. By March 2006, NRSP had 23,310 male COs and 10,575 female COs with a combined outreach of 498,566 members. Establishing almost half as many women's COs as men's COs is an achievement that most would have viewed as impossible in a conservative Muslim culture.

The core model is the same as that developed by the AKRSP i.e. the emphasis on social mobilization to build COs, the key role of local social activists in this process, the role of training to build skills and the role of saving and credit to enhance household incomes. Linkages of the COs, which embody the harnessed social capital, with government, private and civil society institutions and organizations are facilitated by NRSP to enhance the process and so NRSP sees its primary role as a catalyst, facilitator, and provider of social guidance. Thus, the focus in a nutshell is on building social, financial, human, and physical capitals, using linkages as a mechanism when possible, to enhance personal income and community well-being. As with other RSPs, the NRSP COs play an important role in conflict resolution and hence also indirectly contribute to productivity and well-being.

While the core model is similar to that developed by AKRSP, the NRSP innovated in several ways by adopting a very flexible approach. For example, the entry point to addressing community needs and hence mobilizing communities into a CO need no longer be a productive physical infrastructure (PPI) project but could also be training, natural resource management, microenterprises, or a social sector initiative such as a primary school, depending on community needs and resources available. This enables NRSP to be more responsive to community needs that on the plains are likely to vary a great deal from those in the mountainous regions where AKRSP works. Credit is used across the board as an instrument for meeting a social need and for sustaining community interest in the CO for collective action.

NRSP has also made other innovations. While there is a special focus on the poor, the nonpoor are not excluded. As for AKRSP, there could be several COs in a village, but now based on sect, *beraderi* (clan), or *quom* (caste), or on sharing of a common mosque, depending on the expressed preferences of a cohesive group. This again is wise strategy given the greater heterogeneity in the plains.

The head office oversees various regional offices that in turn oversee field units. Male and female social mobilizers, sectoral field assistants, and field engineers are the key personal at the field level and could be thought of as operating on the front lines and hence playing a key role. Interns assist the social mobilizers and are often the pool from which future social mobilizers are chosen and trained via a selective process. Fifty percent of the social organizers in the field are women as are one-third of the professional staff, which again is a major achievement. The NRSP received a glowing interim evaluation from a UNDP-funded team in 1998. One of the main strengths of NRSP was identified to be the professionalism, dedication, and commitment of its staff.[29] Its innovative management systems allow flexibility even as it delivers a standardized package across all districts.

Once the community expresses a willingness to forge a partnership with NRSP via the formation of a CO, a village profile is drawn for establishing a benchmark of basic information and the village then develops a microinvestment profile that includes individual and community plans. Based on this profile, a "resolution" is developed for NRSP and the terms of partnership (TOP) cosigned by the elected community officials and NRSP with the approval of at least three-fourth of the CO membership.

The head and regional office run several programs including National Resource Management, Physical Infrastructure and Technology Development, Rural Credit and Enterprise Development, Social Sector Services, and Human Resource Development. The NRSP Human Resource Development (HRD) unit runs several trainings for the president and managers of the COs including managerial, leadership, motivational, record keeping, and communications. NRSP's

HRD unit also runs these trainings for other RSPs and for activists and officeholders of other grassroots development organizations.

The NRSP has used its financial independence wisely. It has used its resources sparingly and strategically to preserve its financial sustainability and leveraged its funds to draw on government and donor funds to operate on a much larger scale than its recurrent income would permit. Of course, this was only possible because it very rapidly established a reputation for quality and efficiency in engendering participatory development.

It successfully concluded an agreement with Habib Bank to get an unlimited line of credit at the market rate for on-lending to its COs.[30] Many of these loans are for encouraging individual enterprise and so, in character with its flexibility, NRSP is not wedded solely to collective action to enhance the rural standard of living. Recognizing the importance of personal incentives, it has tapped into them to sustain interest in the COs that are then also a platform for collective activity. There are also collective aspects to credit in that group guarantees are required for loans and group pressure for repayment comes into play as poor individual performance affects community access.[31]

In fact, COs have been used very successfully by NRSP to leverage funds from various large public sector poverty alleviation programs including the Khushal (well-being) Pakistan Project and the Pakistan Poverty Alleviation Fund (PPAF).[32] The government of Punjab contracted NRSP under the Khushal Pakistan Project to execute PPIs (productive physical infrastructure projects) such as link roads (farm to market), watercourses, drainage, sanitation, drinking water supply, and schools.[33] The villages overwhelmingly approved of NRSP as a contractor because it put them center stage (from planning to execution and maintenance) and because it cut out the usual contractors who engaged in rent seeking and delivered shoddy outputs for many times the cost. In all cases, the communities made their 20 percent contribution in cash, kind, or labor in a timely fashion and at times exceeded the mandatory contribution. The NRSP field and regional engineers assisted with the planning, surveying, designing, cost-estimation, feasibility studies, and execution, but they ensured community involvement in all stages.

This method of partnership has been used very effectively and, since its inception, by early 2004, NRSP had completed 5165 projects funded by the government and various donors. These projects included 2,064 with Pakistan Development Program / Social Action Plan (PDP/SAP), 915 with the Pakistan Poverty Alleviation Fund

(PPAF), 90 with Khushal Pakistan Project (KPP), 35 with Overseas Pakistani Foundation (OPF), and 16 with Islamic Relief.[34] It has also enabled 383 projects to be directly executed by the COs via establishing a linkage. About 155,239 households have benefited from these projects. More recently, The NRSP along with other RSPs have been approached by the government to breathe life into its plan to devolve power to the grassroots level as explained below.

3.6   Government and Social Capital[35]

The government has tried to contribute to harnessing social capital in several ways. First, it has assisted in the widespread adoption of the AKRSP model in the country as indicated in sections 3.4 and 3.5. Second, those advocating the importance of grassroots or participatory approaches to development continued to find receptive ears among key policymakers in the military government that took control in October 1999. One of its most significant reform initiatives was the devolution of power to the grassroots level. A justification for this complex and ongoing reform was that government service delivery would improve if beneficiaries at the grassroots level were empowered to effectively monitor this service delivery. Also, all the buzzwords of "people-centered development," "participation," and "bottom-up development" can be found in the proposed local government plan as part of the basic principles underlying the devolution.[36] The main institutional grassroots mechanisms to activate social capital for people-centered development and participation include Village and Neighborhood Councils, Citizen Community Boards (CCBs), and Justice Committees or *Musalihat Anjuman*.[37]

In the northern areas where the AKRSP operates, the government requested it to form village councils and to ensure community participation in the election of office bearers. A total of 539 were formed and there was as expected significant overlapping in the memberships of village councils and the prior VOs formed by AKRSP. Khushal Pakistan Project allows village councils to directly access government funds for poverty alleviation projects. Development projects under this program can be identified and planned by the communities and later approved by a district-level committee of which AKRSP is also a member. Communities execute approved projects, so they are involved in all stages of the projects. One of RSPN's challenges was finding the best way of interfacing with the government of Pakistan, Local Government Plan, 2000 at the onset of the devolution process.[38]

A solution seems to have presented itself in the government's desire to see an activation of the Citizen's Community Boards (CCBs). The hope was that civil society would spontaneously form CCBs and bid for district-level funds by leveraging the funds they mobilize and use both sources of funds to deliver physical infrastructure and social services to the community. The obvious danger was that influentials could hijack this process and siphon off funds, given limited monitoring capacity at the district level. There was little movement in the CCB process until the district governments recognized that the VOs/COs established by the RSPs were effectively CCBs that had already established a track record of resource mobilization and collective action for service delivery. Even so, the procedure to register CCBs and "get" projects is tedious and not devoid of corruption within government offices and suspicion and hostility among local level politicians.[39]

The district governments are now tapping the capacity of the RSPs, in the form of a vast network of COs, to deliver on district development on a fairly large scale. Thus the Punjab Rural Support Program (PRSP) signed an agreement with the district government of Rahim Yar Khan to take over 108 of the district's Basic Health Units (BHUs) that were in shambles because the infrastructure was deteriorating, supplies were being misappropriated, and the staff not showing up. By changing the basic power structure in terms of responsibility, giving medical staff more incentives, and instituting monitoring via the COs, the PRSP has managed to make the BHUs serviceable. The number of patients more than doubled, staff reported punctually, and the pilfering stopped. The government of Rahim Yar Khan District's pilot project of turning over 44 nonfunctional schools for control, use, and management to the NRSP met with similar success.[40]

Third, the provincial governments also attempted to "create" social capital by notification of school management committees (SMCs) or parent teacher associations (PTAs). In most cases, there are design flaws, and adequate parental/community capacity building was lacking. Although the social infrastructure is welcome and provides hope for future rectification and effectiveness, research suggests that the objective of making schooling more effective via community participation has not yet been achieved, barring pilot projects where community partnership in schooling has been turned over to an RSP.[41]

This set of initiatives—along with the *Kushali* Bank (well-being or microcredit Bank), which is also a member of the RSPN (although not an active one)—is a key component of the government's poverty alleviation strategy via the harnessing of social capital. The Pakistan

Poverty Alleviation Fund (PPAF) also supports RSPs and other organizations that have adopted the RSP approach for grassroots poverty alleviation initiatives.

Finally, the Government of Pakistan has also been actively wooing the expatriate Pakistani community to assist in Pakistan's development efforts.[42] In the 1990s, the response to these appeals picked up, and one intervention was by an expatriate group of Pakistani doctors who had founded the Human Development Foundation North America (HDFNA) to assist in human development in Pakistan. In 1998, the HDFNA founded the Human Development Foundation (HDF) in Pakistan with a mandate to undertake grassroots participatory development initiatives modeled on the AKRSP approach to harnessing and guiding social capital.[43] Part II of the book represents a detailed case study of the initiation and early progress of HDF.

Summary and Conclusion

The potential benefits from harnessing and guiding social capital need to be put in perspective. A downside is that most new concepts become a fad and some of its advocates become die-hard believers who start to see the concepts as the "panacea." This has been true, for example, for "appropriate technology," participatory development, microcredit, human development, and sustainable development. All of these embody important conceptual and practical breakthroughs and they are likely to make a significant difference collectively. Believers who lend important social energy to one cause easily get disillusioned when unrealistically high expectations are not realized.

Pakistan now has a rich tradition of harnessing social capital and the 10 members of the RSPN have collectively gone to scale based on replicating a model of harnessing and guiding social capital initiated by the AKRSP. The RSP model was adapted and replicated by the HDF (starting with Mardan, Pakistan) with the support of HDFNA, an organization of expatriate Pakistanis.

The partnership of government and RSPs is a delicate one. As indicated in chapter 1, the best option is clearly for the government itself to deliver services for basic human needs. However, such partnerships are a reasonable temporary second best option when the best is not attained due to a lack of capacity, inefficiency, or corruption in government.

The original idea of the RSP model was that RSPs would do the social mobilization (or harness and guide the social capital) and provide the platform, and that the government would deliver the services. It appears that governments at various tiers are viewing the RSPs as autonomous quasi-government institutions that can be used for more effective delivery; they further believe that this path is easier than reform and cultural change of government departments. This raises important issues of scale and sustainability and parallel delivery systems, one redundant and the other active. This partnership is trickier when it moves from the bureaucratic to the grassroots political realm, as the competition for resources to satisfy constituencies is intense and the RSPs could get embroiled in local level political hostilities.

Using an in-depth case study approach, Part II evaluates how successful this RSP model of social capital harnessing and guidance has been in inducing participatory development in Mardan, Pakistan. In so doing, it tests the adaptation and replication of this model in Pakistan, and it simultaneously tests a model for expatriate contribution to the country of origin.

Part II

Case Study: Human Development Foundation, Pakistan

4

Cultural Context

4.1 Introduction

In this chapter, we describe the cultural and historical context in which the Human Development Foundation (HDF) interventions in Mardan were introduced. Mardan is one of the 24 districts of the North West Frontier Province (NWFP), which is one of the four main provinces of Pakistan.[1] Mardan is a predominantly Pukhtun area (see section 4.2) and, as indicated in chapter 1, understanding the local culture and adapting interventions to that is key to success in harnessing and guiding social capital via the participatory development model.

The program interventions at the grassroots have had to contend with existing indigenous institutions. Various Pukhtun institutions interact with the program objectives and influence outcomes. The community initially viewed the project and the project staff as an outside entity and questioned their motives. They saw it as introducing social and economic change that could be inconsistent with their way of life. Thus the project staff needed to be sensitive to the culture they were working within.

In this chapter, we will explore Pukhtuns, Pukhtun society and its social and political organization, and the maintenance of its group identity through Pukhtunwali (Pukhtun code of honor). We will also discuss how global political events, along with local politics, shaped the reaction of the local community to HDF interventions.

4.2 The Pukhtuns

A Pukhtun is a member of a Pukhtun tribe, defined by patrilineage, and behaves according to the Pukhtunwali ideal (see next subsection). Pukhto is the language of the Pukhtuns and the fundamental identity marker for them. In the literature on this ethnic group we see terms such as Pathan, Pukhtun, and Pushtun used interchangeably.[2] Pukhtun and Pushtun are indicative of linguistic dialects; the inhabitants of the Peshawar, Mardan, and Charssada plains use a dialect that predominantly uses the "خ" or "kh" sound, so the person belonging to this ethnic group is referred to as Pukhtun and the language of this group is referred to as Pukhto.[3] The members of this ethnic group that reside in the southern districts of NWFP, the province of Balochistan, and along the Afghan border use a dialect that predominantly uses the "ش" or "sh" sound; thus members of this group are referred to as Pushtun and their language as Pushto.

Another term that has been used to refer to this ethnic group is "Afghan." Pakistani preindependence land records refer to the *qom* (nation) of the landholder as Afghan. In the present postcolonial context, the term Afghan has come to refer to the citizens of the Republic of Afghanistan and also covers non-Pukhtun ethnic groups such as Tajik, Uzbek, and Hazara. Another ethnonym for this group is Rohilla, which refers to those members of this group who live in present-day India. The various ethnonyms for the ethnic group under study are Pukhtun, Pushtun, Pathan, Afghan, and Rohilla.

The origin of the Pukhtuns is debatable; while the Pukhtun genealogies claim Semitic roots, the linguistic evidence points toward an Indo-European ancestry. Pukhtuns claim to have a common ancestor who, according to accepted genealogies, lived 20 to 25 generations ago. The putative ancestor, Qais, lived at the time of the Prophet Muhammad. He sought the Prophet out in Medina, embraced the faith, and was given the name of Abdur Rashid. Thus, Pukhtuns believe they have no "infidel" past, nor do they carry in their history the blemish of defeat and forcible conversion.

Though genealogical interest is considerable, knowledge of accepted genealogies varies both regionally and individually. However, the acceptance of a strictly patrilineal descent is universal.

The Pukhun ethnic group at present is located in a region including the southern and eastern parts of Afghanistan and the western provinces of Pakistan, namely NWFP and Balochistan. The region and its people have been at the crossroad of invading armies, artisans, mystics, economic migrants, and political refugees since time immemorial. History has recorded the movements of the Aryans, Greeks, Turks, Mongols, Mughals, British, and the Russians, among many others, through this region. These movements have impacted the sociopolitical identity of the individual and collective Pukhtun self.

4.2.1   Pukhtun Society

As an unwritten and unrecorded set of norms, Pukhtunwali forms the overarching framework in which various Pukhtun institutions and practices function to this day. Pukhtun society is based on a tribal and subtribal system. The smallest unit of interaction and identity is the *kor* (household) and the largest unit is the *qabeela* (tribe). *Kor* is a focal social, political, and economic unit and the patrilineal law of descent determines membership to this unit.

The general characteristics of Pukhtun society, as described by Caroe (1958), include patrilineal descent, Islam, and custom. A Pukhtun must be an orthodox Muslim and live by a body of customs that is thought of as common and distinctive to all Pukhtuns. Speaking Pukhto is a necessary and critical aspect of being Pukhtun, but, in and of itself, not sufficient because Pukhtuns are more than simply a linguistic group. Pukhtuns have a saying to the effect that "he is Pukhtun who does Pukhto, not merely one who speaks Pukhto," and doing Pukhto in this sense means living by an exacting code, in terms of which Pukhto speakers can fall short. In a nutshell, Pukhtan society is patrilineal and Islamic (predominantly of the *Sunni* sect) and lives by Pukhtunwali.[4] The question of how an Islamic identity was unanimously accepted by a large group of tribes remains unanswered by historians such as Caroe and does not account for various religious minorities who are inhabitants of the region and practice Pukhtunwali in their everyday lives. Our account does not include various non–Pukhto speaking Pukhtun groups such as the Hindko and Saraiki speakers residing in the NWFP. Thus, Pukhtun identity is not as homogenous as mainstream accounts and images would suggest.

Pukhtunwali, as mentioned earlier, is an oral and undocumented code of conduct aimed at maintaining a Pukhtun way of life. Pukhtunwali is defined by various discourses and practices that provide the course of action for the everyday and extraordinary state of being of individuals and groups alike. The literature on the Pukhtuns (Ahmed 1976, 1980, Barth 1981, Caroe 1958, Lindholm 1982) identifies a long list of institutions and practices that constitute Pukhtunwali that we discuss in section 4.3.

For Barth (1981, p. 106) the main objective of Pukhtun society is the maintenance of all aspects of its code of conduct, the Pukhtunwali. "The value orientations on which it is based emphasize male autonomy and agility, self expression and aggressiveness in a syndrome which might be summarized under the concept of honor (*izzat*)."

Barth, suggests that the three institutions of Pukhtuns around which most activity occurs are *melmastia* (hospitality), *jirga* (council of elders) and *purdah* (seclusion and veil for women). *Melmastia* deals with honorable usage of material goods, *jirga* with honorable pursuit of public affairs, and *purdah* with honorable organization of domestic life. Together, these characteristics may be thought of as the "native model" of the Pukhtun. Barth (1981, p. 106) points out that "this model provides a Pukhtun with a self-image, and serves him as a general canon for evaluating his own behavior and that of other Pukhtuns. It can only be maintained if it provides a practicable self-image and is moderately consistent with the sanctions that are experienced in social interaction."

Ahmed (1976, 1980) notes that practices such as *badal* (revenge), *melmastia*, *nanawate* (refuge, forgiveness), *jirga*, *tarburwali* (agnatic rivalry), and *tor* (deviant female) constitute Pukhtunwali or the native model of the Pukhtun. While Pukhtunwali is difficult to pin down, the commonalities are evident in the various accounts.

Interviewees in the project area also had interesting responses regarding what Pukhtunwali meant. According to an elderly gentleman it was *"melmastia, fareeqaino ke rogha kol"* (resolving conflict between two opposing parties), *jang na kol* (not getting into conflict), and *kha lara* (right path)." An elderly female replied in a disgruntled manner that "it is just *zad* (stubbornness) and nothing else." These statements, the latter in particular, capture the complexity of this code whereby all actions are ultimately aimed at face-saving and avoiding backing down; because backing down means admitting fault and a loss of honor.

4.2.2   Social Organization in Pukhtun Society

Tribal structure and patrilineal descent define the Pukhtun. While these are major factors in the Pukhtun social system, the power hierarchies in which they are located differ from region to region depending on geography, economic situation, and political history. At the top of the hierarchy are the khans who are the major landowners. Land is the major resource that determines status in society, depending on whether it is irrigated, fertile, barren, arid, mountainous or flat. It is not only an economic resource but a source of identity and honor as well. Khans also have a documented *shajra* (family tree) in which they trace their lineage to a common ancestor. Thus land and traceable lineage are the commonly seen characteristics of this group.

At the bottom of the hierarchy are the occupational groups referred to as the *kasab gar* (where *kasab* stands for occupation). With a structure that is similar to the Hindu caste system, these groups include occupations such as the *nai* (barber), *zamidar* (peasants, tenant farmers), *mullah* (Islamic clerics), *mochi* (shoemaker), and *jolla* (weaver).

The religious groups are usually referred to as Syeds or Mian. Syed families trace their lineage to Prophet Muhammad through his daughter Fatima, and the Mian families trace their ancestry to a saint; both families are revered by the other social groups on account of that association. The religious groups occupy the space between the khans and the occupational groups and are highly respected by both. They are usually given a small land grant by the khans and are also active in conflict resolution and power brokering.

In the tribal areas, where the state does not have a direct presence and the penal code is not enforced, "malik" is the title for the heads of tribes or subtribes. As a continuation of colonial practice, the political agents to this day operate by working with the maliks who represent the tribe. In the settled areas of NWFP, where the state writ is enforceable, maliks do not have as much power as their counterparts in the tribal belt between Afghanistan and Pakistan, and in the social hierarchy they are below the khans. The nature of their work is that of tax collection and working with state agents in this regard.

The tribes in a particular region form a rigid social structure. However, historical accounts of the Pukhtuns show that they have been very mobile as individuals and groups. Migrations within and outside their area of origin are often in search of better livelihoods or because of *dushmanee* (conflict) or exile. In the postcolonial era, as development makes inroads, urbanization and changing labor markets have altered the social structures and made them region specific. We will elaborate on this when we discuss the case of Mardan in section 4.6.

4.2.3   Political Organization in Pukhtun Society

The sociopolitical organization of Pukhtuns varies from region to region depending on various historical factors, especially the British colonization and the extent of their hold in the areas under their control or influence. The Great Game has had a considerable impact on the political organization of tribes in this region as it has left behind geographical remnants, such as the Durand Line, that to this day have physically if not culturally divided Pukhtun tribes.[5]

The Durand line, named after Sir Mortimer Durand, a foreign secretary of the British Indian government, is a 2640-km border demarcation dating back to 1893 that divided the kingdom of Afghanistan and the then British India. This demarcation was aimed at making Afghanistan a buffer state between the Russian-held Khanates of central Asia and the British-held territories of India. While this demarcation divided Pukhtun tribes, the border has always been very porous and locals and goods have moved across it from both sides without much state control.[6]

The Afghan state evolved from a tribal mode of governance. The monarchy arose from the dominance of the Pukhtun tribe of Durranis, which exerted loose control from the capital of Kabul over Afghan Pukhtun and non-Pukhtun groups such as Uzbeks, Tajiks, and Hazaras. On the Pakistani side, the area of the Puktun populations can be divided into four zones.

First there are the Pukhtun tribal areas in the Balochistan province that for the most part do not fall within our project area.

Second there are the Pukhtun tribes of the tribal areas referred to as Federally Administered Tribal Areas (FATA) and Provincially Administered Tribal Areas (PATA). These tribal areas were another demarcation by the British of zones where tribal and customary law prevailed and the British penal code was not applicable. State control was administered by the political agents through the local maliks selected by the state (British), and this tradition continues to this day. Although the state does not have a direct presence in these regions, which are mostly located on the Pakistani side of the Durand Line, the relations between various tribes are more egalitarian and *jirga* is the main body of conflict resolution.

Third, there are the settled areas, which mostly consists of the remaining parts of the NWFP such as the Peshawar valley and the areas adjacent to it including Mardan. The state, originally colonial and now Pakistani, has a direct presence here and the secular laws of the land are applied through the state machinery along with Islamic and customary laws. Thus, unlike in the tribal areas, a *jirga* works along with the frameworks provided by the administrative and judicial agencies of the state. Pukhtun society in the settled areas is more feudal and practices a distinct hierarchy between various groups, especially the landowning khans and the occupational groups. The colonial experience contributed to the origin of these feudal relations through a number of strategic schemes related to improving and benefiting from the local infrastructure and to "settling" the

Pukhtuns. Using irrigation as a mechanism, the British cultivated a class of client khans to help enforce the writ of the colonial state by encouraging the warring tribesmen from the tribal areas to settle down peacefully in the vast tracts of newly irrigated agricultural lands (see section 4.6).

Fourth, there were the small monarchies such as Swat and Dir located in the north of the province. Again, the British played a crucial role in their creation, especially in the case of Swat where a member of a religious kin group was supported to form a monarchy. These states continued to function independently in postindependence Pakistan until they were dissolved in the 1970s. They were absorbed in the NWFP and the direct writ of the state was established there. The various social groups there are extremely hierarchical, like their counterparts in the settled areas. Swat is the most extensively researched region of the Pukhtuns and it has been studied by anthropologists such as Barth (1959), Ahmed (1976), and Lindholm (1982).

Added to these administrative divisions, Ahmed (1976, 1980, 2004) flagged another division pertinent to the analysis of Pukhtun society: the *nang* versus *qalang*. The *nang* and *qalang* systems of the Pukhtun help clarify the economic and social organization of the community in the project area. *Nang* (translated as honor) is a non-tax paying system found in the tribal areas. *Qalang* (translated as tax or rents) is a system that is accepting of tax paying to a central authority, a system that is found in the settled areas of the NWFP. Settled areas have had an experience of colonial rule with the khans as the intermediaries of the colonial authorities. *Nang*, or the tribal areas, have always resisted the colonizers, such as the Mughals, Sikhs, and the British, and have managed to be free of colonial rule. Thus, *Qalang* societies are characterized by direct experience of colonial and postcolonial states, are more feudal, and are agriculturally productive due to irrigation. *Nang* societies are free of such direct rule and continue to practice their customary way of life and self-governance without direct interference of the state. Relations between social groups in the *nang* are more egalitarian; these groups reside in arid and low-agricultural-productivity zones such as the present tribal areas of Pakistan.

This brief review of Pukhtun sociopolitical structures depicts the heterogeneity of Pukhtun identity. It not only shows how variable Pukhtun structures are but also points toward the role that colonialism played. With this understanding of Pukhtun social and political structures, we move on to briefly review various practices and institutions that are made operational through Pukhtunwali.

4.3   Practices and Institutions of Pukhtunwali

In our discussion of the Pukhtun society, we mentioned the central role of Pukhtunwali in regulating governance of the individual and collective social self. Two important spaces central to Pukhtunwali are the *hujra* and *kor*.

4.3.1   Hujrah and Kor

In this strictly segregated society, there are male and female domains referred to as the *hujrah* and *kor* respectively. *Hujrah* is a public space and focal point for male congregation in the village. Families who own *hujrahs* are wealthy and respected in the village. They are used for maintaining patron-client relations with the tenants, contacts with other social and political groups, hospitality and entertainment. *Hujrah* exists both in the *nang* and *qalang* areas; in the latter its sociopolitical functions conform to and are representative of a feudal existence.

Hujrah also plays a political role in that khans maintain and propagate their political authority through it. As Ahmed (1976, p. 54) puts it, "in Pukhtun areas the *hujrah* provides the platform for political maneuver and tests of strength." Khans have links in the network connecting them with other landlords and also with government offices. These links, along with clients who assemble at the *hujrah*, indicate political strength.[7]

Key Pukhtun institutions are associated with the hujrah. Thus the *jirga* convenes in the *hujrah*. Another important institution attached to the *hujrah* is the *jummat* (mosque). This strategic location depicts the importance of this religious institution in Pukhtun culture and way of life. This is interwoven with times of sorrow *(gham)*, such as death and sickness, and occasions of happiness *(khadi)*, such as births and weddings, when men congregate at the *hujrah*.

Pukhtunwali, propagates gender segregation and encapsulates a polarity. At one end is the *hujrah*, a male domain, and at the other end is the *kor*, a female domain. *Kor* is an institution within which women attain and propagate the Pukhtun ideals. It affects the males because their early socialization takes place here. According to a Pukhto *matal* (proverb), *"khaza pa kor daa ya pa gor daa"* (a woman's place is either in the *kor* [house] or the *gor* [grave]). Thus, *kor* is a woman's domain and her "ideal" abode.

It is through this domain that an important aspect of Pukhtunwali—that is, *purdah* (seclusion and veiling) of women—functions. Age, caste, and class play an important role in this regard. The mobility and *purdah* of prepuberty and postmenopausal women is very relaxed while it is strict for pubescent women and women of child-bearing age. Class plays an important role as women of the higher social classes, such as khans and religious groups, observe strict *purdah*. Exceptions to the class rule are the female members of the *mullah* (religious cleric) occupational group who also observe strict *purdah*. Women of the lower social groups such as tenant farmers observe *purdah* less strictly as they work actively in the fields.

In opposition to the ideal Pukhtun female is the deviant female referred to as *tor* (translated as black). According to Ahmed (1980), a society where the respect and chastity of women is of utmost importance, a Pukhtun male is most vulnerable through the behavior of the women of his house and kin group. Adultery is one crime that does not have to be responded to with *badal* by the concerned parties. A *tora*, a runaway or an adulterous female, brings shame to her family that can only be restored by her death at the hands of her male kin.

4.3.2   Jirga

Jirga is a council of Pukhtun elders that settles various inter or intra-tribal disputes or other matters. This institution has been referred to as the closest thing to an Athenian democracy by Spain (1962). In the *nang* areas, *jirga* represents the interests of the entire tribe and its members are respected *mashars* (elders) and maliks. In *qalang* areas, most members are from the landowning khan families. Religious elders, belonging to the local religious groups, are also members of the *jirga*.

The *jirga* consists of mediators and the two conflicting parties. All are allowed to present their points of view. The decision of the *jirga* is binding on all concerned parties and it may include fines, sanctions, social ostracism, or the giving of women in marriage. The *jirga* makes decisions according to the Pukhtunwali. This is not codified or documented but is the "the way of the Pukhtun" as determined by tradition and precedents. The *jirga* is much preferred by the locals to the state courts because justice is readily and speedily available and at lower financial cost. It is also considered to be Islamic in essence, using the *Qur'an* and *shariah* (derived Islamic Law) as referential authority, which enhances its appeal. While the *jirga* gives no representation to

women, but it makes decisions regarding them in ways that affect
them in substantive ways. Further, women have no say in the whole
proceedings; they cannot even present their point of view.

Many of the settlers coming from *nang* areas talk about the *jirga*
system there as being more permanent. According to them, in their
areas of origin, *jirgas* would at times include representatives of the
whole area and tribe (up to one 100 people). In the *qalang* areas, a
jirga is smaller, of a more temporary nature and is formulated whenever a conflict takes place. While the *jirga* is not as strong as in the
nang areas, it still maintains some prestige as the major informal legal
institution. Currently, the *jirga* operates along with the state courts,
and, even when cases are being fought in the courts, the two parties
may still deal with each other through the *jirga*. All larger issues such
as murder and major land disputes are taken to the courts.[8] For issues
involving women, going to the courts is regarded as shameful.

4.3.3   Tarburwali

Male agnates (cousins) are called *tarbur*. The relationship between
male agnates of the same lineage from a common ancestor is called
tarburwali. Usually, it is a conflicting relationship. Conflict or jealousy
often arises over the distribution of land or other resources. As control
over land gives greater political and economic power, land rights
inherited through patrilineal genealogy plays an important role in rival
relationships. Land and personal identity are interrelated, and so
cousins are often in competition to increase their land holdings.
Tarbur has come to signify the enemy and *tarburwali* is a relationship
of enmity.

Tarburwali is an important aspect of the *pukhtun* social organization. Many traditions of honor, bravery, and prestige function in the
context of the *tarbur*. In the project areas, this relationship was seen as
both unifying and conflict inducing. The conflict manifests itself
within the extended family. However, since a village consists of people
of different origins, each family always maintains its unity relative to
outsiders. In the same vein, various tribal groups unite to form a joint
front when confronted with external threats.

4.3.4   Badal, Melmastia, and Nanawate

Structured on the "eye for an eye" premise, *badal* is essential for a kin
group or individual to take in order to restore their honor. The inability to take revenge against an opponent reflects negatively on the

concerned kin group or individual by making their Pukhtun-ness questionable in their own eyes and the eyes of others. It is because of this that conflicts go unresolved for decades, with opponents settling scores all the time until the *jirga* makes a substantive intervention and arranges a *razinama* (resolution) between the opponents.

Melmastia for guests is an important component of Pukhtanwali whereby the hosts go out of their way to entertain their guests. For Barth (1959), it is through *melmastia* that an individual can create the grounds for personal and political support and maximize it. While Barth's analysis gives a picture of individual choices, Lindholm (1982) shows how it results in wider social cohesion.

Nanawate is the granting of refuge to those who seek it and the ensuring of their security throughout their stay with the host. Added to this is the granting of forgiveness to an opponent who comes to one's door asking for it.[9]

4.3.5   Izzat

The most important component of Pukhtunwali that ties it all together is *izzat* (honor) of the kin group and/or individual. As mentioned earlier, saving face and maintaining and upholding honor with the framework that Pukhtunwali provides its individuals is ultimately the main objective of all Pukhtun actions and reactions. It operates, as in the law of physics, on the premise that every action has an equal and opposite reaction. While this is ensured through *badal*, there are various mechanisms such as *jirga* and *nanawate* whereby truce is ensured while maintaining the balance of honor between the two opponents. Thus, Pukhtunwali not only has conflict prolonging components but also conflict-defusing and conflict-resolving components through the institutions of *jirga, nanawate, melamastia, and hujrah*.

4.4   Pukhtuns of Mardan

The area of Mardan is dominated by the Yousafzai Pukhtuns whose movement into the area is traced back to the fifteenth century. The other main Pukhtun tribes in the area are the Khattaks. There are also sizeable populations of Gujjars (nomads), who are considered to be the indigenous inhabitants, as well as groups of Syeds and Mians who are greatly respected.

The areas of Swat, Buner, and Mardan were collectively referred to as Swat. To this day, the areas of Swat and Mardan are dominated by the Yousafzai Pukhtuns, though the political histories have diverged. A feature of the shared history is the system of land allocation and distribution called *wesh*. This system of land allocations was devised by Sheikh Mali about five centuries ago. He divided the Pukhtuns of this area (comprising of present-day Mardan, Swat, and Buner, and adjoining areas) into nine subgroups and the region into nine areas. Thus, no group had permanent ownership of the land and they changed areas on a rotational basis and this ensured an even distribution of all resources for all the groups. This system is not functional anymore in the project area, since British colonial rule substituted in its stead a system of permanent land grants.

The present district of Mardan is a settled area where successive states have established their writ. Administratively, the district was a part of Peshawar district under the Sikh and the British, until it was made a separate district in 1937. Based on Ahmed's (1976, 1980, 2004) division of Pukhtun tribes into *nang* and *qalang* areas, this area falls in the *qalang* (tax paying) zone. A close look at everyday functions of society shows that these categories are not polar opposites and they overlap in the most interesting manner at times. Geographically, the area lies in the *qalang* system where the Yusufzai nawabs (title granted by the British) of Mardan originally owned the land. But the settlers, who came here to work as tenants, belong to the *nang* system that is dominant in the adjoining tribal areas. The overlap of these two categories has impacted the tribes and social groups residing in the project area.

Historically the society in Mardan moved from the *wesh* system to a more settled and permanent land ownership under the Sikhs and more so under the British. This process resulted in a feudal Pukhtun society such that the relationship between the khan and his tenants became very hierarchical. This relationship was offset when members of social groups with a different culture moved into this area from the adjoining tribal/*nang* areas as tenant farmers.

Historical records show that the British built the Swat canal to run through the Mardan vale. As Baha (1978) points out, this scheme made the *maira*, which was a wasteland, cultivable.[10] While this increased potential revenue and insured against drought and famine conditions, the main reason for its construction was political. It was hoped that the members of the Mohmand and other tribes could be induced by the promise of good crops to settle down peacefully in the British-administered areas. The canal was meant to give the British a hold over the tribes, as the latter's interests became directly or indirectly bound with the canal, and to end the border tension with them. This plan was realized as the lawless tribes, living across the border in the tribal areas, populated waste tracts.

Mardan was a stronghold of the Yousafzai tribe, but with the construction of the Swat canal and extensive farming activity that resulted in its wake, many Mohmand subtribes started settling in the district. While they started off as petty tenants, many have attained a position of economic influence. The Mohmands are now not the only settlers in the area. Many other tribes have also filtered in, such as the Swatis from Swat, Dirian from Dir, Bajauray from Bajaur, and Kohistanis from Kohistan. Other castes such as Sayyeds and Mian and Gujjars (originally nomads) are also a part of this eclectic mix.

According to the local elders, most of them have been coming to make a living due to the lack of resources in their arid area of origin. Some families also migrated here to avoid conflict or were thrown out of their *watan* (land of origin) as a punishment by the *jirga*. At the time of their arrival, they had no or meager belongings and accepted the tenancy on the lands of the khans. Before the construction of the canal, these lands were barren and not utilized, but later, these migrants provided the labor for the agrarian economy of the area.

The feudal land tenure system is operational here and tenant farmers work on the lands owned by khans or others on a sharecropping basis. Prime Minister Zulfikar Ali Bhutto introduced land reforms in the 1970s, which resulted in a peasant movement in this area, usually referred to as the *kissani* by the locals. The Mohmand tenants, who originally belonged to the *nang* system, forcibly occupied the lands they were working on and the houses given to them by their respective khans.

In many cases though, the ownership deeds are still possessed by the khans, but they have no say in operating the land. Over the years, some owners have regained ownership via political connections, legislation, or a show of force while some have sold the ownership deeds to the occupants at nominal prices. In yet other cases, rights to the property still to be decided, but, in the mean time, the occupying tenants still work on it and give little or no *ijara* (land rent) to the khan.

Some of the settlers who purchased agricultural land from local khans at nominal prices have increased its value by their industry. Mohmands are considered to be very tough and capable of vigorous physical labor. In fact, they themselves say that they are capable of getting a good yield even from rocky and barren land because they are not afraid of sweat and toil. The unusual success of this peasant movement needs some explanation.

The community usually identifies an individual or a household by their *watan*. They have strong affinity with their *watan* and also maintain their social links with their families in the area of origin. Some have left behind their ancestral homes and property. For many, maintaining social links is not financially viable but they visit their *watan* on important occasions. Ahmed (1980) refers to this phenomenon as the *dwa kora* (two-house) system. Households, when they get a better opportunity elsewhere, simply shift out and are not tied down by extensive family links.[11]

The *dwa kora* system, along with the *nang*, has been of great advantage to the tenants in the peasant uprising of the 1970s as it positively impacted the psychology of resistance. For example, in other areas of NWFP and Pakistan, the land reforms were not successful as the landlords found legal loopholes and had the political might to resist the reforms.[12] For peasants accustomed to the feudal hierarchy, there was little mobilization and will to seize the opportunity emanating from the populist rhetoric of the political leadership of the time. However, the migrant tenants from the *nang* areas moved their families to live with their relatives in their *watan* as they dug in to occupy by force the land they worked on. Since they were also spread over a vast area, they became a cohesive force of resistance while occupying their individual landholdings. The egalitarian ethic of the *nang* Pukhtun, the refuge for the family in the *dwa kora* system, and the psychology of having nothing to lose but a lot to gain were central in making the *kissani* successful.

After the *kissani*, those occupants who managed to take control of larger tracts of land were accepted as the local khans and opinion leaders. As this is an agrarian economy, agricultural land is the major economic resource and ownership of this resource also determines the socioeconomic status of the individual and his family. This was one reason that the locals were reluctant to report on the extent of their landholdings. There is weariness that the information could be relayed to some sort of taxing authority or state representatives who may take away their hard-fought for possessions.

Landed households prefer to marry their children within the kin or tribe, but, over the years, intermarriages have also taken place between families of different tribes. This has not however resulted in much integration of tribes and they continue to maintain their distinct identities. According to one respondent, "no matter how many intermarriages take place with in us, a Mohmand will always be a Mohmand and a Swati will always be a Swati."

Initially, the *hujras* in the project areas were maintained by the local khans, and the tenant farmers, coming from predominantly *nang* areas, did not maintain any. Over the years, some tenants who improved their economic position by controlling larger tracts of land emerged as the local opinion leaders and khans. They also started to maintain *hujrahs* as a status symbol and to use it as a political, social, and economic platform. While the tenant farmers made the most of their *nang* heritage and roots, they have also emulated the feudal characteristics of their *qalang* counterparts as they enter into patron-client relations with other groups and use their *hujrahs* to sustain their new-found political and economic base.

Baithak (male guest room segregated from the house) is also an emerging trend in the project area, and this is significant for a society in transition. While *hujrah* is more of a public domain, the *baithak* caters only to the family of the house and their close relatives and friends. It was observed that those families who had improved their economic status, by means of income from overseas labor, would make a separate room within the house to serve as a *baithak*. Like a *hujrah*, the *baithak* is a sign of economic prosperity of the family. Tenants and other poor families just have one- or two-room houses.

The land in the project area in Mardan is called a *maira* (high plain), which is intersected by the Swat canal and also irrigated by it. The upper Swat canal, built by the British in 1885, irrigates the land in the project area. *Maira* is characterized by its agricultural economy and there are no markets here. Even agricultural inputs such as fertilizer, seed, and pesticides are purchased from a marketplace in the nearest city or town. Harvested crops are also sent to the market for sale. In the case of the project area, Mardan City serves this purpose.

In their everyday discourse, the community differentiates the "non-market" agrarian economy of their own community from the market-based economy of the city. They refer to themselves as the *mairawaal* and to the city folks as the *bazaari khalaq* (market people). Like any other peasant society, they see themselves as ignorant, uncivilized, backward, bound by tradition, unrefined, fatalistic, uneducated, and unpolished. When asked for an explanation of such a view of themselves, they replied, "but we are *mairawaal*, we are like this." As opposed to this, they see the inhabitants of the city not only as more educated, civilized, cultured, forward-looking, not held back by tradition, more profit-oriented but also more as deceiving in their social and economic transactions.

Certain practices change with a shift in residence. Some families that had shifted to the village from the city stopped their girls from going to school. To a query on this, the typical reply was, "this is the *maira* and here the people are very backward and do not educate their girls." But families shifting to the city from the *maira* would admit their daughters to school because "this is the *khaaria* (city), and here people admit their daughters to school."

Another cultural difference pertains to work. When girls who received their basic vocational training in cutting, sewing, and embroidery were asked if they did any piecework for remuneration in the village, they replied, "that is what people do in the city; in the village, we do it for free."[13] There is a very clear village/city divide and the two societies are viewed to be completely distinct, even though the physical distance between the two is small.[14] The research challenge for us was to explore the potential for harnessing social capital for collective action in this very complex society in constant flux due to outside interventions and with individuals and households between permanent and temporary states of residence.

4.5 Postcolonial Contributions to the Study of Pukhtun Society

Colonial fiction and media usually depicted the image of a Pukhtun as a wild, untamed, treacherous individual who lived by his own law and did not care much for the ideals of civilized society. However, there were also accounts of the hospitable and noble Pukhtun who lived by a rigid code of conduct for a land and home that he would die defending. The anthropological literature has also reproduced this paradoxical picture but based it on an in-depth understanding of the Pukhtun ideal and the various attributes that characterize it (see section 4.3). Given the violent nature of Pukhtun self and society, there has been much emphasis on conflict management.

Barth (1959, 1970, 1981), through his discussion of Swat Pukhtuns, talks about conflict management using game theory and the prominent role of individual agency in maximizing politicoeconomic gains. He analyses how various institutions and practices of Pukhtunwali such as *hujrah*, *melmastia*, and *jirga* are the forums through which political and social capital is gained and sustained. He does not, however, account for the role of the colonial and postcolonial state and its impacts on society in Swat. His focus is on the individual, entrepreneurial, self-maximizing, and, of course, violent Pukhtun. Ahmed (1976) has been critical of Barth's individualistic approach and uses a holistic framework to analyze political action among the Swat Pukhtuns. Even so, his subject matter is still driven by Barth's attention to the conflict management of the Pukhtuns.

Lindholm (1982) captures the interplay of the holistic and individual agency in the everyday lives of the Swat Pukhtuns and is also sensitive to the role of the colonial and postcolonial state and its impact on the Pukhtun self and society.[15] Lindholm (1996) calls to attention the colonial experience and its role in building the paradoxical but mostly violent image of the Pukhtun. For him, the colonial relations with the Pukhtun greatly determined the colonial imagery. During the Great Game, various accounts of British espionage missions portray the Pukhtuns as treacherous and violent tribes. Later, when the British had been badly defeated at the hands of the Pukhtuns, they see a part of their British-ness in them, not only in their phenotype but also in their martial competitiveness to be respected as an opponent.

Lindholm also shows that Pukhtuns treat friends and foes differently. As might be expected, they confronted those perceived as harmful and maintained strong relations with those perceived as friends, regardless of the cost. Toward the end of British rule, Caroe (1958) was viewed as a friend of the Pukhtuns and was immensely popular among them.

Bannerjee (2000), through her work on the Khudai Khidmatgar (Red Shirt Movement) movement, calls to attention the possible nonviolent aspects of Pukhtunwali. This movement was led by the pacifist Khan Abdul Ghaffar Khan who practiced Gandhi's nonviolent creed. He amazingly developed a large and intensely loyal following (almost 100,000 Red Shirts) among the Pukhtuns, including those in the project area, for nonviolent proindependence civil action. Thus for Bannerjee, Pukhtunwali is not a static and fixed concept but a reactionary one. Her research shows how the movement was a different political, religious, and cultural response to the state of affairs at that time in the world, region, and local level. These anthropological interventions are crucial to understanding the dynamics of Pukhtun society today and its reactions to global events and to nonlocal individuals and organizations.

4.6   The Global Context and Local Response in the Project Area

Pukhtun society has been impacted by and has reacted to more recent events such as the Russian invasion of Afghanistan in the late 1970s and the rise of the Taliban, its defeat and subsequent resurgence. The Russian invasion and the attacks in the United States of September 11, 2001 once again brought to the forefront the violent image of the Mujahideen and later the Taliban. Following the political instability in the region and the continuing refugee problem, there has been a convergence of multilateral and bilateral humanitarian organizations in Pakistan and Afghanistan.

The humanitarian aid organizations and Western NGOs are perceived by the Pukhtuns to have poured endless financial and nonfinancial resources into the region. NGOs such as HDF therefore get bunched with this amorphous group with nonexhaustible financial resources. It also confronts the distrust of the West that started with the colonial experience and is continuing as a result of the ongoing military intervention in Pakistani tribal areas and Afghanistan. These issues come up again and again during encounters between HDF and the communities they are trying to mobilize. Thus the HDF field staff takes great pains in explaining the origins of Human Development Foundation North America (HDFNA) and of the role of Pakistani doctors in it (refer to preface).

Project interventions were initiated in 1999 while the bombings in Afghanistan by the Clinton administration were still fresh in everyone's mind. Nawaz Sharif's government was dissolved shortly after in a military takeover in October 1999. Two years later, following the 9/11 attacks in the United States and the subsequent massive military retaliation in Afghanistan, the hostility to the United States grew and this is viewed by political pundits to have resulted in the success of Islamic political parties in the NWFP and Balochistan in the provincial parliamentary elections of 2002.

In this broader context of "Islamization," the question of whether the credit program of the HDF was Islamic or non-Islamic came to the forefront from the onset and has persisted to this day. In the 2005 local government elections, divisions sharpened between HDF-supporting groups and the opposition Islamic groups, and this resulted in the burning of a community health center established with the help of HDF in the project area. Thus, the project has and continues to operate in a very politically charged atmosphere.

Given this social and political context, the activity of the female project staff in the project area and the extent of involvement of women with regard to female community members are other sensitive issues. The context made the interventions and female activity more conspicuous than it otherwise would have been. The project vehicle that transported staff for various meetings and trainings to different villages was very visible. Villagers also saw women congregating for activities, such as development organization (DO) meetings, that represented a new development and a cultural challenge. This, accompanied by distrust of NGOs as trying to impose Western values, greatly impacted the nature of project interventions. The staff, all pathan, was very sensitive to this issue and made sure that packages for females were introduced without disrupting the local gender ideal and relations and were in the context of the existing cultural discourse. Nonetheless, global events and local responses made HDF's social mobilization an uphill task.

Conclusion

This chapter provides a brief overview of the cultural background in the project area. Our main concern was to indicate how the cultural context impacts the attempts of a development NGO such as HDF to engage in social mobilization—their key initiating activity that makes or breaks them. Social mobilization is required to harness and formalize social capital in the form of local organizations that can engage in collective action and participatory development. In the case of Pukhtun culture, for example, social mobilization could be aided by the deep traditions of Pukhtun hospitality. However, an account of Pukhtun traditions and institutions also indicates that social mobilization may be constrained by a suspicion of outsiders, a martial culture, norms of conflict, deference in some cases to khans or "influentials," and the conservatism derived from Islamic interpretations that severely constrain female mobility. In the next chapter, we present details of our research method and the various HDF interventions to give readers a background of the project.

ANNEXURE 4.1

Map of Pakistan with Mardan Highlighted

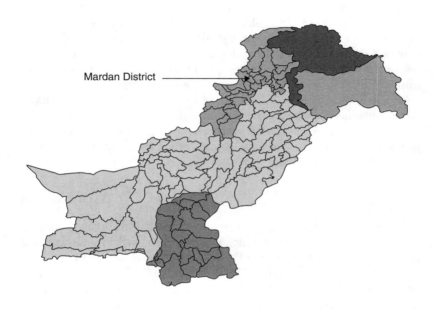

Mardan District

HDF Interventions

5.1 Introduction

As explained in the preface, a group of Pakistani American physicians, who formed the Human Development Foundation North America (HDFNA) in the United States decided to work for the cause of enhancing human development in their home country. The vehicle they chose for this was to register a sister organization in Pakistan called Human Development Foundation (HDF). A unique aspect of this social experiment was to try to forge a partnership with existing NGOs, which had a presence in various grassroots initiatives in the social sectors.

The two logical partners were Association of Pakistani Physicians of North America (APPNA) and Tameer-i-Millat Foundation (TMF). APPNA had been functioning for over a decade and already had widespread interventions in health, including in the project area, and TMF similarly had a significant national presence in education.[1] More important, both these organizations were already partnering with the constituent organizations that founded the HDFNA.[2] HDF took on the development initiatives such as microcredit, training, and establishing linkages with government and other NGOs. Despite some teething problems, it seemed that the partnership approach would yield dividends by drawing on the strengths of organizations with particular expertise, rather than by attempting to build expertise in all fields as usually done in the rural support program (RSP) approach (see chapter 3). The first area of intervention was the Mardan district of the North Western Frontier Province of Pakistan (NWFP) (see chapter 4).

In chapter 1, we outlined the conceptual framework of development organizations (DOs) harnessing and guiding social capital by catalyzing the building of community organizations. The social capital is not the community organizations but rather the trust, norms, reciprocal obligations, and networks that are embodied in them and sustain them. One important point that emerged in that context was that development NGOs need to be sensitive to the cultural context when engaged in social mobilization to harness, formalize (as community organizations), and guide social capital. In describing the Pukhtun culture in chapter 4 and the social mobilization process in chapter 6, the challenges that culture poses become apparent.

These themes are present in this chapter also, but in the context of specific project interventions. Prior to discussing the project interventions, we briefly describe our research method and identify the research issues we set out to examine in the project intervention context. Next, we discuss a number of organizational and institutional issues pertaining to the establishment and operation of HDF as a development NGO. These include a brief description of HDF, interpartner relations, role of community activists, organizational innovations, project expansion, and sustainability issues.

Finally, we describe the project interventions of HDF (training and credit) and that of its partners, TMF and APPNA. Health and education are discussed in more detail in chapters 7 and 8 respectively.

5.2   Research Method and Issues

There are several aspects of our research method that are novel. We sought to study process and the causes of change, rather than just change over time. To capture change, benchmarks were established and data collected again after one year. Also, visits were made throughout the year to observe community organizations and project initiatives and to interview project staff. Follow-up visits were made after one and six years respectively after the completion of the fieldwork (the updates are included in the book as chapters 9 and 10 respectively). This method reveals the dynamic nature of learning and the transformation that development NGOs undergo. Since we, as the staff members of the Sustainable Development Policy Institute (SDPI, the research partner), provided HDFNA with quarterly field reports, some of the suggestions made during this process are reflected in the text of this and later chapters.

Within the limitations posed by social science research, we attempted to study the process of social change, that is, the mechanisms via which the change occurred. The method adopted to observe process was to have a trained and sensitized anthropologist observe and report on both the process of social change and human development and on the interlinkages between the interventions in the areas of health, education, and income generation.[3] This approach also provided the unique opportunity to track interventions and individuals over a period of time, which made the information and analysis much richer than the usual one-shot sample survey or the limited time participatory rural appraisal.

It was equally important to evaluate integration issues at two levels: firstly, how well the various interventions were being integrated with one another, and, secondly, what impact an integrated intervention has on the communities. In other words, whether or not as a result of the interactions between the individual interventions the service delivery was greater than the sum of the parts. In section 5.3.2 and the next chapter, we report how, during the social mobilization process, tension between partners and the lack of coordination resulted in lost opportunities.

In order to double check whether project interventions, rather than broader social phenomenon, were making a difference in the sample villages, we also selected a control village for parallel analysis. Two sample villages were randomly selected out of a list of all villages with project interventions. A control village was selected using the criteria that it should be not only culturally and socioeconomically similar to the sample village but that it should also be far enough in order to avoid project spillover effects.

Apart from process and linkages as crosscutting themes, there are a number of specific research areas we focused on. This study has four components. An institutional analysis was designed to ascertain the incipient "social capital" in the community and how this could be harnessed and used for collective action as a result of the project intervention. Gender analysis was designed to ascertain the state of women in development and how this changed over time. Education and health analyses were designed to ascertain progress in these sectors and also the determinants of this progress. As earlier indicated, detailed chapters are included for health and education as those were the responsibility of APPNA and TMF respectively.

The health analysis focused on the underlying causes of child and maternal morbidity and mortality. Based on the data collected by APPNA, reinforced by qualitative information collected by the field anthropologist, investigations were made to study the cultural and social attributes that shape and define health behavior, especially that of the mother who is primarily responsible for child caring and rearing. In this process, efforts were made to demonstrate how culturally informed attitudes, knowledge, and behavior are modified and transformed by the attainment of health education and the provision of primary health facilities. The main focus of the education analysis was to ascertain children's cognitive skills, as a measure of quality, for project primary schools and how these changed over time due to project intervention. In order to do this, exams were designed to test comprehension and math skills and administered to children in all the schools of the entire project village and the control village at the inception of the project. The same tests were administered to the same students a year later to measure the value added in cognitive skills. Since the school in the control village was a government school, it was possible to compare the relative progress.

Community empowerment is not real or lasting unless it includes women. In order to assess how women were affected by the project, the field anthropologist developed a monitoring approach that incorporated inter alia the following:[4]

1. talking with women in the targeted communities;
2. assessing their decision-making patterns and change over time;
3. communicating with women at different stages of the life cycle;
4. levels of participation in various project interventions;
5. analysis of their perception of change during project activities;
6. their definitions of what change entails and value judgments of the quality of the change;
7. to see if the burden of responsibilities has shifted over time to include more household and community members;
8. intrahousehold time and resource allocation and gender biases in this regard by income group;
9. economic empowerment, women's earning power and access to resources;
10. women's vision for future empowerment;
11. access to information and services offered by the project;
12. and women's assessment of the quality of services and if these services meet their needs.

Levels and distinct groups of women in each community were identified and accessed through formal and informal interviews by the anthropologist. This qualitative approach to project evaluation complemented the quantitative methods of evaluation. The research entailed a range of tools for teasing out relevant information. These included the following:

1. focus group discussions with married women of reproductive age;
2. focus group discussions with women above reproductive age;
3. focus group discussions with adolescent girls;
4. individual in-depth interviews with select women and girls from the above groups to establish life-cycle information regarding access to health and education services, decision-making patterns within the family, participation in project activities, participation in decision-making structures within the community, and the determinants of change over time;
5. individual in-depth interviews with key women in the community who functioned as providers of general information on the above issues. They included teachers, health-care providers, midwives, and women who were associated with the project.

Gender is also addressed throughout the rest of Part II of this book, both as a specific and as a crosscutting issue. Other than health and education, microcredit and training are the key project interventions. An analysis of the project success in providing microcredit and training are addressed in this chapter.

5.3   Organizational and Institutional Issues

5.3.1   Human Development Foundation

HDF was registered in Pakistan in 1997 under section 42 of the Companies Ordinance. The National Rural Support Program (NRSP, see chapter 3) agreed to train project staff, but the plan of having it assume responsibility for the social mobilization, training, and micro-credit fell through. HDF was therefore responsible for these three components. It also had to assume responsibility for gender sensitization and capacity building as Aurat Foundation (a prominent female advocacy NGO) also did not join the project.

HDF initiated its work in Mardan, a district of the NWFP, with plans to expand to other areas based on initial success and funding.[5] On August 26, 1999, a regional office in Mardan was inaugurated. HDF innovated by building DOs that encompassed the existing health initiatives of APPNA and the new educational initiatives of TMF.[6] Thus the designed social organization structure was one where the health and education committees were expected to report to the DO at the monthly meetings. The DO, based on community requests given to it, was also the interface with the project for microcredit, trainings, networking, and for linkages with government line departments.[7]

5.3.2 Interpartner Relations

Given the unusual attempt to forge a partnership among existing organizations to enhance human development, attention needed to be paid to developing a harmonious relationship among them. There are obvious advantages of this strategy because it could take less time and resources to come up to the mark. However, the downside could be that the partnership would not work, due to established identities, and this could continue to have a negative impact on the delivery of project objectives in the long run.

APPNA was initially resentful that, while it had been in the field for a long time, it was upstaged by HDF. APPNA initially lacked a sense of ownership and resisted merging its identity with HDF as a partner. Resentment was also generated from scarce resources and the selective pickup and drop facilities given to HDF staff. Both APPNA and HDF were contemptuous of the other for promising "goodies," while they pursued the correct approach to participatory development by mobilizing and motivating for self-help and collective action. The other partners also resented attempts by HDF to establish oversight on their activities.

This lack of interpartner understanding resulted in operational problems as described in chapter 6. For example, HDF's ability to benefit from APPNA's prior mobilization in setting up DOs was limited. Health Assistants (HA) and Health Committees (HC) should have provided a natural entry point for DO formation, but this did not seem to have happened initially. Even the PTAs were initially operating independently and needed to be more closely integrated with the DOs in accordance with the original conception of the DO.

In fact, the TMF schools, which were—for logistical reasons—in place before HDF, was fully operational, provided an entry point for social mobilization to HDF (see chapter 6 for details). Children asked parents to congregate at the school for the project introduction meeting. Alternatively, the teacher facilitated the meeting and often became the DO secretary. However, while TMF provided this unanticipated benefit of an entry point for social mobilization and a pool of potential activists, the fact that the schools were in place prior to any social mobilization in the community negatively impacted the community's perception of the schools. Thus they were viewed as "official" rather than as community schools to be owned and run by the community.

We had suggested an operational modification, particularly for women DOs. Since female mobility is severely restricted, we suggested that it would make sense to limit the total number of meetings to a maximum of two per month. Thus the PTA and HC could meet once and then report on health and education to the DO meeting and discuss pertinent issues. As the process is very time consuming, this limited meeting schedule could also be adopted for the male DOs.[8] Thus, HDF's decision to pare down monthly DO meetings to two was very sensible. One meeting was designed to discuss DO issues such as development, collective action, training, credit, saving, and linkage while the other to specifically allocate time to the parent teacher association (PTA) and HC reporting in addition to normal DO business.

The interpartner meeting for enhancing interpartner understanding and for giving all partners a sense of ownership and due importance was slow in getting off the ground but subsequently worked well. Talking to the partners over time, we sensed that the tensions had eased and that the partnership was working out well via these meetings and the joint work planning. The other partners acknowledge HDF's leadership. A good sign of the teamwork was that HDF was able to rely on APPNA (who, as indicated above, had been around in the field much longer) to revive a DO.

The registration of the acronym HDF posed a problem. The earlier acronym, HDP (Human Development Partnership), was good as it included HDF and the other partners. The registration of the partnership as HDF gave an identity to one of the members of the partnership, but not to the whole partnership. The reader will note the potential for confusion as both the partnership and the "rural development functions" are referred to as HDF. We suggested that the partnership could be referred to as HDP, and HDF could adopt a functional name such as EDU (economic development unit) or something similar, but this was ruled out due to registration problems.[9]

5.3.3   Organizational Innovations

The main activity of HDF is social mobilization. This process is so complex and painstaking to initiate and so central to the concept of harnessing and guiding social capital that we have devoted a separate chapter to it (chapter 6). HDF's other activities include training, credit and microenterprise formation, establishing linkage with government and other organizations based on need and opportunity and its own limitations and overall coordination and monitoring. While HDF built on the RSP (rural support program, refer to chapter 3) model, it also deviated in a few important ways. As already explained, it attempted to develop an integrated intervention by working with partners rather than first building a DO and then developing integrated interventions. One aspect of this is linking together existing expertise rather than investing in building it up from scratch as part of the development NGO. However, this also entails trying to mesh separate identities into one to benefit from potential synergies. Others issues will be considered further on in this and the subsequent chapters.

Another deviation from the conventional RSP model is that the major interventions—health and education, in this case—were predetermined, that is, they were based on the partnerships, while in the RSP model, they are supposed to be based on a needs assessment of the communities. However, HDF shares with the other RSPs its focus on regular savings and the establishment of linkages with relevant government agencies, civil society organizations, and the private sector based on community needs and available opportunities.

The attempt to link trainings to credit and microenterprise development was an interesting HDF innovation. This was initially opportunistic but was later formalized to identify demand in the local market and tailor training modules to suit that demand, often drawing on locally available resource persons. Subsequently, credit was provided, based on a collective DO request, to develop related microenterprises. Some examples include crafts, fruit canning, and livestock development. HDF even attempted to market the products in an outlet and took some of the risk by purchasing from the community at a fixed price. This was an attempt to both create sustainable livelihoods and contribute to HDF sustainability via the profits.

Another important innovation was an iterative understanding of what a "natural" community represents. Initially, the whole village was thought of as a community. However, the size of the resulting organizations would not have been practicable and neither would the social mobilization on that scale have been feasible. Through trial and error, it was decided that the catchment area of a mosque defined a natural community, many of which existed within each village.[10]

5.3.4   Expansion

The HDF staff made much progress over a very limited time period with limited resources. However, we unanimously felt that they seemed to be under a lot of pressure from the HDFNA, the donor (see preface), to expand to other regions. We also thought that, given the very difficult nature of community development work, much more time was needed for the consolidation of HDF work in Mardan. As such, expansion to other regions before consolidating the work in Mardan and establishing a successful track record may have been ill considered. Not only could it jeopardize nascent trust and partnerships being developed with the communities, if the Mardan efforts did not take off, it could have also adversely affected the overall HDFNA/HDF program as a result of a loss in quality and credibility.

It was reassuring that locals were hired to handle the Shamsabad (Sindh) interventions and that HDF staff from Mardan was not moved. However, the movement of the country director, director finance/admin, and reports officer to the newly created country office in Islamabad appeared to have been a substantial initial loss to the Mardan office. The country director remained optimistic that this transition would be smooth. However, HDF expansion to other areas did slow down activities in some women's DOs.

5.3.5   Role of Activists

A unique feature of the Aga Khan Rural Support Program (AKRSP) model (see chapter 3) was the reliance on local activists to gradually start to shoulder the social mobilization and other responsibilities of the DO, hence freeing up time for project social mobilizers for further DO formation and other activities. Indeed this is absolutely critical for the sustainability of the DO. In this regard, HDF needed to pay much more attention to the cultivation of local activists for community development work. We have acknowledged the cultural problem of deference to the "influentials" and "elders." However, this should not be viewed as an insurmountable problem. Experience from other organizations suggests that ex-servicemen, teachers, and the educated unemployed provide fertile ground for finding and cultivating activists.

5.3.6   Sustainability

HDF planned to use training (fee-for-service) and the profit from the sales of community-made products (e.g., crafts and farm produce) as part of its contribution to project sustainability. The introduction of fee-for-service and its gradual hike to recover recurring costs were sensible. Training is now a competitive business for NGOs in Pakistan, and establishing a market niche is difficult. However, HDF can certainly save costs by doing its own internal training as it started to do. Some of the products we sampled at the HDF outlet in Mardan, including juices and jams, were excellent and there was scope for revenue from these, as well as from craft items, if the marketing was done well.

However, there was a broader issue that the board of HDFNA needed to resolve. Realistically, HDF will always be required to provide subsidized service until the communities in Pakistan reach some threshold level of human development where assistance from the philanthropic Pakistani community in North America will no longer be needed. HDF needs to be provided clear signals regarding how much of the costs it is expected to recover and why. For example, do communities attach value to something that is provided free? Is it that, in principle, communities should be expected to pay enough to recover recurring costs? Clear signals would have released some of the pressure HDF confronted during its very initial stages when it was not only trying to consolidate but also to expand.

HDF planned to use the profit from the microcredit program as well as from the microenterprises to plough back into an endowment fund. This was farsighted given that HDF initiated it in its second year. The risk of marketing was being borne by HDF, since it paid for materials and labor charges. We argued that this was fair and as it should be.

5.4   Project Interventions and Performance

As indicated earlier, most project interventions will be covered in this chapter, but health and education will be reviewed again in greater depth in chapters 7 and 8 respectively.

5.4.1   Health

As its staff often pointed out, APPNA was providing preventive health care to the communities long before HDF arrived on the scene. Child and maternal care, immunization, and reproductive health advice constituted a part of their program. Progress was slow regarding integrating health initiatives into HDF. However, HCs were being formed and it was expected that they would report to the DOs once a month. The linkage with the government for immunization worked well and they had also established a linkage with the hospital for a referral, but that did not work as well.

APPNA staff appreciated synergy being developed via the monthly joint meetings and work planning. However, they pointed out that the introduction of the HDF "package" raised expectations in the community and their social mobilization, based on an appeal to self-help, subsequently became more challenging.

APPNA had its own multitiered *markaz* model that was being implemented in the rest of the APPNA areas in Pakistan (see chapter 7). However, they accepted the DO model of HDF and agreed to work via the HCs when partnering with HDF. However, the problem of conceptually different approaches remained. APPNA, by its very nature, needed to achieve universal coverage while HDF needed to work with those willing to engage in self-help and collective action. The latter approach of course is more geared toward sustainability.

Once again, there was a need for raising greater awareness. Many community members felt that the APPNA's staff was pre-paid to deliver and felt that the service was their right. This reflected a serious shortcoming in social mobilization. Nonetheless, a local traditional birth attendant (TBA) confirmed that prior to APPNA, there was a high incidence of death by tetanus and that APPNA's immunizations had contained this problem. Thus, if the ultimate objective was human development and not necessarily an attitudinal change accompanying it, APPNA had succeeded.

In the APPNA program, the HA (health assistants) doing the hard work were female while the senior health assistants (SHA) were male. The HA felt it was high time that their hard work was rewarded and that the HAs were promoted to the SHA post. We advocated this also, for all female HAs who had suitable qualifications and experience. A project that intends to work for gender justice needs to first attain gender justice within the implementing organizations.

5.4.2 Education

TMF was registered as an NGO in 1992 and has been active in that field ever since. Its initial target was the establishment of thirty schools, fifteen for each gender. These were initially to be one-room and one-teacher schools. The schools were to use standard government curricula, though they were using innovative teaching methods and extracurricular activity. The plan was to have the children complete a five-year primary education program in three years and join mainstream government schooling. The communities were to arrange for a classroom while TMF would provide the material, furniture, teacher, and teacher training.

During field trips, we visited several TMF schools and two government schools in the area. Three of the four TMF schools seemed to be doing very well and this had much to do with the quality of the teacher. The problem of multiclass teaching had already emerged in two of the schools. HDF needed to start planning about what it would do for the fresh crop of students who would want to join. As it was, the teachers were finding it quite challenging to teach at one level to a cohort that varied widely in age. We thought that compounding this problem with an inflow of another class could make the teaching unmanageable. One teacher pointed out how a fresh crop had already entered and that this was proving to be a problem. Another teacher blocked admissions because she said she could not cope.

Another problem that TMF noted arose because a teacher had her own children to tend to and the classroom was part of the family quarters. Teaching her class and looking after her own children competed for her time, and this was unlikely to lead to good teacher performance. In general, a cursory look at the results of the follow-up test showed that there had been considerable value added in the children's cognitive skills due to the efforts of the TMF schools (details in chapter 8).

The PTAs had not yet started functioning as planned in the first year and membership was open to all DO members. This was an important cross-linkage area for the partners. However, even though the PTAs were not operational in the first year, TMF was directly reaching the broader community of parents at its monthly meetings. The objective was to generate a greater sense of ownership and participation by welcoming parents' suggestions. The hope was that this process would also raise DO membership.

When PTA's were initiated, they initially functioned, contrary to design, independently of the DOs. To avoid domination by the teachers, it was sensibly agreed that a parent would head the PTA. However, PTA meetings lacked an agenda. Also, HDF would bypass the PTA in taking important decisions that should have rightly come through the PTA. Thus, HDF's hiring of a very successful and very popular teacher to manage PTAs created much resentment. The decision to shoot a video at a girl's community school for a promotional film, without the parent's consent in a conservative community, created resentment and led to the withdrawal of many girls from the school.[11]

TMF wanted the PTA to help with sustainability as the communities take ownership of the schools. The fact that the communities had accepted a tuition fee was a positive development in this regard. Initially the fee was nominal (Rs. 5), with Rs. 10 charged by the high-performing schools. The community retained the fees collected. Instituting the fee was not an easy task and required persuading and convincing on the part of teachers. The women, who did not have decision-making powers and hence had to get approval from the males, found the fee to be more problematic. Even though there was universal acceptance of the fee, payments were tardy and were forthcoming only after many reminders.

The problem of registration of the schools with the government was resolved, so that government schools could absorb children graduating from the TMF primary schools. However, the problem of multi-grade teaching, that is, handling children of various grades in the same room, remained. At the time of our fieldwork, TMF had left resolving this to the communities; if they were prepared to donate the requisite facilities, the problem would be resolved. Meanwhile, admissions had to be restricted since there was a limit to the number of students that could be absorbed in one room. More awareness raising was clearly necessary. Community members seemed interested in renting school space and there was a perception that HDF had *sarkari paisa* (official money) at its disposal that they had a right to benefit from.

TMF appreciated APPNA's efforts at providing once every month information related to nutrition and hygiene to the students and viewed it as having had a very positive impact—a good example of partner synergy. School children were observed making ORS (oral rehydration salts) for their younger siblings.

TMF viewed some teachers as deserving of more pay since they had higher qualifications. More important, both the communities and the TMF acknowledged that some schools were more successful; communities had even agreed to pay a higher school fee for their children to attend such schools. We suggested that it would be fair then that TMF institute an incentive system that pays teachers of more successful schools a bonus to reward better performances.

5.4.3 Gender

Men have a tradition of collective meetings via the *hujra* (see chapter 4), but this was not the case for women (see chapter 6). Thus, much more training needed to be provided to women on how meetings were to be conducted and minutes recorded to make these meetings manageable and productive. The research team observed a female DO formation process in one of the villages and was very impressed by the enthusiasm and finesse of the social organizer. However, they also observed that the women's DOs were still in a rudimentary stage.

A fall in DO membership in one sample village when a training course was over was somewhat resentfully interpreted by the SO as a self-serving attitude of the communities. A key principle of social mobilization is that individuals join when they see some benefits to themselves and their households. Training was a good entry point to bring the women together. The very difficult and very challenging social mobilization task was to persuade individuals that staying in the DO and using it as a vehicle for collective action was in their and the community's interest.

One drastic step taken by a female social organizer to retain membership was to appropriate community savings and distribute savings of leaving members across those who stayed. We argued that this was an illegal appropriation of private property and that it could have a highly negative impact on future savings. A special effort will need to be made in loan contracts for women as vendors seem to try to take advantage of them. Defective livestock given to women in two separate instances demonstrated this point.

Social interventions can bring about positive cultural change among women and could in turn result in resentment among men as they sense a loss in control. For example, when this happened in Bangladesh in Bangladesh Rural Advancement Committee (BRAC) project villages, religious elements instigated the burning of BRAC schools and dispensaries.[12] HDF was sensitive to such dangers. Members of the abortive United Front had already complained that it was inappropriate for male and female staff to travel together, and that the female staff members had a negative influence on the social environment (see next section and chapter 6).

5.4.4   Microcredit and Islamic Financing

HDF realized that it needed to remain consistent with Islamic modes of finance, given the conservative religious context they were operating in (chapter 4) and the resistance they initially confronted (chapter 6). Thus, they consulted prominent Islamic community leaders and forged a consensus on what would be acceptable from an Islamic perspective. In a nutshell, the advice was that various modes of Islamic finance are permissible, modes that do not explicitly include the payment of interest. The one adopted by HDF (*marahaba*) required them to become party to the transaction by purchasing the goods required and reselling it in advance, to the person taking the loan, at a price that included a premium. The repayment could then be in installments. We feared, however, that there might be more negatives to this mode of microcredit than positives.

On the negative side, first, basic economic theory suggests that fewer constraints result in more individual welfare. Thus, if individuals are provided the cash and asked to use it as best suits their needs, they will acquire more welfare from this than if they are provided prespecified goods by HDF as prescribed by the Islamic financing mode they adopted.[13] Second, individuals have more motivation to get the best buys than HDF has and their time is cheaper. Thus they will expend more energy in searching to get the best prices for the goods they buy, that is, they will optimize better than HDF. Third, this will put the onus of transaction and search cost on individuals, which is where it belongs, rather than on HDF. Fourth, purists reject the idea that this mode of financing is truly Islamic, because HDF prespecifies a fixed return in the advance resale. Although it does engage in some transaction costs, it does not really take any risk or engage in production to justify an ex-ante return.[14] The opinion of the *ulema* (religious scholars), regarding the Islamic nature of the transaction, is divided even within the narrow community in question. Finally, while the community leaders accepted this mode of financing, household views suggested that they would much rather take the cash.

On the positive side, the individuals are shielded from the negative social pressure of the broader community than they would confront if they engaged in interest-based transactions. It may well be that HDF had no option but to engage in such transactions. Nonetheless, we suggested that it should continue to solicit views from the community and jurists and be aware of the costs and inefficiencies resulting from what they were constrained to do.

At another level, HDF may have not been entirely sensitive to the cultural (as opposed to religious) norms of the society it was functioning in. It did not seem to be true that the peer-group pressure of the Grameen model of microfinance would work well in Mardan.[15] First, individuals were at pains to avoid stating what their credit needs were in front of others in the community, as publicly admitting they were needy partly represents a loss of face among Pukhtuns. They would much rather do so in private with the social organizers. However, following the conventional model, the social mobilizers were pushing for a public statement and this probably resulted in an understatement of true need. A simple way to test this hypothesis would be to provide DO members with the opportunity to express their credit needs in private.

Again, the peer-group pressure model is problematic for recovery. Given the history of Pukhtun society, they put a very high premium on conflict avoidance.[16] Thus the decision was made by some male household members to prohibit the female members from signing on for loans. Situations that inherently pit one DO member against the others for the larger interest of the group or community worked to an extent in Bangladesh village communities but seemed contrary to the norms of Pukhtun society. It might have been wiser to focus on individual responsibility and individual sanction rather than on social sanction that the community seems to be resisting.

Credit was a thorny issue for HDF. It went to the extent, as earlier indicated, where a United Front was formed to convey its objections to HDF's credit policy. One DO even tried to have this declared anti-Islamic, but this did not work. Even so, community members were not persuaded that the implicit profit or interest that HDF claimed, as part of repayment at the moment that the transaction is finalized, was fair. The detailed process being followed at the time of fieldwork was as follows: A microcredit collective resolution was received from the DO, following which HDF did the appraisal. If they decided to go ahead with the loan, the product was selected and HDF did the survey. HDF and borrower went to the vendor together and the former paid the vendor and got the receipt. The selling price (price borrower had to pay), including principal, profit, and the installments were mutually agreed upon. There was adequate flexibility so that the terms varied by type of loan.

At one DO meeting, members brought up the terms and argued for a higher principal and for more extended time to make the first installment of repayment. Other objections raised by the community included the question why HDF was not a partner to the loss if it was to be a partner in the profit. This objection was consistent with the profit-and-loss sharing mode of Islamic finance. The latter is the preferred mode but not the one that HDF adopted.

More effort was needed to explain the accounting principles. Community members did not understand why they should be paying Rs. 9,000 as profit on a loan of Rs. 30,000 for two years when they paid Rs. 1,500 for a loan of Rs. 10,000 for one year. They expected to be charged Rs. 4,500 on Rs. 30,000. This lack of clarity resulted in resentment. Subsequently, villagers claimed that HDF should reduce its overheads by using cheaper fuels for their vehicles or public transportation to enable them to provide better rates.

Another problem was the lack of policy consistency that resulted in a loss in community confidence. Initially, HDF provided a choice of Islamic and non-Islamic mode of financing. Naturally, casting it in these terms meant that they would have to withdraw the non-Islamic option. Again, the methodology of calculating the profit rate was changed midstream. These changes were neither surprising nor unexpected for a new development NGO trying to establish systems while coping with its own managerial and administrative wrinkles. Nonetheless, policy changes that do not take the community into confidence can result in a loss of hard-earned credibility.

Overall, HDF did a commendable job in implementing a microcredit policy that was consistent, in as much as possible, with local religious norms (see chapter 9). Community members sensed a weakness at times and tried to exploit it. HDF's decision to stay the course was sensible. However, the fact that some community members used the opposition to interest-based microcredit and decided to call their organization United Front was significant. The name is suggestive of a position that is adversarial to HDF. This was ironic since HDF was in the community to help. We think that there was room for more public relations work to get across the following messages:

1. First, that the microcredit HDF makes accessible is available only at very high rates from moneylenders. At that time, there were no banks in Pakistan that made available such a service, although the Khushali Bank is now partly addressing this shortcoming.
2. Second, that HDF is a partner of the community and is willing to help provided the community is willing to help itself. There is no obligation to make these loans available without scrutiny at completely subsidized rates.

The community somehow had the impression that HDF is not only there to help them as an agent representing outside philanthropy, but that it is also somehow getting in the way of this being done effectively. This may partly explain the adversarial stance adopted by some in the community and also the more congenial, but nonetheless challenging, questioning by even well-intentioned DO members.

There are other observations we made regarding microcredit. First, as Mardan village communities are primarily agricultural, we suggested that it would be worth investing in a staff member with the relevant expertise to interface on advice on agricultural loans and to induce a movement toward organic farming.

Second, the amount of credit was limited and there had to be rationing. Thus, inevitably, several requests had to be turned down, and this resulted in several unhappy households in the communities. The country director and credit officer were deciding who would get the loan. Our suggestion was to leave the onus of rejection on communities. Thus, while HDF could retain a right to veto, it could allocate the total available credit by DO and then let it decide who is the most deserving of getting the loan following a consensual approach in keeping with local culture. HDF did later decide to give the communities (DO) greater say in prioritization and acceptance of credit requests. This was welcome since there was much frustration in communities when credit requests were not fulfilled.

Third, some rationalization of the process was needed as the communities felt that the approval process from resolution to disbursement was too slow. HDF needed to base all policy decisions on empirical investigation to test its assumptions. For example, it was assumed that there was an overlapping of family memberships across male and female DOs. Thus if a man was a member of a DO, it was assumed that a woman of the household was also a member of a female DO. Based on this assumption, a credit policy was framed that ruled that only females would be allowed livestock loans.[17] Naturally, it was assumed that no harm would be done due to the overlapping male and female membership from the household. As it turned out, this assumption was not accurate and the credit policy caused much heartburn among the male DO members who were denied such a loan. It was decided that exceptions be referred to the national office. Finally, vigilance was also called for on the part of the project. In one female DO, four out of the seven loans granted were to one household and naturally this caused resentment among the community members.

5.4.5 Training

HDF Mardan decided to save money and conduct its own training for the Shamsabad (Sindh) staff and subsequently for the Rahim Yar Khan staff in the Punjab. The NRSP training modules were adapted. The trainers did not have the experience of established NRSP trainers. However, the advantage was being able to give an HDF-specific training and draw on the HDF experience in Mardan. We observed the training and concluded that the Sindh staff seemed keen and bright, and one got a sense of an emerging team spirit.

HDF planned to manage both the preservice and in-service teacher training on its own. This was a positive development as long as the master trainers were trained by Adult Basic Education Society (ABES), the new partner in education from Sindh. The Community Management Skills Training (CMST) for APPNA and TMF staff was very well received and contributed to both conceptual clarity about the project and team spirit. Among the lessons learned is that, as the project expands, it should include more such staff-training programs. It was decided that all new field staff (other than drivers and peons) must undergo two weeks' training in all aspects of HDF interventions.

The enterprise skills training tailored to markets and skills in the different regions was arranged for the community. Thus, while training was provided in food preservation, livestock management, and poultry in Mardan, in Shamsabad, training was arranged in crafts (garments). HDF claimed that every one of the beneficiaries of the trainings started successful businesses.

Summary

The conceptual approach to human development adopted by HDF was based on the AKRSP model of harnessing, formalizing (into community organizations) and guiding social capital. Social mobilization is used to catalyze this process to secure successful collective action and to have the DOs provide a platform for project and other government and nongovernment initiatives. Details of the social mobilization, the core activity of HDF, at project inception are documented in the next chapter.

As members of SDPI, the research partner, we sought to study the process of social capital harnessing and its efficacy in engendering human development. Two novel aspects of this research were the attempt to study the process of change by placing an anthropologist in the field for a year. Also, by studying a control village, establishing benchmarks, and having field updates it was possible to identify the extent of change. This was particularly important for the analyses of the health and education interventions(chapters 7 and 8).

Our findings show that much progress had been achieved in a relatively short period of time (about one year) as described in detail in the five chapters that follow. However, our research also compels us to sound a few notes of caution. In the social capital–harnessing approach relying on building community organisations, the role of local culture is often not paid adequate attention to. We found that if this was not carefully dealt with then it could become a stumbling block. For example, since Mardan is part of the conservative Islamic belt, the approach to microcredit had to be different. The project quite rightly sought consensus from the local *ulema* (religious scholars); it was decided that instead of interest, an Islamic mode of financial transaction be engaged in as part of the microcredit initiative. Also, combative Pusthun culture, with its subsequent logical emphasis on conflict avoidance, seems averse to a peer group–pressure model of microcredit. This could also result from the emphasis on face saving, which makes individuals reluctant to identify their true credit needs in front of a group.

There is also a natural suspicion of outsiders and social interventions, even when engaged in by people from the same culture. Thus, whether it was health, schooling, or microcredit, the rural folk wondered if HDF was not somehow coming in the way of resources being bestowed by the government or outside benefactors on the community. These resources were viewed almost as a right perhaps because Islam, like other religions, prescribes that the wealthy support the disadvantaged. Individuals were also looking to gain from the project by renting out their premise for a school, even though it was clearly prespecified that the project would provide support if the community was willing to provide a building.

As explained in the next chapter, harnessing social capital via social mobilization is a slow and painful process and is essentially about winning trust. This is not easily bestowed and there are many local agendas and interests that need to be contended with. HDF could take heart that despite the seemingly individualistic orientation of Pukhtun culture, there were many signs of collective action that it had catalyzed.

Also, despite poverty and reluctance, the communities agreed to a user charge for the schools and were willing to pay more for the schools with better teachers. Thus, villages in Mardan and other areas were ripe for the harnessing of social capital, as are other villages in Pakistan. Patience and cultural sensitivity will go a long way in achieving this objective. We turn in the next chapter to a consideration of HDF's social mobilization in male and female communities in the Pukhtun cultural context described in chapter 4.

6

Social Mobilization

6.1   Introduction

The discussion on cultural context in chapters 4 and 5 needs to be kept in mind as we turn now to an account of the project efforts in mobilizing men and women to harness, formalize, and guide social capital via the formation of development organizations (DOs). These organizations are designed to facilitate project interventions in the two project villages. Social mobilization is the central aspect of the work of rural support programs (RSPs) of the kind described in chapter 3 and hence also of Human Development Foundation (HDF). In this chapter, we first briefly review the RSP method of social mobilization (see chapter 3), turn next to the method as adopted by the HDF, and then to the actual process as observed and documented by our field anthropologist in two randomly selected sites. Finally, we assess this process and conclude with a summary.

6.2   Social Mobilization: The RSP Method

The assumption that a development NGO works with is that if they can successfully harness, formalize, and guide social capital, every community has the potential to bring about a positive change in its present condition via collective action. Social mobilization is a vehicle to harness this potential. The basic premise underlying this exercise is not what the community wants, but what the community has the ability to attain with its limited existing resources.

These resources include human, physical, natural, and social capital. The potential and the capability of a community is viewed as being directly proportional to these resources and the role of the outside agency is to catalyze the effective use and enhancement of these resources within a self-help/collective action and participatory development framework. Self-help is aimed at developing ownership among the community members regarding the development effort initiated in their community. Unless they assume ownership and maintenance responsibility, the activity undertaken is not likely to be sustainable.

Social mobilization relies on building a CO, capital formation, human resource development, and linkages. The CO provides a forum for the community to participate in development-related activities initiated by the CO and other agencies, or those that are engaged on a self-help basis. Capital formation is realized through individual savings, which are pooled in a joint account of the CO. These can be used as collateral for community project loans. Microcredit is provided for small productive ventures in the local economy. Various skill trainings are provided to improve the human resource of the community. Linkages are established with other development NGOs, government line departments (services), or donors to leverage the development platform the CO represents. This is, in a nutshell, the RSP social mobilization and participatory development method. We now turn to an adaptation of this method by HDF.

6.3 HDF Social Mobilization

The HDF social organizers engage in social mobilization. When the project was initiated, the field staff of HDF consisted of one male social organizer (MSO) and one female social organizer (FSO). They mobilized the communities into *tanzeems* (organizations) and registered these as DOs with the HDF.[1] It is through the DOs and its members that various project activities are introduced in the village. Usually only one household member can join the DO but other household members can be project beneficiaries. Thus, each DO casts a long shadow in the community.

Even though the FSO deals with the females and the MSO with the males, the issues across genders within the same kin group are related, notwithstanding the seeming gender segregation. Thus the MSO might work with his DO membership to address female DOs issues such as getting consensus on a venue to conduct training for women. Similarly, since there is a limit on the loans being handed out to each DO, the male members who do not get a loan make their womenfolk apply for loans in their DO. While this enhances the potential benefits derived by a particular household, it also avoids conflict.

At the time of project inception, NGOs were subject to much public criticism. Aurat Foundation, a renowned women's organization, was criticized as being insensitive to the cultural norms of the adjoining Pukhtun areas and it was forced to cease operations. In the adjoining Charsadda district, The Sarhad Rural Support Corporation (SRSC) had the highest default rate of any NGO microcredit program in the country. Thus, HDF was likely to confront an uphill task given the wariness of NGOs in general and of microcredit in particular (see chapter 4).

The process of community mobilization in Mardan consists of the following stages: first contact; (1) dialogue, (2) DO formation and registration, and (3) follow-up meetings. The first dialogue entails the SOs making contact with the community *mashars* (elders) or opinion leaders and resource people that include the Tameer-i-Millat (TMF) school teachers, APPNA health workers, TBAs (traditional birth attendants), and clerics. In this first contact, the aim is to utilize the community links of these resource people to gather the community members at a designated time and place where the SOs make their project introduction.

For males, the forum is a public one, usually a *hujrah* (see chapter 4), a mosque, or any other open space where the local men usually congregate. For women, it is the home of the local elder where womenfolk can readily go. Usually women easily move across houses in the same lane as they belong to the same kin groups. However, movement is not permitted to another kinsman's house that is separated by a neighborhood of another kin group or social group.

Another problem is of conflict within kin groups. At times, women belonging to the same kin group cannot attend DO meeting in households they are in conflict with. Thus, it is more difficult for the SOs to mobilize the women in a village because while men of conflicting kin and non-kin groups congregate in public spaces such as the *hujrah* or mosque, this is not the case for the females.

During the first meeting, the first dialogue is initiated by the SOs to introduce HDF and its objectives to the community. The SOs use traditional and customary discourses about realizing community potential through self-help and collective action. Depending on community willingness, the DO formation might take place in the same meeting. In the case of women, who need to seek the permission of their menfolk, a second meeting date is agreed upon assuming interest in principle in forming a DO.

Once agreement is reached on forming a DO, the next step is for the SO to explain the nature of the likely community—HDF relations. The community members sign a memorandum of understanding (MoU) with HDF. The SO explains his/her expectation of regular meeting attendance and saving by DO members; both are crucial as they have a bearing on loan disbursements and the training provided by HDF. The SO also explains the use of DO registers for recording meeting attendance, minutes, and DO members' savings.

The DO members elect their own DO president and secretary. The secretary maintains the record of the DO as well as the bank account. In the case of women, the FSO maintains the record of the DO because generally female members are not literate. In a few female DOs, the local female TMF teachers, who are also members or secretaries of their DOs, maintain the DO record. In very few cases, the men of the house maintain the DO record. In almost all female DOs, the bank accounts are maintained with the help of close male kin as women do not have ready access to the bank due to low literacy, *purdah* (female seclusion), and distance.

After the DO formation and registration has taken place, the DO's initial functioning consists of meeting twice a month to discuss local issues and depositing savings at least once a month. Once this practice is established, the members can petition HDF for a loan or training. This petition is called a *qarardad* (resolution), which is passed by a majority of its members (at least 80 percent) who sign it and pass it on to the HDF SOs. HDF staff then make their decisions based on a number of factors such as regularity of DO meetings, attendance, savings, and the need of the community. DO registers are a good indicator of community needs and activities.

The difference in perspective between the SOs and community members during the social mobilization and follow-up meetings is notable. The project staff is driven by the ideals of harnessing the potential of these communities for collective action by organizing them into formal DO structures with regular meetings and savings as a form of discipline. The community, however, is overtly incentive driven, and observations of the first dialogues and subsequent interactions between the SOs and community members revealed this tension.

6.4   The Social Mobilization Process in the Project Area

What follows below is a generalized account of social mobilization in the sample villages. A detailed account of the actual process, as observed in

Fazal Killay (east), from program introduction on September 17, 1999 to first credit disbursement on January 4, 2000 is reported in Annexure 6.1.

6.4.1   Sample Villages

Social mobilization was initiated by HDF in late August 1999 in units 4 and 6 of the project area in which APPNA had initiated work.[2] We randomly selected one village each—Fazal Killay from unit 4 and Kandare Jadeed from unit 6—as the sample villages for this study. Fazal Killay is situated off the Mardan-Charsadda road and is one of the biggest villages in the two units consisting of about 250 households. A canal from the Swat river intersects the village and divides it into two parts. The eastern side of the village is called *sharki* and the western side is called *gharbi*. According to the APPNA records, the whole western side and a few houses on the eastern side constituted Fazal Killay A, while the remaining houses on the eastern side constituted Fazal Killay B.[3]

The village was divided into four sections, and each section had its own elder or *mashar*. The whole village was predominantly Mohmand with a few Malikian, Swati and Dirian families. The whole eastern side, where Nasir Khan was the elder and Bashir Khan was second in command, was a section. The western side was divided into three sections: *kalay manz* (village centre), *nehr ghara* (along the canal), and *naako* or *diriano koroona* (households of families from Dir). Social mobilization efforts were made in all the sections of Fazal Killay except for *diriano koroona*. This section was at a distance from the main village, which was predominantly Mohmand. APPNA provided services to this section of the village and considered it as a part of Fazal Killay in their records.

As the nearest female DO was formed in the neighboring village called Said Munir Kotay, some women of this neighborhood were members of that DO and some young girls also took vocational training in embroidery and stitching from there. This oversight took place because of a high turnover of residents and the separate surveys of APPNA and HDF. APPNA provided support to this area, but HDF was not aware of this inclusion in APPNA's program. Their focus was the central section of the village through the TMF schools. An updated survey of the area, with all the field partners involved in the effort, would have ensured rational coverage.

Table 6.1 below provides an overview of project and government interventions in Fazal Killay.

Table 6.1   Government and project interventions in Fazal Killay

Sector	Source of Intervention	Type of Intervention	Quantity	Location of Intervention	Gender
Education	TMF	Informal school	3	western	Male
	TMF	Informal school	1	western	Female
	Government	Primary school	1	western	Male
	Government	Primary school	1	eastern	Female
Community development	HDF	DO	2	eastern	Female
	HDF	DO	2	western	Male
	HDF	DO	1	eastern	Male
Human resource development	HDF	Embroidery training	2	eastern	Female
Microcredit	HDF	Loans	7	eastern	Female
Health	APPNA	Preventive health services	All village	eastern and western	Female and all children < 5yrs

Source: SDPI field survey.

Kandare Jadeed was a comparatively smaller village consisting of about 60 households. There too was a problem of village demarcation. In the APPNA survey and service provision, the village was amalgamated into Charcha, an adjacent village. According to the local residents, this village was formed in the land between two villages namely Charcha and Kandare. This was uninhabited land, but, over the years, a few people from the two villages that flanked it and from outside areas bought land here and settled because it was cheaper. People of both Charcha and Kandare did not consider them as part of their own villages, and this collection of households was called Kandare Jadeed.

When a TMF school assigned for Charcha was opened here, it created resentment among the inhabitants of Charcha. As a consequence, the Charcha villagers thrice uprooted the TMF school signboard. According to TMF and HDF, they were not made aware of the local demarcation, as they had depended upon the APPNA survey. APPNA, however, was of the opinion that they were never consulted in this matter. This again indicates the need for a collective survey by all the partners to ensure identical village demarcation in their program delivery.

Compared to Fazal Killay, this village had a more diverse ethnic mix, with settlers from different areas such as Bajaur, Mohmand Agency, Dir, Kohistan, Akora, Swat, and the neighboring villages of Kandare and Charcha. Haji Shakir Ullah, a Mohmand, was considered the village elder because of his large landholding. There was a lack of ownership of project interventions and the explanation given was that they were not *yo khalaq* (one people) and thus there was no unity amongst them. They kept to themselves and to the households belonging to their own family/lineage and never let their womenfolk visit the households of other families.

Table 6.2 below provides a brief overview of various project and government interventions in Kandare Jadeed.

HDF social organizers were of the view that the APPNA and TMF programs were completely subsidized and thus not sustainable because the community had not developed any ownership for the programs. A discussion of issues arising from the social mobilization implemented in these two villages follows.

6.4.2   Process

6.4.2.1   Fazal Killay (western)

6.4.2.1.1   *Female Mobilization* The entry points on this side of the village, for male and female social mobilization, were TMF schools,

Table 6.2   Government and project interventions in Kandare Jadeed

Sector	Source of Intervention	Type of Intervention	Quantity	Gender
Education	TMF	Informal school	1	Female
	Government	Primary school	1	Male
Community development	HDF	DO	1 (current status is inactive)	Male
Health	APPNA	Preventive health services	All village	Female and all children < 5yrs

Source: SDPI field survey.

which were operational since April 1999. Both the male and female social organizers (SO) of HDF started their work together in the village. On the women's side, the first dialogue, or the project introduction, took place on September 11, 1999, at the TMF girl's school.

There were about twenty women present at the meeting. The SO indicated to the teacher that more women should have attended. The teacher responded that she had told the school children to go out and spread the word. However, they had mostly gone to their own houses and most of the women present were mothers of the TMF-enrolled students. She pointed out that because she did not belong to this village, and because of the prevailing *purdah* (female seclusion) and mobility restrictions, it was difficult for her to go around mobilizing the women. There was no coordination witnessed between the APPNA health workers and the HDF staff. There was no exchange of schedules and programs between the two partners, whereas each partner expected the other to be aware of their program and work. There was a high expectation among the HDF staff of help from APPNA, while the latter were of the view that they were never intimated about HDF field activities, so they could not be of help. A lack of communication and joint planning resulted in disappointments on both sides.

In the inception meetings with the communities, the SO introduced HDF and the partners involved in the project. She dealt with various concepts such as *taraqi* (development) and *ittefaq* (unity) and also gave examples from Islamic history. She provided a cultural context to her work and, as a Pukhtun, tried to establish affinity with the community. Various features of the HDF program such as credit, savings, and various vocational trainings were highlighted.

There were many queries from the women regarding the credit and savings program, especially regarding *sood* (interest) on loans. The SO explained the HDF microcredit program and the issue of *sood* in very simple terms. She explained the concept of inflation by giving an example from the community's own experience. Suppose one of them purchased a buffalo and sold it after a year, would it sell for the same price? She argued that the price of the buffalo would increase over time. The same amount of money, therefore, could not buy the same product worth over time. The women were persuaded by the argument. While, they showed an interest in participating in the program, they indicated they would consult their menfolk and take their *razaa* (advice) and *ijaazat* (permission) regarding this activity.

The project introduction for the males also took place at the same time and according to the MSO, the youth were much exited about the project. At the time of the initial need assessment, the surveyors had indicated that the new program would disburse funds. The community viewed the project as an outside agency with plentiful funds at their disposal and that created high expectations. However, a local *maulvi* (cleric) raised an objection and referred to the microcredit program as *soodi* (interest bearing) and un-Islamic. Distrust was created in the community, among both men and women.

In later visits to the community, it was observed that the women, who were receptive to the project at the introductory meeting, had reservations regarding the credit aspect of the program after consulting their menfolk. On individual visits, the women were willing to participate in the project but no decision came from the community regarding the venue of the DO meeting. The women could not decide in which house to congregate, because, if some were allowed to go to one house, then there were a sizeable number of others who were not allowed to go there by their menfolk. This was because they belonged to a different lineage despite the fact that they were all Mohmand. Since *tarburwali* (see chapter 4) was strong here, young girls were not allowed to go to various houses to attend a meeting or training.

Keeping this in mind, it was decided to postpone the microcredit program. The main focus was upon the vocational training programs and savings to enhance community interest and to gain its confidence. The FSO also followed this strategy on the eastern side (discussed later in the chapter). There was an emphasis on introducing fully subsidized vocational training in the communities. When questioned about the sustainability of this step, the project staff was of the view that, as the community confidence was low at this stage, they had to do this to generate some initial interest. Later, the community would be involved in sharing the training cost.

The HDF field staff was of the view that, initially, the issue of credit raises a lot of problems as some community members think of it as being against Islamic injunctions. This was creating problems for social mobilization because the community leaders held negative views on this issue. During visits to the community, after the project introduction took place, many were questioned about their willingness to participate in the project. The reply was: "We don't know, this is up to the *killi masharaan* (village elders). We cannot do anything unless they initiate it."

Among women in particular, no effort was ever made to get an endorsement for the microcredit program. Later in the year, there were a few attempts made by the HDF to mobilize women, but they failed for different reasons. Death in the village (whenever there is a death in the village, the meetings are cancelled as no one congregates), rain, and a few times the lack of coordination among partner, all resulted in abortive attempts.

In June 2000, HDF again attempted to mobilize women on the western (Fazal Killay) side of the village. They directly approached the community and a project introduction also took place. At the date given for DO formation, women did not show up because there was some construction work in the locality. The women could not come out of the house, as there were a lot of male laborers in the streets. There was no substantive response from the village women as there was no house where all were allowed or willing to congregate.

Also, the men of the village did not encourage this activity and said that their women did not require development-related activities. They were happy with the health and education programs and felt it was enough. Individually, there were cases of women in different house-holds who wanted embroidery training (such as were taking place on the other side of the village) for their daughters and themselves. However, they wanted the training in their house and were not willing to collectively go to another mutually selected place for this purpose.

6.4.2.1.2 Male Mobilization Both the male and female SOs initiated the social mobilization strategy at the same time on the western side (Fazal Killay) of the village. The entry points were the two TMF schools, and the services of the schoolteachers were utilized as they were from among the community.

The teachers in these schools were related to the elders of their section of the village. Shahnawaz—teacher at of the TMF School on the *nehr ghara* (canal end)—was a distant relative of Gul Muhammad, who was the elder or influential (*mashar*) of this section of the village. He took part in the *jirga* (council of elders) and also distributed the *zakat* fund given to him by the district *zakat* committee for dispersal in the village.[4] He was also the support person of the APPNA program in this village. Because of his higher educational qualification, Shahnawaz was elected to be the secretary of the DO and Gul Muhammad was chosen to be the president. As the village elder, it was taken for granted that Gul Muhammad would be the DO president.[5]

This DO was the Fazal Killay male DO 1, formed in September 1999. The MSO, at an earlier stage, had pointed to the lack of internal activists and mobilization in this DO. He was of the opinion that the community was interested in getting as much money out of HDF as they could. In the meetings, they would demand loans much above the HDF limit of Rs. 30,000 and ask the HDF to provide fertilizer and other agricultural inputs for their land. However, they would never come up with an investment plan of their own using their own resources.

Another issue pointed out by the MSO was the lack of genuine leadership in the DO. It was very difficult to bypass the village elders who could highjack the whole process for their own ends. They insisted on involvement, despite a lack of genuine interest in the DO or a willingness to put in an effort to mobilize it. The objection to being excluded was premised on their canny understanding that the DO had the potential to change the power dynamics of the social set up. It takes some time to filter out potential deactivating agents from the DO. Once the process gets underway and the concerned members do not see any direct benefit, they might take a back seat and allow the younger, more active and interested members to assert leadership, assuming they view the DO as nonthreatening.

According to the social organizer, he could recognize such potential hijackers but he could not interfere and remove them from any decision-making position because this may have led to discontentment among the community. At this time, the local institutions were very strong and the project could not openly challenge them. This decision has to come from within the community, and they had to be involved in it to take ownership for their decisions.

The president approached the social organizer and asked for credit for himself. On being refused, he raised objections regarding the issue of *sood* on the loan given by HDF. The community at this time also criticized the microcredit policy of HDF (see section 3). Since the *mashar* is culturally deferred to by the *kashar* (younger), the word of the *mashar* cannot be disputed. The DO chair-holders did not even attend the Community Management Skills Training (CMST) arranged by the HDF in their Mardan office. The president also told the secretary to not to attend, as he was himself not attending the workshop.

Since its inception, the DO was not regular in its meetings, and attendance was also low. As this is an agrarian economy, the DO meetings were affected by agricultural activity, particularly during the sugarcane season between October and January that keeps the men very busy. The secretary failed to mobilize the other members to attend meetings because he had no active support from the president. The DO was considered to be inactive or dead by the social organizer, as they were either not holding meetings or the attendance was very poor.

The nature of leadership that needs to be identified for the program is different for the three partners, as the nature of the package they offer is different. It was a constant complaint of the HDF field staff that the local sponsors and leaders identified and used by APPNA are actually deactivists and not suitable for their social mobilization strategy. They felt that the service provided by the APPNA staff is subsidized and of a door-to-door nature. Thus the model followed by them is of a more inclusive nature because they have to count on the goodwill of the traditional village heads and on their local support and sponsorship. By contrast, the HDF follows a participatory model and they require local leadership that is active and an aid to mobilization. Also, DO members are drawn on a voluntary self-select basis and they, rather than the whole village, are the direct beneficiaries.

With a few exceptions, the traditional leadership of the villages in the project area failed to fulfill the requirements needed by the social mobilization process. One of the reasons given by them for not actively participating was that they were too busy in their own work-related activities and did not have the time for organizing the DO. As these leaders saw little individual benefit for themselves, they were not motivated to act on behalf of the DO to motivate the community members.

The youth of the village, though more receptive toward the project, took a more passive position in the DO meetings in conformity to local traditions. The idea of having an age limit on the DO membership or youth organizations was not upheld by the project staff, because this would limit the activities and outreach of the DO. There were a few examples from the project area where the youth had actively participated in the DO program as chair-holders and their DO was very active. In one instance, a youth was asked why the *tanzeem* did not do well in their village and he replied, "it was all in the hands of the *masharaan* (village elders) and, since they are old fashioned and have limited understanding of the mobilization process, they did not do much in this regard."

The project needs to wait for a longer period of time to filter out the potential DO "hijackers" and "deactivists." This is where internal DO monitoring needs to be institutionalized such that the DO chair-holders are accountable for the position they hold. In the beginning, they acquired the position by tradition, but as the process goes further, they should have to earn the right to retain the position held by them. They have to be held accountable to the DO, irrespective of their social status, and this is where internal performance evaluation needs to be introduced along with internal elections at the end of a certain predetermined period. Since such a practice clashes with the existing culture, this will be a slow process a dynamic community would need to be willing to initiate.

In September 2000, HDF staff developed a questionnaire for planning at the DO level. This was designed to collect information regarding the current status of the DO savings, credit, training, education, and health-related activities. It was also designed to acquire information regarding the future plans of the DO: estimated annual savings, loans required, investment in new enterprises, amount of internal lending, and increase in membership; potential for DO formation in the vicinity and for economic development not involving finance from HDF; and plans for sustaining the TMF schools and improving the health program.

The exercise was aimed at developing planning skills at the community level and giving the DO objectives to follow through on. This was to be a joint effort and the social organizer at a DO meeting was to fill the questionnaire after a mutual discussion with the community members present. During discussions, the HDF field staff was of the opinion that this activity would lead to even greater expectations on the part of the community from the project and was of an unrealistic nature.

The second male DO on the western side was made in the section of the village called the *killay manz* (village center). There were two TMF schools in this part of the village, and they were usually referred to by the names of their teachers as Jameel's school and Iqbal's school. As Jameel's father was the *mashar* (elder) of this section of the village, the community members automatically took him to be the president of the DO. As earlier indicated, the elder of the community needs to be included in the project, especially in the beginning, as this gives it social acceptance. Also, they are to be made the president because this position is seen to correspond to their already existing social prestige in the community. After a few months, the president delegated this position to another person he nominated because he was too old and sick to participate in DO related activities.

The social organizer was not satisfied with this DO either, but it was performing better than its counterpart on this side of the village. During the winter season, the meetings and attendance were not satisfactory due to agricultural activity. Even this DO had reservations about the microcredit program of the HDF, and this was the cause of their irregular meetings and slow response to the mobilization efforts of the HDF. They were of the view that HDF was not consistent in their credit program and that the policy was changing all the time, which led to a lack of trust in the program. As these reservations persisted, the community could not capitalize on various training opportunities such as welding and computer training.

The social mobilization strategy of the HDF required the DO members to hold regular meetings and register savings at the end of the meetings. Members absent without any valid reason in more than two consecutive meetings had their membership cancelled. Every resolution coming from the DO required signatures of at least 80 percent of the present members. On several occasions, the DO reached a decision and drafted a resolution that could not be forwarded to the SO because the DO attendance fell short of the required 80 percent. This slowed down activity, because the DO had to wait for two weeks until the next meeting took place.

The SO was asked by community members to remove the names of the members who were consistently absent from meetings. This way, all those members not interested in the activity would be filtered out, and DO meetings would be more productive. Also, delay would not be caused by a lack of quorum. The SO's response was that the members should take steps on their own to remove such delinquent members from community self-governance.

Once again, this is where one has to keep in mind that this is a culture where members practice conflict avoidance. *Badal* (revenge) is a very important aspect of Pukhtunwali (Pukhtun code of honor) and, because of this, conflicts can take a very nasty turn (see chapter 4). Conflicts not only persist over a long period of time with the two parties trying to outdo each other in an attempt to save face, they are also violent and economically taxing. This is why the DO members do not openly challenge any one's membership or remove them from the DO. At times, members approached the SO separately to inform him about another member's unreliability. This is an important tool used by the SO to crosscheck unreliability of members regarding various DO matters, since the members do not openly get involved in a discussion in meetings regarding fellow DO members.

6.4.2.2   Fazal Killay (eastern)

6.4.2.2.1   *Female Mobilization* The response to social mobilization conducted on this side of the village yielded better results as compared to the other side. There was no prior education-related intervention on this side and, because of the mistrust between the APPNA and HDF staff, the social organizer did not involve the Health Assistants in this effort. On September 17, 1999, the project introduction took place at Nasir Khan's (a village elder) house. Unlike her project introduction on the western side, her presentation here did not introduce the HDF credit package. Her main focus was on livestock, embroidery training, and uses of savings.

RSPs operating in Pakistan (see chapter 3) often do not introduce any program packages to the community during the initial dialogue. They only talk about what the community can do on a self-help basis. This is more of a "finding out" dialogue aimed at judging the willingness of the community to help itself. Packages related to credit and training are introduced at a later stage. The HDF project introduction is, however, more package-oriented. By immediately introducing the community to what HDF can do for them, they gave the image of a donor organization, thus giving rise to high expectations. When these expectations were not fulfilled, it led to discontentment on the part of the community. That is one of the reasons why the community at times complains that the project is slow in service delivery.

An important factor contributing to the success of the participatory model is the presence of community activists. There was no community activist in this part of the village who could mobilize women. As such, there was no one willing to give this project sponsorship. As earlier mentioned, another drawback was the lack of coordination between the partners at the field level. As there was no joint planning or a regular exchange of plans, any social mobilization–related activity in this part of the village could not be dovetailed with related partner activity.

6.4.2.2.2   *Male Mobilization* In the village Fazal Killay (eastern), the DO was formed on January 22, 2000, with seventeen members. During the project introduction and DO formation, the members welcomed HDF with great enthusiasm. They made a movie of the project introduction and gifted a copy to HDF. In the second and third meetings of the DO, attendance and saving of the members were encouraging. In the fourth meeting a resolution was passed to give credit worth Rs. 20,000 to Zardad, a member of the DO.

During the appraisal meeting, Bashir Khan, the president of the DO, told the members that the loan would be repaid without interest or "profit," which was in any case against the HDF credit policy. The SO again explained the whole procedure and the HDF credit policy to the DO members. But Bashir Khan time and again told the members that the HDF credit would be repaid without profit. He tampered with the DO terms of partnership (TOP) and changed "with profit" to "without profit." He showed the changed TOP to the DO members, and told them that HDF had mentioned in its TOP that the loan was without profit. As a result of his antics, credit was refused to Zardad.

After this, Bashir met with the office bearers of other DOs and told them that the HDF credit program was interest-based and formed a United Front against HDF. He attempted to forge a partnership with other DOs in the project area to oppose HDF credit policy, given that his personal request for a loan was turned down. He also gave negative projection to other project-related activities in the village and later also blamed the social organizer for not explaining the program properly or cooperating with him.

HDF decided to form a cluster organization of the DOs in order to tackle this situation. Their hope was that the cluster organization would institutionalize the social mobilization activity that was taking place in the community more broadly and also create the basis for collective action to address the needs of several DOs at the same time.

There were some reservations on part of the field staff regarding the cluster formation. They were of the opinion that the DOs were not mature enough for the time being. The potential "hijackers" in the DOs could also filter into the cluster and jeopardize the whole process. The experience of other RSPs showed that cluster formation took place after a minimum period of about three years. By this time, the COs attain a certain level of maturity and have ample experience of the participatory process, and they have by then also acquired the community management skills through various trainings. Thus, in their view, HDF needed to proceed with caution, as many DOs did not meet the maturity criteria required for cluster formation.

By the time the United Front issue arose, on April 2000, many grievances had accumulated against the HDF in the community. One complaint of the DO members was the unbecoming conduct of the female staff of the three project partners in that they traveled in project transport with male staff members. Later, in a meeting in June, when the United Front had fizzled out, the SO had a long meeting with the DO members in which the SO addressed all objections.

The allegations against the female staff were proven wrong and the community reaffirmed their support for them. The SO was unable to convince the DO in principle regarding the issue of interest in the microcredit package of the HDF. However, the community decided not to avail this package but decided to utilize other facilities provided by the program such as training, health, and education. They also decided to reorganize themselves and start holding regular meetings. However, they told the SO that they did not require a female DO.

Later, in an individual encounter with the social organizer, the president told him that he did not want to take responsibility for other members in the DO for taking loans and thus he did not encourage the practice. Now, he was willing to make another DO consisting of only his direct family members as he could take responsibility for their loan allocation. The SO discouraged this course of action as the project does not cater to individual families and because this was viewed as a dubious self-serving suggestion. Consequently, the DO remained inactive as of September 2000. Meanwhile, feeling rebuked again, Bashir invited *mullahs* (clerics) from the surrounding areas to declare the HDF credit program as interest-based but he again failed in this effort. During this period, he met with the RPM (regional program manager) and requested a job in HDF. This demand was also turned down and he was told to respond to a job advertisement when one was placed in the newspaper. The Fazal Killay–III DO remained inactive, and all the efforts to reactivate it had been in vain during our fieldwork.

There appears to be a thin line between activists and "hijackers" in the RSPs. From the conversations of the SOs, it seems that the activists are hard to come by and are very crucial for the success of the intervention based on social mobilization. At the same time, if the activists start taking control of the initiative or learn to figure out the system to get maximum benefit for their household, lineage, or DO, they become dubbed hijackers in the internal project language. The distinction from the local leader's point of view seems to be one of ownership and control while from the project's point of view it is one of individual versus collective benefits.

6.4.2.3   Kandare Jadeed

6.4.2.3.1   Female Mobilization   In the initial contact that took place in early October 1999, there was confusion regarding the parameters of Charcha. The first contact was to be initiated through the APPNA health assistant (HA) and the entry point was to be the health support group they had established there. The initial contact could not take place as there was a lack of coordination between the SO and the HA. The convening time given to the women by the HA was not suitable for them because at 2:00 pm they were busy working in the fields and getting fodder for the cattle. Attendance at the meeting was very poor and the SO waited an hour for the women to assemble. As Kandare Jadeed was separated from the main village, Charcha, the HDF SO decided to initiate the project intervention herself and decided to have the project introduction at the house of Haji Shakirullah. As the HDF staff was conducting a field survey at the village, they were utilized to spread the word around the village regarding the project introduction.

The project introduction by the SO was brief as compared to the other ones. In the introduction, she did not touch on the issue of credit, as that would have led to controversy. Her strategy was to initially introduce the training package of HDF, as women readily accepted this package and it helped in gaining trust. Thus, her strategy was to first gain trust and then introduce the credit package. A potential activist was identified in this first meeting. After the SO finished her dialogue, she invited them to join the project. Women were interested in training in embroidery and sewing and told the SO that they would consult their men and, if permitted, they would join the organization.

In the last week of October, during the field survey of Kandare Jadeed, the women were again asked whether they wanted to participate in the DO or not. They were very indecisive about this and were waiting to see how the male villagers would respond to this initiative. The men, however, showed little interest in this social mobilization process (next subsection).

All the interested women were supposed to congregate at the house of Haji Shakirullah on October 27, 1999. However, nobody showed up because of a death in the village. Some women later informed the SO that they were interested in forming a DO but they were waiting for a response from the other women in the village. One woman said that the men did not talk about this issue and that when one woman asked, she was reprimanded.

6.4.2.3.2 *Male Mobilization* On the male side, the PTA formation of the TMF School was used as an entry point for the HDF project on October 13, 1999. The first project introduction took place and the members of the PTA were used to help spread the word around and collect people. The meeting took place at a local elder's (Adam Khan) place. There were two households in the village that were of equal socioeconomic standing: those of Haji Shakirullah and Adam Khan. It is for this reason that Haji Sahkirullah did not attend the meeting, but his son was present. All the participants were very enthusiastic and indicated a willingness to form a DO. They all decided to congregate again on October 20, 1999, to form the DO.

In this second meeting on October 20, 1999, all the interested individuals gathered in the mosque but Adam Khan backed out at the last moment. As in the case of the PTA formation, he had initially shown full support for the expansion of the TMF School but was later concerned that he would end up shouldering all the responsibility of building the school. Based on consensus, Rehmanullah, son of Haji Shakirullah, was chosen to be the president of the DO, as Shakirullah backed out due to old age and sickness. Another educated young man in the village was selected as secretary. Though Adam Khan did not attend the meeting, all of his sons became members of the DO. A week after this meeting, the president and the secretary attended the CMST at the HDF office.

Attendance at the third meeting of the DO in the first week of November was affected by rain and only nine members were present. However, the SO was very happy with the way the DO secretary and president conducted the meeting and utilized the knowledge they had acquired at the training course. They explained various concepts such as savings and other uses of DO formation to the members present.

At the fourth DO meeting, no member turned up except for the secretary and the president. They were questioned about the attendance, to which they replied that they had gone from house to house to remind the members about the meeting the day before and even so no one turned up. They had decided to convene another meeting at the mosque to discuss the issue of attendance.

The SO was meanwhile contacted by other people of the village who told him that the present DO would not work because most of the members in the village do not accept the leadership of the current president, Sharkirullah's son, who belonged to a different lineage. In characteristic Pukhtun fashion, during the DO formation, Shakirullah absented himself and the others endorsed the leadership of his son. Adam Khan's sons supported the son in public to avoid antagonizing

Shakirullah but later they and their supporters voted with their feet to indicate how they felt about the leadership.

6.5   Assessment of Social Mobilization

Social mobilization is particularly difficult in this community due to a cultural suspicion of outsiders, poverty (and subsequently the primary concern for making a living), and the deference to influentials. Different development NGOs have different strategies to deal with the dominant role of "influentials." HDF needs to give this more thought particularly as it appears that, culturally, the young in Pukhtun society generally defer to the "elders" and even avoid speaking before them. Experience seems to suggest that once the "elders" establish their prestige-based claim to hosting DO meetings, they have little time for the DO and the more energetic and enthusiastic are prevented from participating fully. Also given the history of peasant struggles for land in this area (see chapter 4) the khans or influentials were vary of any mode of organization that brought the peasants together and hence tried to discourage it.

We interviewed the ex-head of a now defunct DO who had forged a grouping called the United Front against interest on loans. There was little he said that left an impression, except for his complaint that the TOP provided by HDF to the community was a fait accompli with the community having no say in the matter. This was notable and something that HDF should think about as participation is central to the model it purports to be following. While there are obvious complexities involved with tailoring the TOP for individual DOs, it still needs to have them viewed by communities as a partnership they understand and value rather than as one imposed on them. This particular community had subsequently shown an interest in DO formation and the community view was that credit was only one component of the package and, a component they did not have to opt for. That the HDF responded positively speaks well of the flexibility and persistence of the field staff.

HDF had encouraged an initiative of the community to form a supra-DO organization in the form of a cluster organization. This was done by the AKRSP and BRSP (Balochistan Rural Support Program) in the context of marketing. Here it is important to follow the principle of "subsidiarity." Thus any issue that can be resolved effectively at the DO level should be, and any issue that involves inter-DO relations should be part of the cluster organization mandate. A good example of a cluster organization collective action came up while we attended a DO meeting. The community members were expressing their resentment at a local landlord who was using his land as an open dumpsite for making fertilizer. This had multiplied the fly population and was perceived as having increased the incidence of disease. As this issue concerned several DOs, collective action at the cluster level was an ideal way of tackling this problem.

It was encouraging to see that collective action at the DO level was working in the well-functioning DOs. The community proudly pointed to the dredging of the watercourse and the road repair that they had done on their own initiative. Another example we encountered was the community collectively providing water supply for the school. However, in general, social mobilization is clearly an extremely difficult process to initiate, as it requires winning trust, and even more difficult, to sustain it. Some examples will explain this statement.

The deference to the elders was a potential discouragement and impediment to the participation of the young men. Also, various hostilities in the community played out in the various forums created by HDF such as the parent teacher association (PTA) and Health Committee for both men and women. Selecting an appropriate time of meetings for both genders was of utmost importance. Given the agrarian economy, conflict with the agricultural activity calendar meant almost no attendance. Similarly, cultural obligations such as attending marriages or funerals took precedence over DO meetings and the SOs have to be sensitive to such issues.

The task of the women social organizers was made difficult by the near complete female illiteracy. Several mosques were present in a large village and so several DOs, both male and female, were created in a village. The mosques were used for *ailans* (announcements of meetings). Defining the community based on mosque catchments was even more relevant and important for women because of severe restrictions on female mobility, even across the village, and because congregating at the house of someone from a different lineage, particularly if there was clan enmity, was not acceptable.

Another problem confronted by FSOs was the complete lack of experience women had of meetings and the basic norms governing them. Thus, ensuring order at meetings required a very assertive social organizer. Beyond that, the complete dependence of women on men and therefore having to refer back all key decisions to men slowed progress. The cultural resistance among women to playing any social role beyond being mothers and homemakers required the SO to constantly appeal to cultural and religious symbols for social mobilization. This included referring to the conduct of profitable business by Prophet Mohammed's wife.

It was painstakingly difficult for the SO to get across the importance of taking responsibility seriously. Thus, women found it difficult to understand that being DO members required attending meetings and engaging in regular savings; that it really was a big deal when someone tried to gatecrash a training without being a DO member; that their staying on in the meeting to sign a resolution for a DO member to get credit or training really was important even if they personally were not interested in the training. Changing old attitudes and individually motivated behavior into those conducive to collective consciousness and collective action is difficult. Thus, enthusiasm for membership was high while there was the promise of embroidery training, but it immediately slackened when the training was over.

The challenge for the SO was to be constantly alert to sustaining the momentum of social mobilization. Quickly disbursed credit sparked attention, but the real challenge was to be able to persuade the women that collective action could in small ways improve their quality of life in tasks such as keeping the neighborhood clean. The social mobilization remains superficial until the internal dynamic for such collective action is kindled based on community social capital.

Summary

This chapter establishes two main points. First, that development NGOs need to understand the cultural context for success in harnessing, formalizing, and guiding social capital in a participatory development framework. Second, even with that understanding, the process of social mobilization for building and sustaining village DOs that formalize, embody, and extend social capital is extremely difficult.

Some of the difficulties that the Pukhtun culture posed include the deference to the influentials or khans. The latter were more concerned with preserving social order and keeping their authority intact and consequently showed little motivation and energy in the leadership position and impeded the young and enthusiastic from assuming it. In one particular case, denial of a loan to an influential resulted in his starting a campaign against HDF using Islamic injunctions against interest charged on microcredit. Thus, this potential leader, when it seemed that his own ambitions were being thwarted, formed a United Front against the project on the pretext of fighting the practice of collecting interest (*sood*). This group also created a situation by getting the community to object to the joint traveling of HDF male and female staff in the office vehicle. However, communities have horse sense and resilience and they were able to bypass this person when they felt persuaded that the project was making possible individual and collective benefits via a participatory, self-help, and collective action approach. For example, one community got together and built a drinking water facility for the school and another community collectively dredged an irrigation channel.

For project success, as much depends on winning and retaining community trust, our word of caution was that consolidation and slow and measured expansion should be the approach to social capital harnessing via social mobilization. However, based on donor pressure, HDF expanded within the first year of its existence to establish its presence in other provinces as well.

The Pukhtun culture places a premium on being strong and capable of avenging an injury. As such, it is more individualistic than collective in orientation. In such a society, the cost of conflict is very high in terms of loss of life and other costs. Hence, in "group" behavior, there is an attempt to avoid confrontation. Social organizers need to handle both delicately and strategically information that might be volunteered to them privately.

The frustrations confronted by the women social organizers were much greater. Women were illiterate and had little sense of how meetings are run and had to be taught from scratch. In addition, the limits to mobility in a conservative and conflict-prone society and the deference of all key decisions to men made decision making slow. Like men, women were often motivated by what they could get from the project and many lost interest if that was not forthcoming or once it was received.

In addition to these problems, social mobilizers confronted suspicion, inertia, and initially an unwillingness to spare time from daily activities for meetings. At times, this was because of conflicts between the timings of agricultural activities and that of NGO-related programs, and at other times due to culturally mandated attendance of events such as funerals and marriages or an unwillingness to engage in collective action or accept the leadership of others from a different lineage. APPNA had been working in the area for over a decade and could easily have created the goodwill for the social mobilizers, but tensions among partners and the need for different mobilization strategies limited the benefits of an effective entry point into the community.

As a health program, APPNA served the whole village while HDF needed to define the community in a more operational sense, for example, all those going to the same mosque formed a DO. Even within this community, HDF needed to work with those volunteering to become members. As a consequence, HDF staff pointed to the APPNA program as welfare oriented whereas they viewed themselves as the truer embodiment of participatory development for catalyzing collective action. There were similar counteraccusations from the APPNA staff. As a consequence, the lack of communication and joint planning resulted in field inefficiencies.

APPNA staff resented having been upstaged by HDF, in the sense of its not being in the coordinating and leadership position and its staff not having better facilities, such as transport, even though they had a long prior presence in the field. The TNF catchment was also broader, like that of APPNA, but given that they owed their presence in the area to HDF, there was closer cooperation between them and HDF. TMF teachers often served as an entry point for social mobilization by getting the parents together for an initial meeting and by also serving as DO secretaries.

Apart from the difficulties posed by the cultural environment and the nature of the social mobilization process itself, the HDF social mobilization strategy compounded the difficulties. One disaffected village leader made a telling point by indicating that the TOP were not discussed or participatory in any way and that this was presented to the community as a fait accompli. While tailoring the TOP to each community would not be possible, better communication may have helped. Also, HDF realized that they had to offer something to create an interest, but again the communications strategy may have been faulty as very high expectations were created in communities about *sarkari paisa* (official funds) and that HDF was somehow coming in the way of their due.

Given the cultural and other obstacles to social mobilization, the lack of interpartner synergy in the initial period, and mistakes that are inevitable for any development NGO as it gets established, it is remarkable that HDF achieved as much as it did in its first year (see chapters 9 and 10). It is important to keep in mind that our account is based on two randomly selected villages out of the initial six they made interventions in. In the concluding chapter, we narrate how HDF has become a national project, highlight some of its achievements, and provide an indication of the cost-effectiveness of the project. We turn now to a review of the health and education interventions of APPNA and TMF in the next two chapters.

ANNEXURE 6.1

A More Detailed Account of the Social Mobilization

Fazal Killay (east): First Contact, September 13, 1999

Fazal Killay (east) did not have a TMF school like Fazal Killay (west), which had both a boy's and a girl's school at the time HDF started its social mobilization there. A few days earlier, a first contact had taken place in Fazal Killay (west). This was facilitated by the TMF girl's school teacher, not a local resident, and APPNA contacts. The FSO was not happy with the turnout, only 20 women showed up, and they were all mothers of students enrolled at the TMF School. Since the FSO had already introduced the topic of credit, the discussion had veered onto *sood* and it being *haram* (prohibited in Islam). This, along with male disinterest, negatively contributed to the female DO formation. The men believed that since they would participate in all the activities, such as credit or trainings, it was not necessary for the women to participate. Women took little initiative and they would not even decide on a meeting venue.

The FSO decided to focus instead on the other (east) side of the village that lay across the canal. The teacher of the girl's TMF school had told her that a number of women did not come because they were on the other side of the village and did not come to this side except for *killee ullas* (relations of social reciprocity—attending weddings and funerals). The FSO ascertained the *mashar* of the other side from the MSO and the APPNA traditional birth attendant (TBA), who was a local resident of Fazal Killay (west).

She visited the *mashar*, Nasir Khan, and spoke to his wife and his elderly father who was referred to as "baba." They seemed interested and the FSO gave them a date and time on which she would make her project introduction. She asked them to collect as many females of the village as they could at their house. Baba was a patriarch and would usually be present in the *kor* (house) instead of the *hujrah*. The women of the village and the project staff did not observe *purdah* from him and spoke to him very openly and in a relaxed manner. As there was no DO activity of males on this side, it was baba who initiated it by asking the female staff that they should have a similar *tanzeem* (organization) for men as well on their side of the village.

Fazal Killay (east): First Introduction September 17, 1999

As agreed, the HDF FSO arrived in the program vehicle at Nasir Khan's house at 9 am. As she entered the *kor* (house), avoiding the livestock that was tied in the open in the central courtyard, women of the household come forward to greet her. As this was a joint family, the wives of Nasir Khan's brothers and his daughters and daughters-in-law were all present. However, no other village women were congregated in the courtyard and this irritated the FSO as she had insisted that the womenfolk and baba (who was lounging on a charpoy in the veranda) gather the women by 9 am.

Nasir Khan came in and spoke to the FSO and said that he had been busy with a local *jirga* but will make an *aillan* (announcement) on the mosque loud-speaker to beckon the women. He also mentioned that as the women were likely to be busy with their chores and preparing lunch, some time might ensue before they arrive. The FSO decided to visit the TMF school on the other side of the village and said she would return in about an hour.

When the FSO came back by 10 am, about 13 women were sitting in the courtyard on charpoys and at 10:10 am, she started her dialogue. She stood up and asked the women to assemble the charpoys in a circle. She started with the recitation of a Quranic *Surah* (verse) and then went on to introduce her-self, HDF, APPNA, and TMF as the project partners and also their work in the field. She told them that although it had been about fifty years or more now since independence, their condition has changed little. There are no roads, proper schools, health facilities in their village. APPNA started their program here with the help of a few Pakistani doctors in America and the community has benefited from that. The women all nodded in agreement. She said that the same people have again collaborated and drawn on their earnings to help improve the economic conditions of this area, adding that the project's success depends on the women's willingness to help themselves. She clarified that she did not come as a representative of the government.

The FSO asked the women, "What is *taraqi* (development)?" Nasir Khan's wife replied that

> it is a condition in which no one is *mohtaj* (dependant) on anyone. We are not here to give out alms but to help guide you, the FSO continued. A car has four wheels and an engine but without the steering-wheel you cannot direct it and control it. In the same way, HDF is like a steering-wheel and we will help guide you in your efforts to improve the quality of your lives.

She continued,

> we are all Pukhtane (Pukhtuns) and come from Pukhtun households. We are not here to break the traditional norms but to maintain them. Keeping within the limits of Pukhtana (Pukhtunwali), we will help you realize your goals. We do not want anyone to be a *pardagee* (one who violates *pardah*) and you will not be asked to leave your homes or village without the con-sent of your menfolk. However, you will be able to participate in the activ-ities of the *tanzeem* (DO) and improve your lives. This will be like a women's *hujrah*. All this time, the women listened to her very attentively.

The FSO then said:

you must be wondering "*da tanzeem se balla da?*" (What monster is this *tanzeem?*). *Tanzeem* means *ittifaq* (unity) and our religion states "*ittifaq ke barkat de*" (there is blessing in unity) and the *jirga* is also based on *ittifaq* through which we can solve our various problems. Just as the *jirga* needs a *mashar* to help resolve issues, the *tanzeem* also needs *mashars*. A *tanzeem* needs two *mashars*, a *sadar* (president) and a secretary. You know how we women waste our time in gossiping and "*tawail mawail*" (you said, I said) or in our homes mothers-in-law and daughters-in-law fight with each other. We have *mashar* women whose experience can be utilized in the *tanzeem*.

A *tanzeem* has a lot of benefits such as trainings for maintaining livestock as all of you own some livestock. You can also learn sowing and embroidery and you will also be saving money, which you can use later as one never knows when the need may arise. You know that you cannot go to the town or city for such trainings and no one is going to come here and give you trainings at home. You also cannot go to the bank, but you can bank through the *tanzeem* and reap many benefits. We are not asking you to leave your homes and we know the menfolk will not like that and we are not asking you to do that and create problems for you at home.

If you make any product for the *bazaar* (market), you cannot sell it directly and a middleman buys it from you at a very low cost and sells it for high profit. We will help you with this marketing and make sure you get good prices. Women in Islam, such as *Bibi* Khadija (Prophet Muhammad's wife), who was a business woman, have been very entrepreneurial.

She went on to explain that a *tanzeem* was very important and if they run it well they will reap its benefits:

The *tanzeem* has to meet regularly twice a month and you have to save regularly as well, at least once a month. So if you want to go ahead with this then let me know. To this Nasir Khan's wife replied that this was indeed very good for all of them and that their menfolk knew all about it. Also, some of them have children at the TMF schools and all benefit from the *doctaraan* (referring to the APPNA staff) who visit them. They decided to go ahead with forming a tanzeem.

The FSO asked them about who will be the *masharan* (elder). The women looked at Nasir Khan's wife and said that as she is their *mashar* already, they see no reason why she cannot be the *mashar* in the *tanzeem*. Nasir Khan's sister-in-law (brother's wife), who lived in the same household, was nominated as the secretary. As no woman among the congregation that had collected there was literate enough to maintain the DO records, the FSO decided to maintain them. She told the president and secretary that they had to take care of the registers and also ensure that women attend all the meetings. She filled out the registers and entered the names of the women and made entries in the *karavai* register (minutes register) for the day. She assigned the date and time for the next meeting.

Fazal Killay (east): First DO Meeting, October 6, 1999

When we arrived at Nasir Khan's house at the assigned time for the meeting, no one was present. The women said they will get the meeting announced via the mosque loudspeaker and also sent out children to call the women from their homes. The president of the DO was asked by the researcher what she understood from the last meeting and her response was "nothing, I do not understand or remember what the FSO had talked about." Meanwhile, an announcement was made from the mosque loudspeaker asking the women to congregate at Nasir Khan's house as "health workers" who were dealing with the *bachat* (savings) scheme had arrived.

As the women started coming in, some told us that they remembered the meeting but were waiting for the announcement. Others said they did not remember or were doing chores such as cutting grass for their livestock. The secretary did not remember the meeting and was visiting family. The young girls in the growing congregation were excited about the embroidery trainings they had heard about. As the number of women reached about thirty, the FSO started the proceedings.

She talked about the *tanzeem* formation saying that

now that you have formed one, you must take responsibility for it. I had asked you that if you cannot attend meetings, then do not become members but you all decided to join. However, today your behaviour has contradicted your stated intentions. It is not possible to make announcements and send people after you begging you to come each time; you have to be serious about this. Those of you who cannot commit to attending meetings should take your names off the registers. You remember wedding dates but not meeting dates and that is because you think these are a waste of time and you are not serious about them.

After this reprimand, she again explained the savings process and issued individual savings booklet to each member. She also introduced the HDF credit package but avoided details. The women asked when the trainings will begin and the FSO queried them about an appropriate place where the training could be held so that all the women could easily come.

Nasir Khan's wife said that her household had no space for this activity. Her sister (Galoona), who lived about fifty yards away in the same neighborhood, replied that she had seven daughters, her sons were very young, and her husband was in Saudi Arabia as a laborer and therefore her house was a *khazo kor* (women's house). Thus, women could easily come and go all day as they pleased (she also had an empty room available). The FSO noted that since the membership of this DO had become too large (over 40), she would divide the DO into two and Galoona could be the president of the other DO. She agreed to the trainings being held in her house and said that members of both DOs could attend.

Fazal Killay (east): DO Division, October 9, 1999

The FSO arrived at Nasir Khan's house. A few women were already present and the women of the house made the children run out and call the others. In a few minutes, about thirty women had congregated. They were all talking among themselves, and the FSO called the meeting to order. New members were also added to the already long list of DO members. The FSO reminded them that due to large membership, she was dividing the DO and hence two DOs were formed in Fazal Killay (east): Fazal Killay I, whose president was Nasir Khan's wife and Fazal Killay II, whose president was Nasir Khan's sister (Galoona). Names were called out and the women chose the DO they wanted to be in and those not present were allocated to one of the two DOs on the basis of their proximity to the houses in which the DO meetings were to take place.

The FSO gave a meeting date to the women of Fazal Killay II and asked them to leave, while the women of Fazal Killay I were asked to stay. She took the savings cards of DO members to note the change. After this activity, the FSO spoke to the women about the conduct of future meetings. She said bringing infants to the meetings is fine as long as they do not create a disruption. She expressed her appreciation for the fact that the women had congregated without an announcement. She then asked them to place the charpoys in a circle so that everyone would know what is going on. The president and the secretary are to maintain decorum. The women are to kindly refrain from talking at the same time; everyone will be given a chance to voice their views but one at a time. To this, one of the elderly participants noted, "*da de mairay khaze dee, doee se katale nadee*" (these are women of the maira, they have not seen much).

Toward the end of the meeting, the FSO made some announcements. She focused on the fact that training is not the aim of the *tanzeem* and that there are other aspects of it that need to be paid some attention. In particular, the members need to hold regular meetings and save regularly and later they can use this *tanzeem* (as it strengthens) for other benefits. Finally, she took attendance using the registers provided by HDF (the members indicated presence with thumb prints) and announced the date for the next meeting.

Fazal Killay (east): New DO Formation, October 11, 1999

The FSO went to Galoona's house at the announced time. She skipped the project introduction speech, indicating that the women present had already heard it. She tallied the women present with her list, gave them their own register and noted the savings in the booklets. New booklets were handed out to the new members. This activity took a while. Galoona recommended that another elderly lady, who lived next to her house, should be the president as she was a *mashar* and that she should became the secretary instead. That notwithstanding, the DO came to be known by Galoona's name among the HDF project staff who continued to deal with her.

Fazal Killay (east): DO I and II Meetings, November 8, 1999

The last meetings of both the DOs were cancelled by the FSO as there was a death on the western side of the village. She assumed that the majority of the women would not be able to attend the meeting. The FSO was told by the DO president and secretary that they thought that the *tanzeem* and HDF had been disbanded because Prime Minister Nawaz Sharif's government had been removed by the military. The FSO clarified that HDF has nothing to do with the comings and goings of various governments and they are here to work.

It again took some time to bring together the members who complained: "We are tired of signing all these papers (referring to the attendance and savings registers, and the resolution for trainings) but nothing is happening. When is the training coming as the nearby village had already started one?" The FSO replied with a question: "Did you make the *tanzeem* only to get training?" The women asked who was eligible for the trainings and the FSO replied that all the members and their dependants were eligible. She clarified that dependents do not have to be DO members.

There were a number of questions in this meeting and women were comparatively more vocal. They wondered if the *tanzeem* and training were separate and the FSO clarified that the training was a benefit of being a member of the *tanzeem*. They asked how much and how many times do they have to save? The FSO answered that they have to save only once a month and as much as they can afford. Another participant asked that as she was not attending the training and was only saving could she just send her savings, through someone else? The FSO replied that attendance was a very important part of the *tanzeem* and two consecutive "absents" will result in cancellation of membership. However, one woman cancelled her membership on the grounds that she could save in her piggy bank at home and that as she was not going to avail the trainings, there was no need for her to get into this activity.

Savings were collected and the FSO did all the paperwork for it and handed the money to the president of the DO. Neither the president nor the secretary was yet clear about managing the savings. It was decided that the secretary's husband (Nasir Khan's brother) should help manage it as the women were not literate.

By now, the women were getting impatient about the training and asking openly when it would start. The FSO replied that the training can be initiated as soon as they identify a place where the training can be held, even tomorrow. The residence of Galoona, who was now secretary of Fazal Killay II, was identified as the training place for Fazal Killay I also. Nasir Khan's family, once informed accordingly by the FSO, had realized that no rent was to be paid for the room provided for the training and so they were not forthcoming in providing a room themselves. Guloona agreed to her house as the venue for Fazal Killay I training. Once the location was decided, the FSO wrote out a *qarardad* (resolution) and the members present attested it with their thumb prints. The names of the nominees for the trainings were also decided and noted by the FSO.

Once the decision about training was finalized, the women themselves broached the issue of credit: "*daa de karze se chal de?*" (What is up with this credit/lending?). Women were interested in taking credit for their husbands to initiate some economic activity. Some women wanted to speak to the FSO in private about credit, but the FSO insisted that all discussions pertaining to *tanzeem* activity must take place in an open forum and in front of all members. She said that she will have a detailed discussion on the topic of credit in the next meeting as the decisions made that day were enough.

After concluding this meeting, the SO and researcher walked over to the close by Fazal Killay DO II meeting place. A similar question-answer session took place there as well. Women wanted to know who would provide the sewing machines, could they be retained once the training was over, and would HDF pay rent for the room? The FSO clarified that HDF would provide the machines, but it is not a government organization and does not donate the machines as some government organizations are known to do. Instead, once the training ends, they will take away the machines which are HDF property (and will be used for other training). She also clarified that HDF will not pay any rent for the premises.

After this, the FSO did some housekeeping. She reduced the DO size, in accordance with HDF policy, by removing the names of young dependent girls whose mothers were already members. After this, she gave a similar talk on the conduct of meetings as she had done in Fazal Killay I. A similar resolution requesting training for the members was written by the FSO and was attested by the members, thereafter nominations for the training were noted.

Fazal Killay (east): Embroidery Training, November 11, 1999

The first embroidery trainings for the two DOs were initiated soon after. This brought up a number of issues as many girls wanted to attend the trainings but there was not enough space in the class. The nominees were mostly young girls whose mothers were DO members but many more, such as their cousins, who lived in the same household, too wanted to avail this facility. Many girls had siblings who wanted to take the training but could not as only one of them could according to HDF policy. This put the DO *masharaan* (elders / presidents and secretaries) in a very difficult position in their community. The FSO publicly reprimanded them for allowing more girls to attend the trainings than stipulated. Later she mentioned that she had to do that to take the pressure off the DO *mashars* so that the community does not hold a grudge or any ill-feeling against them.

Fazal Killay (east): First Credit Demand, December 11, 1999

Within a month of the training being initiated, a credit demand came from Fazal Killay I. Anticipating this, instead of the FSO, the female credit officer attended this meeting. She explained the credit process followed by HDF to the DO members and fielded many questions regarding its Islamic nature, the difference between credit given by HDF and a bank, and the mode of repayments. The credit officer explained that HDF loans are a business relationship of HDF with the community as permissible in Islam. She further stated that no bank comes to their village to engage in such business with them and local moneylenders charge exorbitant amounts in interest. HDF, however, is willing to do *karobar* (business) with them and brings all other facilities that a bank might offer to their doorstep. However, there is a cost of such service delivery, such as staff payrolls, rents, and transportation, and HDF covers this with a service charge. These are nominal amounts and are consistent with Islamic teachings (in the way that they are executed).

Five requests for credit were made ranging from Rs. 2,000 to 20,000 from the two DOs. Four of these were for initiating some businesses by the husbands of the female members and one was for the purchase of livestock. By December 30, 1999, the credit officer has conducted the credit appraisals for these requests with the concerned members.

Fazal Killay (east): Credit Disbursement, January 4, 2000

The first two credits were disbursed by the HDF credit officer in the female DOs of Fazal Killay (east). After these disbursements, the demand for credit and with it attendance went up in both the DOs. However, the DO members openly stated that they were not willing to take responsibility for anybody else. Also, questions about whether they were being charged too much and whether the transaction really was Islamic started to be voiced by the credit recipients. Nonetheless, following the disbursement to the female DOs, HDF received a request from the men of Fazal Killay (east) to form a DO as well on January 19, 2000.

7

Health

7.1 Introduction

As explained in the preface, APPNA Sehat (APPNA) is the partner responsible for the health interventions as part of the Human Development Foundation's (HDF) integrated development interventions in Mardan.[1] Also, as mentioned earlier, APPNA's interventions in the project area pre-date HDF's entry, and the project's design anticipated that APPNA's prior presence would facilitate HDF in introducing its integrated development approach to the locality. APPNA's mission is to work on preventive health care programs in rural areas, with an emphasis on maternal and child health care.

In sections 2 and 3, we describe APPNA in some detail as one of the three constituent partner organizations in Mardan. This includes a description of its operating philosophy, project description, and broad accomplishments in the country. We turn next to our project area, and in section 4 we outline our research method. In section 5, we report our findings (based on a survey) and the anthropological investigation that we utilized for assessing the health interventions. We end the chapter with a summary and our recommendations.

7.2 APPNA Sehat: Operating Philosophy and Project Description[2]

APPNA Sehat was founded in 1989 to work on preventive health and, by 2000, was active in Mardan, Sahiwal, Murree, and Badin districts. It expanded rapidly, and by 2000, was serving about 140,000 people in 91 villages, with a staff of about 180, 80 percent of who were women. Five doctors, who served as regional coordinators, were among this staff.

The areas of intervention were selected after much thought on identifying the major causes of morbidity and mortality and included immunization of women and children, growth monitoring and counseling, sanitation, and drinking water.

The main goals of APPNA were to improve health behavior through health education, reduce morbidity and mortality among population groups at greatest risk, identify and solve health problems utilizing existing resources, demonstrate how collaboration between public and private sectors can result in marked reductions in serious health problems, and to successfully demonstrate a model of sustainable Primary Health Care (PHC) that could be replicated by institutions and organizations working for improving the quality of life in rural Pakistan.

The personnel are generally recruited from the project village and there is a strong focus on hiring and training women. Community involvement is a strong feature of the project. Dr. Frederick Shaw is credited for substantial contribution to the conceptual model in use and Dr. Naseem Ashraf was a moving force behind the founding of the project.

The main conceptual breakthrough was premised on the realization that prevention was much more cost effective than cure. The philosophy is that there should be no dependence of the community on the project and that the community capacity should be built by mobilizing existing resources. The communities are expected to participate in a fundamental way. Thus, village health committees (HCs) were to have a real say in decision making, including firing of staff not conscientious or responsive to the community. The sustainability of the behavior modification for preventive health is premised on the revealed benefits of the changed behavior and the immediately experienced costs of deviating from it (e.g., moving to unboiled from boiled water). A simple village model for health care was founded called the Village Improvement Model (VIM). This model was successfully piloted in four rural locations in 1989 and then replicated as Village Improvement Projects (VIP).

The APPNA program is carried out in units, each comprising of several villages of varied sizes ranging from 83 households in Mansab (Unit 1) to 1,272 households in Muslimabad (Unit 5). On average, a unit constitutes about 1000–1200 households. The APPNA staff consists of

1. two health assistants (HAs) for every unit responsible for home visits,
2. two traditional birth attendants (TBAs) for every unit to assist HAs in maternity services,

3. one lady health visitor (LHV) for every three units to provide care to high-risk pregnant women and for family-planning services,
4. one male senior health assistant (SHA) for every two units to maintain a record of the community demographic profile, to carry out community mobilization among men, and to assist in hygiene and sanitation work,
5. a regional program coordinator (RPC),
6. a volunteer who acts as a facilitator and engages in social mobilization.

After the initial identification of a unit, a household census is conducted to gather basic information including health behavior, education, income, and other resources. In case the unit gets included in the project, this information then constitutes a benchmark and a means to identify the target groups. Apart from the baseline survey and community mobilization, the program activities include PHC household visits and health education, tetanus immunization, antenatal care, safe delivery, postnatal care, family planning, childhood immunizations (EPI—the Federal Government's Expanded Program of Immunization), breast-feeding promotion, growth monitoring, nutrition education, control of diarrheal diseases and acute respiratory infections, first aid for injuries caused by accidents and other reasons, women's literacy, water and sanitation, and personal hygiene.

For each activity, such as immunization, the target group is registered and the information updated every month. Male and female HCs are formed and their activities focus both at the household and at the community level. A fairly elaborate structure for participation has been devised. Ten community organizations are formed per unit with about one representative per five households. In the unit committee, there are two representatives from each of the community organizations. On the regional board there is a representative from each unit committee, and on the national board there are two representatives from each regional board. The idea is to facilitate both a sense of participation and the flow of information. The male and female community organizations and HCs are formed for work-related to community mobilization, health education and preventive care. Ideally, HCs are also expected to engage in other development work via collective action.

TBAs are locally trained women. Other staff members are recruited more broadly, are at least matriculates (grade 10), and are trained by APPNA. Transport facilities are not made available to the field staff by the project. The HAs are provided blood pressure apparatus, weighing scales, thermometers, and registers. Vaccines are obtained from government health facilities and contraceptives are purchased from the government and private sources.

Mothers are provided growth and EPI cards to maintain the health records of their children. These cards have some basic health information for mothers in easily understandable *Urdu* language.[3] In general, women are trained to interpret the findings based on the monthly weight and height data generated for the registered children. Malnourished children are referred to an appropriate source for assistance.

The project has field offices in community-donated spaces where meetings of the Health Committee and support groups are held and demographic data on the community as well as some health education material in *Urdu* is displayed. Government and private health facilities are at commutable distance and are used as referral facilities when needed.[4]

Monitoring is rigorous and based on a detailed implementation plan (prepared by each unit) that is based on joint monthly work-plans of the field teams. The monitoring is based on both assessing knowledge and skills of the field staff and also relative to outputs implicit in the work-plans. Inadequate skills can form the basis of further field training. The field reports, based on targets achieved are compiled and passed up the hierarchy from the unit to the regional and on to the head office. Thus considerable paperwork is involved in the field worker's duties. However, an interesting aspect of the reporting is the expectation that there will be follow-up reporting on action that is implicit in a deviation from targets set in the last report. Apart from ongoing evaluation to assess and troubleshoot the meeting of project targets, impartial outside evaluations are also conducted.

7.3   Achievements in a National Context

APPNA claimed that the annual cost per beneficiary of its project interventions was US$1.1 in 2000. For this very frugal social investment, it reports many accomplishments in the project area relative to the health statistics in a control area or the rest of the country. Because of antenatal and postnatal care, maternal deaths in APPNA villages are now virtually nonexistent. Also, by teaching families how to prepare and administer oral rehydration salts (ORS), dehydration related deaths due to diarrhea have almost been eliminated so that mortality resulting from diarrhea, one of the main child killers in Pakistan, has been reduced to 0.4 percent. In 1989, 14 percent of the population was found to be suffering from various illnesses in project areas. This was reduced to 1.5 percent by 2000. Similarly, illnesses among children less than five years were drastically reduced.

Between 1989 and 2000, APPNA managed to raise the full immunization of children in the project area from 32 percent to 95 percent and to raise women's immunization against tetanus from 1.5 to 90 percent.[5] In the control group, the estimated increase was to 63 percent and 15 percent respectively. Safe drinking water was made available to 70,000 children. The results were evident in the improvement in the human development indicators.

The CDR (crude death rate) was reduced by 67 percent while the reduction was 21 percent nationally (including urban areas). The infant mortality rate (IMR) was reduced from 110 to 29 per 1000 live births, while the national IMR was reduced by only 10 percent in the period in question to 95 per 1000 live births in 1998.[6] The under five mortality rate (U5MR) declined by 50 percent to 80 live births per 1000, while the decline at the national level was by 16 percent to 136 live births per 1000 in 1998.[7] The maternal mortality ratio (MMR) was reduced from 600 per 100,000 live births to 79, compared to an approximate national average of 450 per 100,000 live births, projected from past data. These achievements were partly the result of an additional 70,000 people having access to safe drinking water. The crude birth rate (CBR) was reduced by 59 percent compared to the national reduction of 21 percent. Thus, the population growth rate was reduced from 2.8 percent to 1.7 percent in 2000, while the national population growth, also decelerating, was still 2.2 percent.[8]

As earlier indicated, APPNA's program focused on preventive care. However, they were under pressure from communities to also address their curative needs. In partial response to this identified need, it had embarked on a pilot project called *sehat markaz* (health center) in Murree district to treat minor illnesses, monitor growth and immunization services, give antenatal care, and look after deliveries other than cesarean sections. *Sehat markaz* represents a clinic developed with community partnership, with the latter providing a place, financial management (after training), fund raising via fee for service, discussion of issues in the unit HCs, and monitoring and evaluation. The program provided furniture, funding for two years (on a declining basis), and training and joint monitoring. For referral, a linkage was established to the nearest hospital. The success of the first clinic in Murree resulted in a call by the community to open a second clinic and one was also established in Mardan.

Given this record of accomplishments, there was an initial reluctance by APPNA to give up its independent identity and merge into the HDF structure. Contrary to expectations, they did not provide entry points into the community to facilitate HDF's social mobilization efforts for a while (see chapter 6). However, in many localities, both APPNA and HDF staff managed to work together well, in spite of these reservations. The formation of HCs as viable structures renewed APPNA's commitment to the project as they were seen as potential foundations on which to establish their planned Health Centers in the community. The routine of regular joint meetings and provision of Community Management Skills Training (CMST—refer to chapter 5) to APPNA workers also increased their interest in providing support to HDF.

7.4 Research Method and Sampling

Two project villages were randomly selected to assess prevalent health practices and behavior in the study population of mothers with at least one child under the age of five years. The focus was on immunization, growth monitoring, family planning, breast-feeding, diarrhea, acute respiratory infections, smoking, chronic illnesses and disability, AIDS, use of iodized salt, and mothers' knowledge of health. Respondents were also asked to rate the performance of the APPNA workers.

Anthropological analysis, based on the observations of a field anthropologist, who lived on the project site for a year, was central to the health research. We also associated a medical doctor with the field team to facilitate the data collection and analysis. A sample survey of 10 percent of households in the project villages was conducted. This amounted to 41 respondents in the two intervention villages that had both APPNA and HDF interventions. For comparison, a 10 percent sample, amounting to 32 respondents was also drawn from a control village that had only an APPNA presence, but not an HDF intervention.[9]

HDFNA's earlier assessment of APPNA suggested to them that there are limits to improving health indicators if it is not done in the context of overall social and economic development of the village. This in fact was one of the main motivations for pursuing an integrated multi-intervention approach. The purpose of including a control village with an HDF presence was to see if villages with integrated intervention perform better on health indicators. However, since the intervention had been in place for only one year, this is being put forward more as a method for future use and as a benchmark, rather than as a true indicator of the relative advantages of a specialized versus an integrated approach. However, as done earlier, we will also be comparing district-specific project achievements with that of the country as a whole to get a sense of APPNA's achievement in relative terms.

7.5   Findings

7.5.1   Survey Data Analysis

The relative health performance of the study and control village is likely to be determined only by the quantity and quality of APPNA's health activity in these villages as other interventions were not present or were not effective. Naturally, this is in part determined by how responsive the villages were to a given level of effort and in part by the quality of the particular health workers. The distribution and regular maintenance of immunization and growth charts was indicative of both health worker effort and community responsiveness. These charts were distributed to and being maintained by almost all the respondents in the sample and control villages. Even so, there were differences on several health or health-related indicators across the study and control villages.

For example, the utilization of family planning in the study villages at 44 percent was almost twice that in the control village and compared very favorably with a national average contraceptive prevalence rate of 17 percent.[10] We also explored the incidence of various diseases. Children in almost two-thirds of both study and control village households suffered from diarrhea. Half or more households were aware of ORS and used it. However, these use rates were below the reported national average use rate of 97 percent.[11] The incidence of other diseases is reported in table 7.1 below.

Table 7.1   Incidence of diseases among household children in the study and control village

Disease	Study Villages		Control Village	
	number	*percentage*	*number*	*percentage*
Acute respiratory infection				
(previous year)	37	80	21	66
Pneumonia (ever)	8	17	7	22
Hepatitis (previous year)	16	42	8	31
Malaria (previous year)	16	42	7	22

Source: SDPI sample survey.

About a fifth of the children in the sample had contracted pneumonia at some time in their lives. Also, the incidence of acute respiratory infection was quite high across the board, considering that contending with these is an explicit part of APPNA's program objectives (see section 1). The incidence of malaria was quite high, considering that the national average of reported cases was 54 per 100,000 people in 1997.[12]

Other APPNA objectives include promotion of breast-feeding and dissemination of health information. In this regard, they have been very successful across the board as indicated below in table 7.2.

There is near universal practice of breast-feeding and there is knowledge of iodized salt and immunization among almost all mothers, which is highly commendable. About three-fifths of mothers in the study villages know about AIDS. Although this is much higher than the national average, as evident from poll results reported in the national press, more awareness needs to be created about this disease.

Table 7.3 shows the mothers' rating of the APPNA program.

Table 7.2   Health knowledge among mothers

Practice/Awareness	Study Villages		Control Village	
	number	percentage	number	percentage
Practice breast-feeding	44	96	32	100
Aware of AIDS	27	59	14	44
Aware of iodized salt	43	94	32	100
Aware of childhood immunization	40	98	29	91

Source: SDPI sample survey.

Table 7.3   Mother's rating of APPNA program

Response	Study Villages		Control Village	
	number	percentage	number	percentage
Fair	1	2	1	3
Good	13	31	31	97
Excellent	28	67	0	0
Total	41	100	32	100

Source: SDPI sample survey.

In the study villages, mothers rated APPNA's program as good (31 percent) or excellent (67 percent) and in the control village, 97 percent rated it as good. This really is an unusual degree of client satisfaction, and APPNA's performance in this regard has been outstanding. In the study villages, half the households were visited by the health workers once a month and about half of them twice a month. In the control village, it was once for over two-thirds of the household, twice for about a fifth, and more for the others.

7.5.2   Analysis Based on Health Component of Anthropological Study

Anthropological analysis was carried out to get an understanding of the social changes taking place due to project interventions. The anthropologist was able to serve as the eyes and ears of the research team and helped provide insight into many important aspects of the study. Based on her periodic reports, further questioning on topics of interest by individual researchers, as well as her assistance in getting information on important developments in the study villages, many interesting facts about the community dynamics and prevalent health attitudes and behavior in the community were revealed.

As in the quantitative responses, the community expressed satisfaction with the work APPNA was doing and attached much value to the program of home visits. APPNA workers were their main source of information on health matters. The APPNA field staff generally made regular visits, but some irregularities were also reported. Due to the heavy workload, the HAs sometimes collected mothers and children in one location to provide services. Many mothers were unable to attend such sessions due to other engagements, hesitation to visit the household designated as the meeting place due to strained family relations (see chapter 4), or lack of prior notice. This resulted in delays in getting timely care for important services such as immunization and family planning.

APPNA staff maintained links with the school system as well and attended PTA meetings as recommended by the program. They also started conducting monthly health education sessions in the TMF schools on topics of hygiene, sanitation, and healthy lifestyles, and these were well received. Many APPNA support groups and HCs were not perceived as very active and functional. The newly formed HC under HDF gave impetus to the program, and workers were interested in attending the meetings. The committees (male and female) were mandated to assist in achieving the goals and objectives of APPNA, raising funds, strengthening linkages of the program to government and to other NGO services, and establishing Health Centers.

Other than on weekends and holidays, there were some additional gaps in program coverage. When a health worker was on leave, sometimes her position was left vacant for long durations. Newly hired replacements were trained on-the-job but were not ready for sometime to take up full responsibility. There also appeared to be a lack of a focused approach to deal with emergencies, as observed during a reported measles outbreak that was handled mainly in the routine daily visits. A more concerted approach and active participation of the male health staff and male members of the community could have been helpful.

Although there was good teamwork among APPNA workers, they were unable to perform beyond a certain capacity due to a heavy workload, incommensurate remuneration, and a perceived lack of promotion opportunities. There were some complaints, especially by TBAs, about not receiving salaries on time.

Even though APPNA is an elaborately planned program, there are apparent gaps and a lack of a structure in the design of its training and fieldwork components. Some senior HAs had been provided LHV training and others were nominated for it, but a detailed formal training curriculum for the rest of the health staff was not available. Also, the teamwork in the field was unorganized and lacked specific guidelines for various steps in carrying out individual interventions and interstaff coordination. This may partly be the reason why staff members felt they were overworked.

The health workers had good rapport with the community. Their interaction was mainly with the females, as there was strict gender segregation and observance of *purdah* (female seclusion, see chapter 4). They were aware that the sensitive nature of their work took them deep into a conservative and traditional community and were cautious in maintaining a good reputation and being nice and courteous. For the same reason, they avoided a strong or confrontational stance in persuading mothers to accept healthier lifestyles.

The community viewed these workers as paid employees, and this restricted their sense of ownership of the program. It was hoped that the functioning of the Health Committee may promote greater participation and ownership by the community leading the community to in turn assume responsibility for sustaining the program.

Mothers maintained the growth charts and EPI cards well and understood their significance. In some households, fathers assisted in maintaining these records for the children if mothers were unable to comprehend them. Most of the workers were experienced and had a good understanding of the basic concepts and practices of their work, an understanding that they were able to communicate successfully to the mothers and their coworkers. Even though the use of radio and television was common in the community, they did not seem to be important sources of health information.[13] Diseases were generally identified by their salient features/symptoms or by local terms rather than by their medical names. As such, most mothers could recognize two to three EPI diseases.

The use of iodized salt in the community was very limited and some rumors about its link to family planning existed. In spite of this, there seemed to be a lack of focus on promoting the use of iodized salt in the health education campaign. Also, given the novelty, shops were either not carrying it or selling it at higher prices. Thus the familiar noniodized salt continued to be preferred by the community.

Many traditional health practices were prevalent. These included the use of *ghutti* (applying a little honey or another traditional local product to the tongue of the newborn), provision of special care and diet to pregnant and postpartum women, warming up the bed for women during delivery in winter by placing burning coals under the bed, avoiding baths during menses and in the postpartum period, and licking mud (*gachni mitti* or a special type of clay) during pregnancy. The community also believed in spiritual cures provided by religious mendicants.

There also existed some gender biases such as celebrating the birth of a child only if the newborn is male, belief that a female child should be breast-fed longer (i.e., up to two and a half years compared to two years for a male child) as they needed to be buttressed for postmarital work. Most mothers started breast-feeding soon after birth; they mentioned that previously, when they were not educated about it, they used to delay it. Young mothers generally breast-fed until the next conception. Mothers were aware of the optimum duration of breast-feeding.

Mothers mostly reported their deliveries to be normal and preferred staying home for their deliveries. This is because they were averse to the inconvenience of travel and the long waiting periods associated with hospitals. Many relatives and elder ladies in the household assisted with deliveries and TBAs were called if a risk of complication was encountered. LHVs followed up high-risk pregnancies but did not handle abortions if asked for. A considerable number of mothers interviewed complained of minor irregularities in menstrual periods.

The communities still preferred a large family. Most married women of thirty and above had four to six children. As a rule, young mothers did not use family planning so that they could complete their families, unless they were very weak or had closely spaced children. Tubal libation was not popular due to the perceived inconvenience of stitches. Those who had tubal libation sometimes spread rumors about associated symptoms such as backache, headache, and abdominal pain. Injectable contraceptives were popular, although some users considered some symptoms, such as backaches, to be linked to them. Health attendants provided education on family planning to mothers openly and frankly and advised them to get consent from their husbands in such decisions, which was usually not a problem. Mothers were hesitant to obtain contraceptives from a commercial source because they felt shy to access such outlets.

Diarrhea was common during summer months, especially in young children. Many mothers reported that children often did not like homemade ORS, and they were advised by health workers to add *sherbet* (flavored sweet drinks) for taste. ORS was available in shops and local dispensaries and flavored brands were popular. There was some use of medication for diarrhea, usually obtained from local dispensaries, because mothers believed this helped.

Other diseases commonly reported in children included acute respiratory tract infections (in winter) and skin infections (in summer). An outbreak of measles was reported close to the end of the fieldwork. The community was apprehensive, as they did not believe it to be possible in the presence of the EPI. Delayed measles immunization could have been a contributing factor.

Among adults in the community, skin infections were common. There were also reports of tuberculosis (TB) and hepatitis. A TB control program was reported to have started around that time, perhaps as a result of the cases detected. No case of goiter was detected in routine fieldwork. It was difficult to estimate the prevalence of smoking in the community by talking to women, since men avoided smoking inside homes in the joint family system as a mark of respect for elders. The use of *huqqa* (dong) and *naswar* (a local tobacco-based intoxicant pitted under the gum) were common among males.

The community relied mostly on APPNA workers for health services. Those who could afford private providers preferred it over government health facilities, for the latter meant travel inconvenience. The locally residing dispensers, who worked at clinics and hospitals, were also the preferred health care providers and they dispensed common medicines. The community referred to them as "doctors." TBAs were well respected and trusted for maternity care. Government Basic Health Units (BHUs) were not functional, even though the local ones had their staff strength and facilities enhanced. They provided vaccines and coordinated with APPNA workers on polio days. Referral and patient follow-up were not very strong components of the program.

APPNA had revised some data collection instruments to obtain more detailed information on maternal morbidity and mortality, occurrences of diseases such as TB and hepatitis, age-specific information on immunization, growth monitoring, and family planning. This was expected to strengthen the referral system of the program, among other knowledge-related health care services.

The hygiene and sanitation conditions in the village were not very good even though APPNA had been working in the area for many years. Animals were often housed very close to the living quarters and sources of water. Refuse was commonly dumped outside houses, to be used as fertilizer. Water was obtained mostly from hand pumps, and more than one household often shared one pump. People thought the water was portable and were thus reluctant to boil it. However, HAs promoted the practice of boiling water because the water sources were likely to be contaminated by the unhygienic surroundings.

Summary and Recommendations

APPNA started work in 1989 to promote preventive health care with a focus on maternal and child health care, and Mardan was selected as one of the areas for intervention. Vaccines are obtained from the government health facilities, as a backup, and contraceptives purchased from government and private sources. In this regard, APPNA as a constituent part of HDF in Mardan, represented a good example of government-nongovernment partnership. APPNA trained staff including health attendants (HA), TBAs, LHVs, and senior health attendants (SHA) for the purpose.

This study relied for its findings on two randomly selected project villages and one nearby control village that had an APPNA unit but not an HDF intervention. Ten percent of the households were randomly selected in the sampled villages. The field reports of an anthropologist, who lived in the project area for one year, also contributed to the findings and analysis of this chapter.

The utilization of family planning in the sample villages at 44 percent was about twice that in the control villages and considerably higher than the national contraceptive prevalence rate of 17 percent. However, the diarrhea prevalence rate in both the sample and control villages was high (about two-thirds). Half or more households in both sample and control villages were aware of ORS, but this was considerably below the reported national ORS-use rates. The incidence of acute respiratory infections, hepatitis, and malaria was also high.

However, APPNA had been very successful in promoting health knowledge and awareness among mothers. There was near universal practice of breast-feeding and knowledge of immunization and iodized salt. The mother's rating of the program was also very high: 98 percent "good" or "excellent" in the sample villages and 97 percent "good" in the control village. APPNA's fieldworkers were experienced and had a good grasp of the basic concepts and practices. They also successfully communicated these to the communities with whom they had a good rapport. Finally, they were sensitive to the culture they were operating in.

APPNA was initially reluctant to merge their identity with that of HDF and the level of cooperation was low. However, they understood that the concept of HCs, promoted by HDF, for community mobilization, health education, and preventive health care, was consistent with their own program delivery needs. The monthly meetings and joint work planning also raised the level of trust and comfort among the partners. The APPNA field staff's delivery of health education sessions on hygiene, sanitation, and healthy lifestyles in TMF schools was widely perceived as a success and a good example of synergy among the partners. Thus the children became the instruments of introducing better practices in the households. This was needed as hygiene and sanitation practices in the villages continued to be very poor.

Once again, some old themes reemerged as we studied APPNA's interventions. Although APPNA's field workers were appropriately sensitive, as earlier indicated, in some ways they could be more so. Thus the attempt to initiate group gatherings for heath education, to save health worker time, failed because of the severe mobility constraints women faced. There was also the broader failure of the program communication strategy in that APPNA workers were also perceived by the communities as paid professionals delivering a service that was the community's right. However, the community approval rating for these workers was extremely high.

8

Education

8.1 Introduction

This chapter explores the relationship between educational inputs, in a broad sense, and outputs to explore the determinants of students' cognitive achievements. Doing so provides the context for studying the impact of Tameer-i-Millat Foundation (TMF) on the cognitive skills of children over a one-year time period. In the next section, we introduce TMF as the organization responsible for the implementation of the education component of the Human Development Foundation (HDF) project. In section 3, we briefly report on the survey details and data collection. In section 4, we describe the analytical method used and in section 5, we discuss the findings based on the quantitative data analysis and reports of the field anthropologist. We conclude with a summary.

8.2 Tameer-i-Millat Foundation[1]

Like APPNA Sehat (APPNA), TMF was founded in 1992 by a non-profit foundation group of Pakistanis living in the United States. In this case, the goal was to help enhance the quantity and quality of education in Pakistan. TMF's stated goals are to

1. educate every person without any discrimination of race, sex, color, or religion;
2. set up a sizable chain of state-of-the-art educational institutions in Pakistan and abroad;
3. search and mobilize all possible resources (i.e., academic, intellectual, financial, or otherwise), locally as well as internationally, for the promotion of education at all levels;

4. promote character building of students in the light of the teachings of the Holy Qur'an and *Sunnah* (teachings and traditions of the Prophet Mohammad);
5. establish Institute(s) of Education and Research to improve the quality of teaching skills and techniques;
6. open a Teachers Development Institute to organize preservice and in-service teachers training programs;
7. open libraries for the benefit of the students, staff and the general public;
8. hold seminars and conferences on educational themes, encouraging creative work and exchange of ideas among educationists and other professionals at the national and international level;
9. publish books, brochures, journals, periodicals, and pamphlets for continuous education of the students, teachers, and the public at large;
10. provide scholarships, stipends, grants and loans to brilliant and deserving students.

TMF has been supported by a number of foreign (including HDFNA) and local organizations, including various governmental organizations such as the Prime Minister's Literacy Commission and the National Education Foundation.

By 2002, TMF listed a number of achievements based on one decade of operation. It had opened 22 formal schools with 7,025 students, and 119 nonformal basic education schools with 3,567 students. It claimed that, in public examinations, 100 percent of its students passed, many with distinctions. Teachers were trained continuously through seminars, workshops, and Allama Iqbal Open University Courses. Quality improvement was ensured via educational co-coordinators, a monitoring and evaluation system, and school management committees.

Like APPNA, TMF was working in various communities prior to the initiation of HDF but it was not present in the Mardan area. TMF was assigned the task of setting up 30 schools in the project area, and it established 26 schools by May 1999. These were one-teacher, one-room schools, for which the communities provided rooms and TMF provided the material, furniture, teachers' salary, and teacher training. In some cases, teachers provided rooms for the schools. The schools used standard government curricula, alongside innovating with teaching method and extracurricular activity. The plan was to have the children complete five-year primary education in three years and join mainstream government schooling.

As mentioned earlier, HDF selected two units, out of the existing 10 units that APPNA was active in. TMF started its operations in

Units 4 and 6 by opening schools in the villages Fazal Killay and Kandare Jadeed (see chapter 6). The number of schools that were opened depended on the village population size: four schools were opened in Fazal Killay and one school in Kandare Jadeed. Local teachers were hired, and in all but one case, these teachers provided the school premise.

8.3   Study Design, Survey, and Data

We explored various aspects of the educational intervention of the project. The main focus of the analysis was to ascertain children's cognitive skills at a particular point of time (benchmark) and how this changed over a one-year period. In order to do this, exams were designed to test comprehension and mathematical skills, based on the syllabi introduced by TMF. These tests were administered to children in all the project area schools at the inception of the project. The same tests were administered to the same students a year later to identify the value added in cognitive skills. A total of 161 students were given the test, but our analysis was based on 121 students because the rest, who were present in the school in the initial tests, were not present during the repeat visit for the follow-up tests.

Since, the increase in cognitive skills could be attributed to several factors including household, community, school, and teacher attributes, background data on these factors were also collected. In addition, we used the same statistical model to observe changes in cognitive skills in control village government schools during the course of our study. This is the key element in the analysis of the effectiveness of the TMF schools.

To avoid any spillover effects of the project intervention on the control village, the latter was purposely selected to be at a reasonable distance, but close enough for the comparison to be valid. Thus, the other cultural, institutional, and socioeconomic factors needed to be the same for a valid comparison. Household data were collected based on a census of all households in the three villages.

8.4   Analytical Method

We use the education production function approach to estimate the input-output relationship mentioned in the introduction. This is summarized by the equation below:

$$VA = F (TC, HHC) \tag{1}$$

Where
    VA = Value added in cognitive skills test (math and comprehension tests)
    TC = Teacher characteristics (qualification, experience, salary)
    HHC = Household characteristics (parental education, family income)

The equation takes into account individual teacher characteristics, such as his/her salary, qualification and experience, and household characteristics that can have an impact on student performance. However, we were unable to account for some of the possible explanatory variables such as teacher skill, behavior, and motivation, which affect the precision of our estimates. A literature review of educational production functions is included as Annexure 8.1.

8.5   Findings

8.5.1   Quantitative Data Analysis

8.5.1.1   Achievement of Students in Cognitive Skill Tests

As indicated earlier, students were given tests for math and comprehension, and, to observe value added in cognitive skills over time, the same tests were administered to the same students one year later. All students showed considerable improvement in their mean scores over a period of one year (table 8.1). Part of the reason for such a high percentage improvement in scores is that students had got very low scores in the first round of tests, as they had entered the schools quite raw. Also, they were familiar with the format of the test the second time around. However, the performance for the children in the control

Table 8.1   Mean scores by subject and school

School	Math		Comprehension	
	1999	2000	1999	2000
Jarande (control school)	10.7 (4.5)	17.6 (5.3)	14.8 (4.8)	22.7 (2.4)
Fazal Killay	19.2 (8.5)	35.7 (8.4)	18.2 (6.2)	21.0 (3.1)
Kandare Jadeed	20.3 (10.0)	33.1 (6.8)	12.7 (6.1)	21.2 (4.7)

Source: SDPI Survey.

Note: The maximum possible scores on math and comprehension tests were 46 and 26 respectively. Figures in parenthesis are standard deviations.

government school was much lower in math in the base year and the percentage improvement (64 percent) was also not as large as the TMF schools (86 percent).

Mean scores in math and comprehension were higher for girls compared to boys as is evident from table 8.2 below. TMF primary schools primarily cater to female students who were not being sent to the government schools. TMF's reputation of being a religiously oriented organization, the use of female teachers, and the schools' physical proximity to the communities is likely to have induced parents to send their daughters to the school. The community also welcomed the teaching of the *Qurani Quaida* (religious primer) and prayers.

Our data shows that more than two-fifths of the students (41.5 percent) who enrolled in TMF schools were earlier studying in government schools. This is a very high percentage and challenges TMF's/HDF's contention that they are only catering to students who slip between the cracks and are not displacing existing public education. A more charitable view on this obvious displacement could be that TMF schools provide the government schools with some needed competition. However, this would make a difference if the loss in enrollment has some quality consequences for government school teachers and managers.

The move to the TMF schools from government schools is a puzzle because TMF schools have higher student-teacher ratios, lower teacher qualifications, and worse school facilities. One possible explanation for the shift in enrollment to TMF schools is their much more convenient location. As TMF caters to a cohort of very young age of between 5 and 8 years, parents may prefer the proximity of TMF schools. The other explanation is the good reputation these schools have acquired, compared to the general view that attending government schools is a waste of children's time.[2]

Table 8.2 Gender differential in mean scores in math and comprehension tests

Name of School	Math		Comprehension	
	1999	2000	1999	2000
Male	13.2 (9.3)	28.2 (11.2)	15.3 (4.7)	20.4 (6.1)
Female	21.1 (8.7)	35.6 (6.4)	17.4 (3.9)	21.7 (6.4)

Source: SDPI Survey.

Note: Figures in parenthesis are standard deviations.

8.5.1.2   *Associating Inputs with Outputs: The Educational Production Function*

We estimated equation 1 (see section 8.4) to identify the determinants of value addition in math and comprehension. The results are reported in appendix 8.2. Adjusted R^2 for value added in math was 0.40, which is reasonably high for cross-sectional regression. The variable for type of school is very significant and shows that the project schools did much better than the control government school in the sample in generating value added in math cognitive skills. The value of the coefficient is 6.42 and, to put this into perspective, this is 44 percent of the mean value added in math cognitive skills. One possible explanation for this result is the better oversight in the project schools as demonstrated by Khan et al. (2005). Another notable finding is that greater teacher qualifications are not necessarily associated with greater acquisition of student cognitive skills.

8.5.2   *Anthropological Analysis*

As in the case of the health chapter, the anthropological analysis complements the quantitative data analysis. The standard participant-observation method of using key informants was utilized. The one-room schools posed a problem for TMF, as they were unable to enroll new students in the second year of their operation. Having just one room also means that teachers have to cope with multigrade teaching that can be distracting both for the teacher and students, and detrimental to the educational progress.[3] HDF signed a Memorandum of Understanding with Adult Basic Education Society (ABES), their educational partners in the Punjab Province, to provide multigrade teacher training, as an interim solution.

HDF induced TMF to form parent teacher associations (PTAs) that were made a part of the development organizations (DO). The terms of reference for the PTAs were to overlook the functioning of schools, including teacher and student attendance; to motivate parents to send the out-of-school children to school; to devise ways and means for school sustainability, as the project intended to exit once they decided that the intervention was self-sustaining; to take stock of the existing quality of the TMF schools and take necessary steps to improve it.

According to the anthropologist's field reports, only two PTAs were formed in both these villages and neither was very active, especially the one in Kandare Jadeed. A PTA was formed on October 13, 1999, in the latter village. As the teacher was a male, the PTA was to be constituted of the fathers of the girls. There were only ten parents present at the meeting, although all the parents had been invited. The reason for the low attendance of parents was that the timing clashed with the sugarcane harvesting and most parents were busy in the fields. Out of ten parents present, seven agreed to become members of the PTA. Although one of the project objectives is that PTAs should bring up educational issues at the DO meeting, this did not occur in either project village.

The PTAs also made no effort to draw unenrolled children of school-going age into the schools. In both the sample project schools, there was no effort observed to improve the quality of education at the TMF schools. The enrollment data show that the number of students enrolled in TMF schools went down from 180 in July 1999 to 162 in July 2000. This is not indicative of a serious effort made on the part of the PTAs to enroll "out-of-school children."

HDF mentioned that some PTAs had persuaded communities to pay a monthly fee per student of Rs. 5, and in some cases even Rs. 10. Tapping into such community willingness to pay is certainly good for the sustainability of the schools, a stated objective of the PTAs. But, PTA deliberations in both the sample villages indicated little inclination toward instituting a fee.

Thus, in the first year of the project, PTAs were not accomplishing any of their assigned tasks. The possible reasons could be the low level of social mobilization and subsequently the lack of a sense of ownership among the community of the TMF schools. TMF schools pre-date the HDF social mobilization efforts to set up DOs in which the PTAs were to be integrated, and therefore the community did not perceive these schools as a self-help venture. Thus, while the schools provided an entry point for the social mobilization in several cases, the community ownership of schools suffered from the lack of such social mobilization prior to the setting up of the schools (see chapter 6). To address this shortcoming, HDF hired a female education officer. Prior to this, teachers were entrusted with social mobilization tasks, but lacked any training or incentive to deliver on them.

HDF also did not demonstrate adequate sensitivity to the communities they were working in. In two instances, the project alienated or fragmented the communities due to an intervention that did not take the community into confidence. In one instance, TMF posted the most outstanding school teacher to the TMF office in Mardan to help manage the female PTAs. This transferring of a popular teacher led to resentment in the community, particularly because it was not party to the decision.

Another conflict surfaced because of prior tension between the wife of the owner of the premises in which the school was located and another PTA member. Contrary to the rules, the wife of the building owner had been made a PTA member even though none of her children studied in the school. At the time of the PTA formation, this was not pointed out to the social organizer who ducked the issue. The upshot was that the owner's wife refused to let the other mother enter the school premises and attend the PTA meetings and so the regular operations of the PTA were adversely effected. As the newly appointed female PTA co-coordinator thought that she was not capable of mediating, she called the education coordinator from HDF to help her resolve the conflict.

Another problem that surfaced was incidentally related to education but had more to do with project coordination. Thus, while the project perceived a school as belonging to Charcha, the school was actually located in Kandare Jadeed. As the signboard said Charcha, the inhabitants of Charcha thought that the school was meant for them and that it had been hijacked by Kandare Jadeed.[4] This created considerable resentment among the Charcha community who on two occasions removed the school signboard that referred to the school as belonging to Charcha.

Summary

TMF was established in 1992 and by 2002 it had provided education services to about 7025 students in formal schools and 3,567 students in nonformal schools at 22 locations in various parts of the country. In the Mardan area, TMF opened nonformal schools to supplement the economic development and health interventions. We selected two project areas and a control village and administered tests in math and comprehension at the start of the project and revisited the same schools and administered the same tests to the same students a year later. This was the main analytical exercise we conducted to gauge the success of the TMF schools relative to the control government school. Compared to the control government school, the TMF schools attained 44 percent higher value addition in math cognitive skills.

TMF started opening informal schools prior to HDF establishing its presence in Mardan. Thus, the informal schools were made operational prior to any sustained social mobilization. TMF uses a service delivery approach, and its conception of participation was limited to the community providing the premises for the school. In view of this, a more comprehensive sense of the schools it founded as being community schools was not established. The community's ownership of the schools was limited and, in fact, some sought to benefit from the founding of the schools by trying to rent their premises. Other community members saw it as an opportunity for employment and the two teachers in the two project villages we studied provided the rooms in exchange for getting employed.

It is always difficult to create a sense of ownership ex post, and attempting to do so can create resentment. Thus, the communities perceived these interventions as a right and were quite reluctant to pay a user fee to contribute to school sustainability. Nonetheless, this was achieved once HDF social mobilization picked up, as was the establishment of PTAs to ensure monitoring and constant improvement. However, one year into the project, these PTAs had not achieved a visible impact.

Once again, culture played an important role in the success of the schools and TMF easily adapted to this community requirement as they were predisposed in that direction anyway. Thus, the use of female teachers to cater to village girls not attending government schools, the use of government syllabus, the overt imparting of religious education were all perceived as positives by the community. That TMF was able to found the schools in the heart of the village so that the girls did not have to travel much was a major factor in its ability to enroll and retain girls. However, TMF also managed to build on these advantages. As an NGO, it adopted flexible timings that were in harmony with the agricultural calendar. It also drew on a national organization to provide teacher training. In the next two chapters, we provide updates on the project's achievements in various areas (including education), based on follow-up field visits one and six years later and on information gathered from the national and field offices.

ANNEXURE 8.1

Review of Literature on Educational Production Functions

The multiplicity of inputs and outputs in education makes estimating the statistical association between the two, more rigorously referred to as the educational production function, very complicated. For one, it is difficult to obtain good measures of both inputs and outputs. Expenditure per pupil, class size, student-teacher ratio, teacher education, experience and salaries are some measures of inputs and student performance on cognitive skills test, educational attainment after school and earnings of the students in later life are measures of output.

The Coleman Report (1966) is the pioneering study in this field of associating education inputs with outputs. This report concluded that family and peer group characteristics were more instrumental than school system characteristics in promoting student achievement. However, there has been an ongoing controversy in the literature on educational production functions about whether school resources have significant effects on output. Some of the major contributors include Hanushek (1986, 1996), Card and Kruger (1992, 1996), Hedges, Laine, and Greenwald (1994), Heckman, Layne-Farrar, and Todd (1996), Dearden, Ferri, and Meghir (1997), Angrist and Lavy (1999), Hoxby (2000), Feinstein and Symons (1999), Levin (2001), Wilson (2001), Hanushek and Luque (2003), Coates (2003), Kremer, Miguel, and Thornton (2004), and Glewwe and Kremer (2006).

According to Monk (1990), despite the fact that production function studies have not yielded much useful insight and face serious obstacles to doing so, it is premature to jump to the conclusion that education production functions should be abandoned as a research tool.

The empirical literature shows mixed results. Hanushek (1986) concluded that there is "no strong evidence that teacher-student ratios, teacher education, or teacher experience have an expected positive effect on student achievement" and that "there appears to be no strong or systematic relationship between school expenditures and student performance."

Studies using more refined measures of teacher inputs have found more consistently positive results. For example, Monk and King (1994) reported that teacher subject matter preparation in math and science does have some positive impact on student achievement in those subjects. Measures indicating how selective teachers' colleges were also showed a positive association with student achievement (Ehrenberg and Brewer 1994). Also, some studies have found a positive association of teacher's verbal ability with student achievement (Coleman et al. 1966; Ehrenberg and Brewer 1995; Ferguson 1991). Unfortunately, teacher motivation, enthusiasm, and skills undoubtedly influence students, but these traits are very difficult to quantify with accuracy and thus are omitted from the analysis, hence resulting in biased estimates due to the missing variable problem.

Many studies that include teacher and class characteristics use variables that have been aggregated to the school level. Often teacher characteristics in many studies are not those of the individual teacher of the students in question, but rather school level variables such as mean years of experience or mean teacher salary. There is a considerable variation in teacher and class characteristics within schools and so using aggregate variables becomes virtually meaningless. Such aggregation can lead to dramatically different estimates of the effects of school resources on achievement. Akerhielm (1995) found this to be the case in estimating the impact of class size.

Hanushek (1996) found that, despite ever increasing school budgets, student performance had stagnated. He proposed that to reverse this trend, efficiency of the resource use be increased, performance incentives for schools, teachers and administrators be introduced and the pace of experimentation with educational alternatives be increased. He referred to this as a continuous learning process.

Heinsen and Graversen (2005) investigated the importance of school inputs in primary and lower secondary school for later educational achievement and found that expenditure per pupil in primary and lower secondary school had a statistically significant but very small positive effect on the probability of eventually passing upper secondary school or vocational education.

Many education production function studies have major deficiencies in methodology and data. Some have omitted key variables, or some have used crude proxies of teaching ability, such as teacher degree levels and years of experience. Over time the studies have become much more sophisticated to account for various methodical and statistical shortcomings although the results remain mixed.

ANNEXURE 8.2

Determinants of Value-Added Math (VAM) and Value-Added Comprehension (VAC): OLS (Ordinary Least Square) Regression Results

	VAM	VAC
Teachers' education		
FA	6.805* (3.87)	−5.072* (3.62)
BA	−7.394* (3.19)	−4.673* (2.53)
Income groups		
Rich	−2.214 (0.60)	−3.222 (1.10)
Middle	−1.985 (0.99)	−0.714 (0.44)
Poor	−3.087** (2.10)	−2.542** (2.16)
Other		
Gender	1.224 (0.74)	0.272 (0.21)
FEDU	−0.178 (1.16)	−0.197 (1.61)

Continued

Annexure 8.2   Continued

	VAM	VAC
RSIB	−0.851 (1.74)	−1.431 (1.03)
Jarande	−6.422** (2.25)	−0.241(0.11)
Farmer	−0.466 (0.30)	−1.074 (0.88)
Constant	15.132	10.988
Adj. R^2	0.41	0.18
F−Stat [10, 110]	9.26*	3.56*
N	121	121

Source: SDPI Survey.

Notes: VAM = Value added math
VAC = Value added comprehension
FA = Higher secondary
BA = Bachelors'
FEDU = Father's education
RSIB = Ratio of other school going to total siblings in the household
Jarande = Control village with government school

The base categories are metric (grade 10) for teacher's qualifications, extremely poor for income group, project village schools and nonfarming occupations. Parenthesis contain t–statistics.
 *: Significant at the 1% level.
**: Significant at the 5% level.

Field Update 2001[1]

9.1 Introduction

At the end of December 2001, almost a year and a half after the initial fieldwork, the field-team revisited the project site. This was done in view of an unavoidable delay in documenting the findings of the earlier two rounds of fieldwork. However, we perceived the delay to be also an opportunity to investigate how some of the main issues raised in chapters 5–8 played out. A checklist of questions was developed and the study included an extensive set of interviews with all members of the field management and social organizers (SOs), and visits to schools and to the field involving participation in DO meetings (both male and female). The findings are reported below by key categories (including institutional issues, social mobilization, education, health, microcredit, training, and linkages) discussed throughout Part II of the book. In many, though not all, cases there is evidence of much project learning and institutional innovation.

9.2 Findings

9.2.1 Institutional Issues

Association of Pakistani Physicians of North America's (APPNA) prior work in the community and the goodwill that they achieved was now acknowledged by the Human Development Foundation (HDF) to have been invaluable both in giving them an entry point into the community and also in helping to mediate potential conflicts. At the field level, the partners were getting on well. While joint work enhanced bonding, the joint monthly meetings were discontinued and coordination meetings were held only on a need basis. The new regional program manager (RPM) had quite effectively established his authority, and the office gave the impression of being a going concern.

Another important aspect of the synergy between the partners was the role played by Tameer-i-Millat Foundation (TMF) teachers as activists. As indicated in chapter 6, they often served as the secretary in the development organizations (DO) and were an important link of the project to the communities. The platform that TMF provided to APPNA for its monthly talks in schools on hygiene, nutrition, and preventive health care were continuing and welcomed by TMF and well received by the community. We were informed in the field that the finances to the different organizations come from the parent organization, rather than from the HDF field office as was actually the case, and this could be a potential roadblock to continued synergy.

One attempt at institutional sustainability was to market the products of the communities in a project outlet and put the project share of the profits in an endowment fund. Thus foodstuffs generated from trainings in preserving and canning and from craft goods were marketed. However, the revenue generated was not adequate to recover costs, particularly the high rent, and this initiative was going to be discontinued. The women contended that they used high-quality inputs, as a result of which the product prices were higher than the current market rates. The costs went up further because finishing touches had to be given by the project staff. We were told that in Mardan people preferred to buy the lower-quality and lower-priced products. The project staff felt that it was difficult to market products in the project area, as most people are self-sufficient in those products. The earnings from the credit program continued to be put into the endowment fund, which exceeded Rs. 1 million by the end of 2001.

New staff training took place as an orientation activity, and it was designed and executed by the HDF head office. While this was viewed to be quite successful, the SOs, who are pivotal in any rural development NGO, felt the need for on-the-job training on various aspects of the development activities that they motivated the communities to be part of.

The project worked out an interesting exit strategy. Thus the goal was to form DOs, forge them into Village Development Organizations (VDOs), and then create an Integrated Development Organization (IDO) at the unit level (such as the *sehat markaz*, refer to chapter 7), which would be registered with the Social Welfare Department and would represent six to seven villages. The plan was that this apex organization would be able to take over the task of HDF in a particular unit, and HDF could then move on to other units.

9.2.2 Social Mobilization

Village-level representative cluster organizations (VDOs), comprising members of DOs, were to be formed. Since DOs are community organizations, rather than village organizations, there can be several in a village. This would be on the pattern of the APPNA village health committees (VHC) prior to HDF moving into the area. It was realized that the health committees (HC) that HDF asked APPNA to form to report to the DO had actually split up the VHC that was already in existence. As this was perceived not to have worked well, given the door-to-door nature of APPNA's activities, the VHC would report to the VDO but there would no longer be a HC reporting to the DO. The DOs would continue to meet twice a month and review education and economic development activities such as trainings, credit, and linkages.

Both the male DOs in the sample villages that had earlier been visited were nonfunctional. In Fazal Killay the lack of an influential seemed to have been the problem according to the SO, since the villagers were not willing to follow anyone. The reasons that the villagers gave were lack of unity among themselves and their poverty that forced people to stay immersed in their own affairs to make a living. One of them suggested that perhaps the project should provide the leader and things would then go well. The project suggested giving the young, energetic, and enthusiastic men a chance to run the DO. An example was given of the young president of a highly active and well-rated DO. However, it was quickly pointed out that his father was the influential in the village. Also, the young president pointed out that success was achieved through a lot of effort and awareness campaigns.

The other DO failed because the locality had two khans and the problem of one group's unwillingness to meet at the other group's meeting place persisted. The project resolved this impasse by calling meetings at a public place. However, when a president was selected from one group, the other boycotted the DO and it collapsed. In both villages, we witnessed the willingness to try at DO formation again, now that benefits in neighboring communities were becoming evident. However, while the khans still call the shots in many ways, the DOs were providing opportunities for much wider participation in decision making.

There were fresh signs that communities were capable of and willing to engage in collective action. In one of the two study villages, a

DO officeholder, who had bought a goat with project credit, resigned and turned the goat over to the DO. This was taken care of and proved to be quite lucrative. The man subsequently asked for the profit, and when this was refused, he burnt the savings register. The community decided to go to court, but the social mobilizers persuaded them to first try and resolve the issue at the community level. The man was threatened with a social boycott unless he paid a fine of Rs. 2,500. This worked, and the person apologized and paid the fine that was used for food for a social gathering. Another example of collective action was demonstrated in Fazal Killay, where a woman gave her own house to be used as the school, the neighbors provided electricity, the community together had two fans installed, and another member of the community provided a hand pump.

There were about 42 female DOs in the area, but no female VDO had been formed. Conflicts and the lack of unity among the community was the main retarding factor. If the men did not get along, the women were also not allowed to interact. Thus, although three VDOs were planned, due to these intercommunity conflicts, none materialized. Two women VDOs were planned for the year 2002, each comprising of three DOs.

The attitude of the community toward the project varied from one area to the next. When the project staff moved into a new area, the community initially is wary. Their worries and fears about the true motives of the project include being taken away from their religion. One of them feared that because the funding originated in the United States, their daughters would be taken away from them and sent to that country.[2] Thus SOs have confronted even abusive language, until things had been explained to the community patiently. In areas where the project had been functioning for a while, people started trusting it and the level of acceptance went up. In these areas, the perception concerning the project—that it brought in *sarkari paisa* (official money) for *them*—was changing.

In keeping with this slow acceptance, savings were low. Once people understood that it was for their own well-being, they started saving more. In some female DOs, the savings had even gone up to as high as Rs. 100 per month. One of the reasons for the low savings was that communities had a recollection of being exploited in the past by unscrupulous NGOs. Savings were collected twice a month and people contributed according to their ability.

As in the case of the male DOs, female DO meetings were normally held twice a month.[3] They remained casual affairs and were not very orderly. The typical agenda for the general discussion included problems faced by the community with respect to the schooling of their children, the available trainings, or credit-related issues.

To sum up, there were major difficulties in successfully mobilizing communities so that the social capital could be formalized in DOs and successfully harnessed and guided for collective action to alleviate poverty and enhance community welfare.

9.2.3   Health

The HCs were functioning well and were quite effective, although, as indicated earlier, they were to be dissolved into the VHC and so there would no longer be a HC reporting to the DO. The HCs dealt with issues pertaining to family planning, vaccination, and hygiene and sanitation, with the emphasis on preventive health care. The community continued to want curative health care facilities also and the newly opened *sehat markaz* (health center) at the unit level was to address this demand.

The HC could not directly hire or fire employees. Recruitment-related decisions had to go through the proper channel to the regional office. In case of hiring new staff members, they could make suggestions but were not authorized to hire field staff directly. Also, no female HA had been promoted yet to a senior health assistant (SHA) position. The reason given was that due to the prevalent cultural norms, women are normally not taken seriously, and their word was not given due weight. It was also argued that the SHA position involved much monitoring and moving around, so it would not be very practical for female staff members.

The community view was that internalizing preventive health care is part of a self-help effort and continued to be appreciative of APPNA and its staff. We had identified the problem of having no backup for APPNA staff if they were to suddenly quit. This represented a big setback to the community, which had started to depend on these services. TMF had addressed this problem by having a reserve teacher in the system. In the same way, APPNA could design for some excess capacity. One option suggested by the regional project manager (RPM) was to hire interns based on the same rigorous standards as for regular APPNA field staff. These young women could get trained and could move on when they got other jobs. However, should a vacancy arise in APPNA due to a sudden departure resulting from a staff member getting married or from any other reason, the interns could quickly step into the position as trained backups.

9.2.4   Education

The school facilities were still very rudimentary, even by government school standards. Generally, TMF operated "one-room one-teacher" schools while operating two or three classes. Often, to accommodate an additional class, the community built a makeshift space, such as an overhang.

Multigrade teaching was still going on in schools. The teachers felt that their attention was being divided and at times they could not cope with two classes at a time, so they asked one of their brighter students to tend to the junior classes. This was slowing down the teaching process and reducing its effectiveness, and they felt they could have performed better if there were more than one teacher. The problem of teaching to different age groups was further compounded because the more mature students picked up concepts much more quickly and the weak students were required to repeat the class.

The teachers were satisfied with the training being given to them, including that on multigrade teaching skills. Language and basic teacher training was organized for newly appointed teachers. These included teaching annual work planning and daily lesson planning. To enhance their teaching skills, the project staff also provided on-the-job training and discussed the teachers work-related problems. TMF also held a workshop on joyful learning in 2000.

Seventy percent of the students were still girls. Even so, both culture and cost of conveyance prevented females studying beyond the primary level. At times, the girls themselves felt that primary school was enough and at other times there was parental opposition. In one case, a parent stormed into the classroom and tore up a girl's books saying all this learning was useless and that she could do much better by helping the family in the fields. In another case, a father got his daughter, who had picked up basic mathematics, to maintain his business books and accounts, saying she had learnt enough to be of use to him. TMF was trying to persuade him to let the girl continue to study part time.

Contrary to what was expected, there is no statutory requirement for an NGO school to be registered for its students to appear in a board exam after grade 5 in order to enter grade 6, an exam that is arranged for all primary students by the government educational board. However, some community members thought otherwise and, to placate them, one of the schools had been registered. All the students who appeared for the government exam were to be fielded through this school and other TMF schools were shown as branches of this registered school. This was because registration was quite demanding in terms of the staff and facilities that had to be in place. Thus, the schools are only implicitly recognized by the state. The project also made sure that a migrating family received a school-leaving certificate signed by the district education officer (DEO) so the child could be admitted to a government school.

PTAs were being formed in every school and they no longer reported to the DO. Each PTA had seven members including the teacher, a DO officeholder (who reported back to the DO), and five parents, generally mothers. The members were appointed during a general body meeting at the time the school is founded and subsequently met biannually to review the progress of the school. The effective and involved PTA members stayed on while the others left, making way for new more committed members. For new schools, a five-year plan was chalked out, during the course of which it was hoped that the community would completely take over the school. Mothers attended regularly, but we were told that as they could not make decisions on their own, decisions were often deferred to the next meeting.

A typical PTA agenda included problems relating to absenteeism (of both student and teacher), dropouts, high fees and other problems faced by the students. If the teachers were not performing their duties well and the community members were not happy with her performance, she could be replaced by a competent teacher. Decisions were made collectively and everybody's consent was sought.

Communities closely monitored the teacher and one was removed due to community dissatisfaction. In this particular case, the community settled for a local male teacher, despite cultural reservations, because the female teacher was often late. As a result of the male teacher's good performance, students who had dropped out returned and many others as well were drawn to the school; all in all, the total enrollment went up. There was an extreme shortage of educated females locally and so attempts were made to recruit from places as close by as possible to minimize both cultural differences and costs in terms of transport and time.

A School Management Fund (SMF) was established for each school, and parents were encouraged to deposit small sums (Rs.5–Rs.10) into it on a monthly basis. In addition, parents were expected to pay a similar amount in tuition fee. The hope was that eventually this fund would make the school self-sustaining. About 50 percent of the parents contributed something. Some schools managed to accumulate about Rs. 3,000–4,000 and a bank account was to be opened for these schools. The signatories were to include a teacher, a PTA member, and a TMF representative. A monthly matching contribution from the project was to represent an incentive for the community to build the fund.

The government schools had much better facilities and much better student–teacher ratios. TMF was however much more confident of its superior techniques and assured of a better outcome. There were good relations between the TMF field management and government teachers. We were informed that the government teachers had adopted monthly tests based on TMF practice and advice. One of the main advantages of the TMF schools, relative to government schools, was their willingness to be flexible. This applied across the board, but was particularly advantageous during the harvesting and processing seasons.

The anti-NGO sentiment whipped up in the wake of the September 11, 2001 attacks in the United States resulted in community members pulling their children out of schools. The local imams were still hostile and could incite community suspicions. APPNA now had the trust and goodwill of the community, as they had been delivering door-to-door service for the past 13 years, but, even so, communities were ever watchful.

Good teaching was rewarded via moral incentives—a certificate was issued to them. However, in view of the low pay of teachers— Rs. 1,500 for the matric level (10 grades), Rs. 1,700 for the intermediate level (higher certificate of education requiring 12 grades), and Rs. 1,900 for undergraduate qualifications—the TMF management felt that even a low bonus as an incentive would be helpful.[4] Since teachers invigilated and graded each other's tests, they thought this would not be difficult to administer.

Several communities had requested a high school because they do not want the girls traveling long distances. The project's response was that their mandate was primary schooling, but that if the community provided the building and teacher's salaries, it would facilitate the process and also provide the teacher training.

9.2.5 Microcredit

Loans continued to be based on the Islamic principle of *marahaba* and were given in kind. The community still viewed the HDF credit policy as a disguised form of interest-bearing loans and also continued to think of the "commission" charged as being too high. Although this was factually incorrect, as the credit was subsidized, it would take a skillful communications strategy to get the point across. In any case, several DOs were not utilizing the microcredit facility. Quoting a religious teaching, they said, "those who take interest and give interest are equal in their sins." In most of the meetings, the issue was brought up in one way or the other.

Another problem was that much of the credit was tied to trainings and these were delivered to individuals. This limited the benefits to the larger community. For example, credit was linked to training in garment making and the women were given loans to buy machines. Similarly, in case of livestock and poultry management, loans were given to buy chickens or buffaloes. To address this problem of individual versus collective benefit, HDF was planning to enter into joint business ventures with the communities, and these are completely acceptable from an Islamic perspective. The preparatory work in computing the returns for various joint ventures was completed with the RPM personally taking much interest in this.

The plan was to use the monies in DO savings and the school fund and match those for an investment. The profits would be shared on a pro-rata basis depending on who invested how much and the loss was to be accordingly shared.[5] We cautioned that this is risky, as the community may question both the amount of profit made and the scale of loss. Also, risking the school fund did not seem wise.

Given the high transaction cost of the current credit policy, HDF had sensibly hired a full-time credit officer who was responsible for purchases. The credit policy also required that the initial two or three credits given on the recommendation of the DO be paid back before fresh loans were approved. Thus peer group pressure was being utilized in some form despite our earlier concern that it may not work for cultural reasons in this project area.

Out of the 210 loans granted, only 2 were in default. In one case, a lady who had taken a loan of Rs. 15,000 started engaging in a highly lucrative smuggling business. On her way from Lahore (the capital city of Punjab province), the police confiscated all her goods and so she lost all her investment. The community had paid one installment on her behalf, and she was hoping to pay another installment by selling eatables. In the other case, a man was arrested on a criminal charge and he was continuing to try to arrange installments.

The community was now deciding who would get the loan, and at the time of giving a loan, the community—after verifying that the borrower was trustworthy—undertook to be the guarantor. In one case, the DO had difficulty in refusing an influential and tried to get the project to run interference. The DO officers suggested that the DO president would write a coded letter to the project to refuse a recommended loan. The project did not go along with this subterfuge, preferring that the DO take responsibility and do so by following transparent procedures.

9.2.6 Trainings

The joint venture strategy was an attempt at spreading the benefits that were being confined to individuals via trainings and subsequent credit. Thus, computer or welding training and the credit associated with that benefited only individuals by enhancing their skills to start profitable ventures, but HDF felt that the benefits should be more widespread. Some of the training also ended up being "certificate chasing" with little chance of follow-up. Thus computer skills courses, without a computer at home, often meant that the trainees were unable to practice those skills and hence lost them. An individual we met at the time of our field visit was learning how to drive and was paying half the cost himself.

The assistant director of the livestock department provided a course for women on poultry and livestock management. This had to be a very basic training with pictures, since virtually all the women were illiterate. The community asked for training in making washing powder, since it was a high expense item in the household budget. A resource person, who had picked up this skill in Islamabad, was identified. Based on one two-hour training for DOs, many households were making their own washing powder, and the knowledge was spreading fast.

In the previous year, the project offered trainings in livestock and poultry management, washing powder making, candle making, and garment designing (embroidery, stitching, cutting). These trainings were well received by the community women and the attendance was high. The women faced difficulties in accessing inputs, and, due to lack of exposure, they were not aware of the latest trends prevalent in the market (in case of garments)—this made their products very hard to promote. Another problem highlighted by the women was that even if people brought them work, they refused to take it up as it did not pay well.

9.2.7 Linkages

Linkage had slowed down because the line (government service) departments were in a state of uncertainty due to the government devolution (of power to the grassroots) plan.[6] Most were in a "wait and see" mode until there was clarity on the powers and functions of the new local government officials relative to the line departments. However, even resolutions from the communities that entailed linkages were not forthcoming. The project has thus adopted a more proactive role in this regard and did a "needs analysis" in the communities.

There were examples of successful linkages including linking communities to a welfare organization that facilitated operations for polio victims. Another linkage had facilitated vocational training for the disabled. A third linkage was on the back burner because the communities were very busy with sugarcane harvesting and processing. However, the plan was to have members of the Sugarcane Research Center, located in Mardan, to provide capacity-building workshops for DO members. The linkage with the Education Department ensured school registration and school transfer for students and the one with the Livestock Department ensured livestock vaccinations and veterinary assistance.

One of the problems being confronted by the project was the attitude of potential resource persons in the line departments. NGOs were perceived as cash cows that were flush with donor funds and so the lower-paid government servants demanded, and sometimes received, a very high daily fee. HDF was on a tight budget, but found it difficult to negotiate this fee down. There were also expectations that HDF would accommodate the trainer's relatives in various jobs and the culture of merit-based appointments was difficult to explain to demanders, as the broader environment functioned differently.

Summary

The project had developed an interesting exit strategy for the future: a cluster organization at the village level was to be formed and called a VDO. The DOs would report to the VDO, rather than the project NGO. Several VDOs would then be forged into an IDO as an apex body. The IDO would be registered and hence capable of fund-raising and would then engage in the support function by the use of linkages and capacity building. This would then enable the project NGO to move to other units.

It was also realized that APPNA really needed a village-level organization and the HCs that reported to the DO actually were splitting up APPNA's VHCs and undermining its effectiveness. Thus, HCs were slated to be abandoned. Similarly, PTAs no longer reported to the DO but included in their meetings a DO representative to report back to the DO. Thus the project demonstrated learning and adaptation.

Our earlier observations about the challenging aspects of social mobilization for cultural and other reasons were borne out and remained relevant. Women's social mobilization continued to be seriously influenced by conflicts among men. However, the project was slowly winning the trust of the community and having a positive influence by means of DOs on collective action, several examples of which came to our notice during questioning. These included the use of a social boycott and collective contributions to a school building.

As earlier indicated, several problems remained unresolved, including the problem of multigrade teaching in what were essentially one-room schools. Not surprisingly, across the board, culture continued to have a powerful impact on the project. For example, there was pressure on girls to discontinue their education after puberty. Even though dearth of locally available educated female teachers meant that teachers needed to be brought in from the outside, getting teachers from neighboring villages was problematic because of travel constraints. Similarly, TMF was quite careful to ensure that the Islamic education was part of the curriculum. This is not only consistent with the TMF approach but also warded off the potential opposition from the local imams.

An interesting institutional innovation in education was the establishment of a SMF into which about half the communities were contributing at least small amounts. The project was providing a matching grant as an incentive. The TMF management cooperated with the government schools and had persuaded them to adopt their monthly examination system. The teacher training, including a module for multigrade teaching, was intensive and well received by the teachers. TMF also adopted a flexible schedule during harvesting season to minimize dropout rates. Such flexibility among TMF schools is a great strength relative to government schools.

The PTAs had started functioning and parents were empowered to discontinue the services of an unsatisfactory or tardy teacher based on consensus. Similar empowerment was not evident in practice among the HCs, although APPNA claimed this was the case in its national project documents. In practice, the complaint had to be put up via proper channels to the regional office.

Despite objections, no female HA had been promoted to a SHA position. The project justification was again an appeal to prejudices that women SHA would not be taken seriously in the current cultural norms and would find it difficult to travel. Although TMF had dealt with the problem of having a backup on hand by hiring a reserve teacher, such excess capacity was still not built into the APPNA program. The RPM was contemplating initiating an internship program to address this problem.

Another unresolved problem was the continuing discomfort of the community with the implicit *sood* (interest) involved in the microcredit program. Several DOs were working with the project on other interventions, but avoided microcredit. The RPM was contemplating an alternative profit-and-loss sharing transaction as a joint venture with the community. Although this was acceptable in Islamic terms, it entailed high risk. However, the RPM felt this would work and also address the issue of loans that benefited the individual rather than the broader community. As all loans required an endorsement by the DO, which agreed to be a guarantor, and earlier loans needed to be returned to qualify for new ones, the peer group pressure model had become operational.

Thus, our return visit to the field revealed a great deal of leaning, adjustment, and institutional innovation. Naturally, not all issues flagged as actual or potential problems in chapters 5–8 were resolved, but most were addressed and progress on several fronts was clearly evident. The prominent effect of culture on the project was again evident.

Field Update 2006

10.1 Introduction

Our follow-up fieldwork was greatly facilitated by fortunate circumstances.[1] We got approval from the head office to visit the regional office in Mardan and interviewed the regional program manager (RPM) and other field staff at the regional office—including the social organizers (SOs) and the engineer—and also visited the original sites where we had done fieldwork in 1999. Annexures 10.1 and 10.2 provide an account of what we learnt from the original sites of the female and male social mobilization and DO formation respectively.

We conferred after the first day of fieldwork and realized that we were not getting a holistic picture of the project by returning only to the original sites and decided, based on resources and time available, to explore other project interventions using a stratified random sample (8.5 percent) of 14 DOs (eight male and six female) for follow-up research.[2] HDF had started work in 1999 in two units in Mardan and had formed 31 DOs; by 2006, it was working in six units and had formed 403 DOs.[3]

We fielded a follow-up questionnaire in the male and female focus group discussions (FGDs) in the sampled DOs, primarily to get a sense of social capital and induced and autonomous collective action.[4] We also used the field registers of the sampled DOs, which had been active for over a year, as another database to get a picture of the field presence of the project. DO registers provide a detailed record of attendance, minutes of meetings, credit, savings, project work, and induced or autonomous collective action.[5]

Thus, this update is based on interviews in the regional and head offices, project documents collected from the field and the head office, visits to the original field sites, follow-up FGDs in the randomly selected DOs, and a review of their register records.

10.2   DO Update

While the original DO was defunct, the young men in the Fazal Killay village had formed a new one that was quite active. However, since they continued to regard *sood* (interest) as problematic, this time around there was no credit program and the members concerned themselves with training and other aspects of the broader HDF project.

Even so, this was a very significant development indeed, considering the dominance and also nonfunctionality of the village elders six years earlier. It was also significant that while the earlier DOs met only in the presence of the SO, because they viewed nothing of adequate significance if it did not involve the SO, the new members met regularly (once every two weeks) with or without the SO. Thus community issues were now viewed as having import significant enough to be discussed and handled by the community on its own. This is precisely the outcome that HDF wanted to achieve and in this case they were successful. The survey of male DOs also indicated that the DOs held meetings as per requirement, without the presence of the SO.[6]

This spirit of collective action was also evident in the newly formed female DO in Kandera Jadeed. It stood up to TMF and threatened to close down a school if the decision on the transfer of a popular teacher out of the community was not reversed. The lack of female mobility continued to be a problem and, in the case of one woman, discouraged female savings because of dependency on men to manage the accounts, a dependence that made the funds less accessible.

We also learned that the National Rural Support Program (NRSP, see chapter 3), which had a prior presence in the area, tried to organize the same community. This effort failed, as the NRSP revolved program heavily around interest-based credit. This also reveals the potential problem of overlapping catchments for development NGOs.

10.3   Other Institutional Issues

We explored the issue of what motivates DO formation in our follow-up survey and it appears that a number of factors were instrumental, prominent among them was a spillover effect. Thus if adjacent communities had DOs and individuals and the community appeared to be benefiting from it, they approached HDF to form a DO. In these cases, social mobilization is easier since the members are already motivated. The female DO formation was more influenced by the presence of a TMF teacher in the neighborhood or by the male members of a DO endorsing this activity for the females they were associated with. Some respondents were quite categorical about the personal benefits they expected to derive from the DO formation. All except one of the female DOs faced negative public pressure with regards to DO formation and were even told that by involving themselves in NGO-related activities they were engaging in sin (*gunnah*).[7]

As indicated earlier, the HDF presence in Mardan had expanded to 6 units and a total of 403 DOs and 25 village development organizations (VDOs) had been established. The criteria for establishing a DO was the same, and VDOs were cluster organizations formed when DOs in a village represented 80 percent of the village households and they comprised of 2 nominees from every DO. Smaller villages may have only one DO and this could be converted into a VDO if it represented 80 percent of the village households. The purpose of the VDO was collective action across DOs in the village or linkages with government or other agencies—particularly in the context of the government's devolution of power plan (see section 10.5). A unit development organization (UDO) had also been established, with two nominees from each VDO, to address unit level issues. Candidates were also successfully fielded for local government elections and 12 succeeded in winning positions at the union council (the lowest) tier of local government.[8]

Nonoperational DOs were referred to as "dead" in project language, although a proposal was afloat at the head office level to grade DOs. This was to be based on a maturity index comprising of "objective criteria" such as attendance, savings, credit received, and recovery rate based on the DO files in the regional and head offices. We view this "objective criteria" as mechanical and subject to manipulation and as a poor substitute for the knowledge and insight of the SOs working in the field.[9] Our analysis of registers also demonstrated that villagers met and saved according to their needs. Thus there was a decline in savings when *Eid* (religious festival) expenditures picked up and DO meetings would pick up when the community felt the need to solicit HDF's assistance for some project, activity, or training. Thus regularity in saving and attendance could be viewed as a superficial and "input"-oriented method of judging maturity rather than as an "output" or collective action–oriented method.

HDF anticipates that this might improve DO performance by creating competition among DOs because the higher-graded ones would get priority on requests. Based on the Aga Khan Rural Support Program (AKRSP) model (see chapter 3), community physical infrastructure (CPI) projects were being mediated by HDF and funded by the Pakistan Poverty Alleviation Fund (PPAF).[10]

Similar to the criticism of the maturity index, another criticism of the Rural Support Program (RSP) model is that it is very target driven such that just forming the DOs (inputs) become an end in and of itself rather than a means to an end (collective action). This could be one part of the explanation of why about two-fifths of the DO's had not succeeded even by the regional office's own criteria. In HDF's case, annual targets for DO formation are set jointly by the regional and head offices.[11] The regional office proposed the targets based on its field assessment of needs and subject to the approval of the head office.

Instead of a conventional Monitoring and Evaluation Section, a performance improvement program had been put into place. Monthly and quarterly assessments were based on a review of target achievements, both quantitative and qualitative, based on field visits, a review of regional office records, assessment of social mobilization, and punctuality in report submission. The work of the regional offices was graded and available in a consolidated hard copy report and on the HDF Web site so as to create healthy competition among regions, with response to resource requests acting as incentive.

10.4   Collective Action

Collective action engaged in at the DO level is discussed in the monthly DO meetings and the record maintained at the DO level. Information on linkage-related collective action was sent to the head office in the monthly reports and documented in the HDF annual report. There were some interesting examples of collective action at the grassroots level in Mardan.

Some villages had decided to save on transactions costs by pooling electricity bills and have one person at a time pay them all. A VDO addressed, in an emergency meeting, the crises of an electricity transformer that blew up. They delegated members to lobby the power department and managed to have the service up and running the very same night. Another case was that of a mutual signing of a legal bond (with a Rs. 400,000 penalty) by DO members and a heroin dealer, enforceable by the court, to prevent local sales that had become very disruptive in the community. Another case was that of a UDO that accosted the power authority's alleged overbilling. A mutually agreed solution was the installation of village electricity meters to monitor consumption.

The male DOs that we surveyed had all initiated self-help interventions. Five of them had organized and participated in the community cleaning of the distribution canals (*khal*). One had initiated a fundraising drive and collected Rs. 8,000 for a drainage project and another had their village water pump repaired.

10.5   Project-Community Partnerships

This is something that the first regional manager had conceived of as a way of utilizing community savings for profit. On an experimental basis, HDF matched the collective savings of a local DO that had accumulated a substantial saving by local standards (Rs. 500,000) and jointly established a fertilizer purchase and sale dealership as a *musharika* (joint venture).[12] There was to be a discount for DO members. HDF trained the community in managing accounts and stocks, and this was discussed at DO meetings. The project initially worked well and turned a profit but was eventually abandoned when DO members decided that the opportunity cost of time spent in this activity did not match the return.

HDF is also currently considering a "one-village one-product" marketing joint-venture strategy based on building on the existing excellence and specialization it discovers in different villages. The one attempt at this based on the highly profitable *khaddar* (indigenous rough cotton cloth produced with handlooms) failed. While the product is extremely profitable, the attempt at a joint venture by HDF did not work, partly because one family, which was reluctant to engage in the partnership, was largely deriving the benefit. HDF's attempt to provide broader training to other DOs was also not successful because *khaddi* production is viewed as a lower-caste activity.[13]

The attempt to get communities to invest in the one-room community primary schools was also not successful. HDF tried to persuade community members to build verandas that would provide space for some grades and shelter in inclement weather. As the schools were run from the house of the teacher, this was seen as upgrading property in private rather than community ownership.

10.6   Public-Project Partnerships/Linkages

The military government introduced its local government devolution of power plan in 1999 (see section 3.6) and we explored how this interfaced with HDF in the project area. One provision of the devolution plan is the encouraging of grassroots work through the establishment of citizen community boards (CCBs). The district provides 80 percent of the funding of approved projects of the CCBs and the latter has to raise the other 20 percent. As many of the villages in the Mardan area had been mobilized by HDF, social activists in the project area were successful in having 12 CCBs registered.[14] However, funding was generally based on political patronage and so establishing a CCB was a necessary but not sufficient condition for actually getting a village-level project; by mid-2006, only one (in Unit 3) had procured such a project by utilizing its saving of Rs. 240,000.

A second source of partnership with the government was through the PPAF, designed for grassroots microcredit-driven projects to alleviative poverty. In practice, the PPAF operates like a bank providing funds for on-lending to grassroots development organizations at a markup. This has been a wonderful opportunity for HDF because, once again, they were well positioned to solicit this funding using the DO platform. The PPAF funding has been used for CPI projects. After the social mobilization and the formation of the DO, the community can send a request for a sanitation-related, hand-pump, watercourse lining, or a street pavement project as part of the CPI program.[15]

The general procedure of working with the communities for infrastructure projects has been formalized. The community puts up a request via the DO, given 80 percent attendance, and this request is vetted by the SO in terms of its social viability (composition of beneficiaries, community contribution, maintenance capacity, maturity of the DO, and weather a contractor might be involved) and by the project engineer in the regional office to ensure the technical and environmental viability.[16] This process is completed by way of three formal dialogues with the community and a TOP (terms of partnership) signed during the third dialogue. Once the project proposal is completed, it is sent to head office and then on to PPAF for approval. The approval process takes about two months and has so far always been forthcoming. HDF then establishes a joint account with the community, a check is provided in a DO meeting, and the funds are accessible to the community nominees (president / secretary) with HDF as a cosignatory. The payments are staggered based on project monitoring.

The community contribution is 25 percent of the total project cost, mostly in labor and some occasionally in cash.

An integrated model village project had been implemented by a VDO based on the above procedure and this included all infrastructure components (sanitation, hand-pump, watercourse lining, and street pavement) and also composting. The village contributed Rs. 3.1 million in skilled and unskilled labor and cash, and PPAF contributed Rs. 2.4 million. The work was good, as was the maintenance, although the drains were clogged during our field visit. In accordance to specified procedure, the VDO had established a village project/purchase committee, audit committee, and a maintenance committee. HDF hoped for replication and diffusion as other communities observed what had been achieved.[17]

HDF had also been collaborating, as a contractor, with the government's *Khushali* (well-being) Bank by engaging in the social mobilization to construct DOs for the Bank's interventions, much as NRSP was initially considered as a project partner to do the social mobilization for HDF (see chapter 5).

10.7   Health

APPNA was no longer a project partner in the project area. The HDF regional office mentioned that this was based on their exit strategy of leaving once adequate preventive education had been provided and a community health center (CHC) established. The departure was phased such that that the community would take over the CHC in five years and fund it by means of out patient revenue.

APPNA retained a presence in Mardan and our discussions with them revealed that they viewed the partnership, as initially and wisely conceived, at the field level to have been very valuable and complementary. They viewed the termination of the partnership as a very unfortunate result of conflict of egos of the first HDF regional/country manager and the regional head of APPNA.

We learned from the HDF head office that the pulling back of APPNA operations was made by the board at Chicago and that the impact was nationwide. Thus, APPNA was no longer a partner in any of the HDF units across the country. HDF had taken over the APPNA functions arguing that this service was needed in the project area to continue achieving higher human development. The communities had not taken over the APPNA CHCs as envisaged. Thus, in addition to the preventive functions described in chapter 7, HDF had taken over the CHC and added a curative facility to the health program in two of the six units. A doctor, who worked with a lady health visitor (LHV) and a dispenser as an assistant, headed this facility. The LHV supervised four lady health workers (one per 250 households). Thus these services were available to the general public as were the services of the periodic (three until mid-2006) medical camps based on invited specialists.

The nutritional training in the TMF schools was taken over by the LHV who also directly tended to or referred sick children. Visits to the school were monthly in the two units containing the CHC and quarterly for the other units, and meticulous records for all the children were maintained. Creating the demand for reproductive health information in a very conservative community was viewed as a singular achievement of the health program.

10.8   Education

TMF continued to work with HDF as a project partner; the one-room schools, with a teacher willing to provide a room and working for a salary, remained the basic building block of the project's education provision.[18] Thus multigrade teaching continued to be a problem. HDF provides the teacher training, books, and teacher salary.[19] There was now two-way traffic of students between government and TMF schools. While 23 of the 45 schools were girl's schools, 60 percent of the total 2,461 children enrolled were girls. The regional office viewed the female teachers as having more successfully adopted the "joyful learning" methodology that TMF teachers (master trainers—regional education officers) are trained to receive at head office. The field-level training is by means of the master trainers with the HDF head office trainers present to provide backup.[20]

In 2006, 14 TMF schools had fielded 75 students in the government's grade 5 external board exams and 69 had passed. This pass percentage of 92 percent compares well with a pass percentage of 76 percent of children from government schools appearing from the same center at the same time. Seven TMF-HDF students had secured among the top three positions in various centers. HDF acknowledged this achievement in a prize-giving ceremony.

HDF had acquiesced to community requests to start three secondary schools, but none had been registered due to the onerous government registration requirements. The plan was to have the students matriculate privately, but this kept enrollments low. Tuition fees were being paid, based on capacity, into a school management fund that had accumulated to Rs. 292,000.[21] The parent teacher associations (PTAs) meet once a month, with the education coordinator or his assistant participating, and monthly reports were sent to the regional office. Among other school-related issues, appropriate tuition fees and delinquency in payments were discussed.

10.9   Microcredit

The credit program continued to experience problems. Communities continued to posture against interest (usury), notwithstanding the use of *murahaba* (markup) that has Islamic sanction. However, this did not prevent the taking of loans.[22] The RPM acknowledged recovery problems in certain areas, even though the overall cumulative recovery rate was estimated to be 87 percent for Mardan and 89 percent across all units for 2005. The RPM attributed some stuck-up loans to SOs who did not follow procedures and hence unduly favored some recipients.[23] The HDF CEO argued that enhancing the well-being of poor communities, rather than recovery rates, should be the main objective. Also, his view was that not many individual projects at the grassroots level could realistically bear a return that can cover the organizational transaction cost of the loan. HDF field staff claimed that their culture of "humanized loans," which protected the dignity of the recipient, was also a cause of the relatively low recovery (by microcredit project standards) in some project areas.

The practice during our fieldwork was that the mark-ups recovered were sent back to the head office. The remaining capital, as determined by the head office, was maintained at the regional office as a revolving fund. An alternative incentive driven Special Micro Credit Incentive Package (SMCIP) targeted at entrepreneurs had been launched. The idea was to target loans to "the best category of borrowers" at a subsidized rate using HDF's revolving fund. Once the DO nominates a member, the terms and conditions including the installments due, markup, and the technical viability of the loan are discussed with the SO in the DO meeting. There is then a credit appraisal based on the reputation of the person taking the loan and the case is prepared and sent to the head office. Again, if there was a default by any member of the DO, no new loans were approved so that the peer pressure model continued to be in use. This package entailed more careful appraisal and had improved recovery to about 100 percent. That recovery statistics continue to be cited suggests it is difficult for a development organization to move away from conventional target assessment despite its own better judgment.

10.10   Training

HDF continues to engage in Leadership Management Skills Trainings (LMST) and Community Management Skills Training (CMST) for community officeholders and in addition provides technical training based on community requests. Between August 2004 and July 2006, it provided trainings, mostly lasting two to three days, to 594 persons (of which 533 were female). Apart from LMST and CMST, these included livestock extension worker training (with knowledge shared with DO members), basic garments training (sewing/stitching), poultry management training, poultry farming training, and tailoring for men.

Our survey of male DOs indicated that they had, facilitated by HDF, availed of electrical-maintenance, first-aid, and computer training in a vocational skill training center. Lower level of literacy and the long commute meant that women were not yet availing these opportunities. However, apart from the usual LMST and CMST training for officeholders, women benefited from embroidery, sewing, livestock, poultry, fruit preservation, tie and dye, and detergent-making training.

The officeholders of one DO used the training to sew clothes for the women of the village at nominal charges. While HDF is no longer engaged in the direct marketing of such products, it continues to make linkages of the community with the private sector.

10.11   Local Perception of HDF

This was one of the questions we included on our questionnaire for the follow-up FGDs because we had witnessed community suspicion and wariness of the project during its start up. DO members were unanimous in stating that the negative perception of HDF among communities had abated across the board. The school, health, and infrastructure schemes were changing community views. One respondent stated that: "Earlier, neither MPAs (Member Provincial Assembly), MNAs (Member National Assembly), nor district government did anything for us; only HDF has come to us and worked with us. So people were generally happy about project interventions." This view appeared to be broadly shared. The women in the follow-up survey were equally positive about the project. One response captured this well: "Women have learnt some skills and have figured out how to generate incomes; if it was not for these people (HDF) who would come to us illiterate village folks."

10.12   Sustainability and Exit Strategy

The marketing of community products to build an endowment fund did not work. The technology for sealing juice and jam bottles was not sound and so products perished. While there were individual successes with regard to embroidery, the project's attempts to market for liveli-hoods and project sustainability did not work. The competition kept costs lower with bulk purchase and ensured better quality.

The original conception of trying to make a school self-sufficient in five years with the development of a school management fund was found to be overambitious in practice. In all cases, the interest on the capital accumulated was not enough to pay even the teacher salary, leave alone the school's running expenses. These funds are continuing to accumulate as joint accounts with community representatives and HDF as cosignatories.

HDF's broader exit strategy was linked in 2004 to the UNDP's mil-lennium development goals (MDG) that are set for achievement by 2015.[24] However, just as there is acknowledged slippage in the attain-ment of the MDG virtually across the board, the management recog-nizes that as long as poverty remains and funds are available to credibly address it, HDF is likely to continue to have a field presence in some evolving form. By mid-2006, HDF depended on HDFNA for between 70 and 80 percent of its budget and raised the rest locally through partnerships.

10.13   What Makes DOs Succeed?

An important issue we confronted was why social mobilization did not work in 157 out of 403 cases, why some DOs die while others suc-ceed, and whether harnessing social capital is central to success. The SOs viewed social capital (as described in chapters 1 and 2) as relevant but indicated that based on their experience, this was more likely to be found in communities that were homogeneous, that is, from the same clan or tribe.[25] The RPM attributed success or failure to the quality of the community social activists or community leadership. As community social activists are cultivated and mobilized by the SOs, one could view the quality, dedication, and commitment of the SOs as another factor. The response at head office was that the key was to empower communities and having adequate resources to keep them engaged. As the project interface and resources are likely to be roughly similar for all communities, the issue of why some succeed and others do not remained unanswered.

We included questions on this issue on the follow-up survey FGDs of the functional DOs. The conventional measurement of social capital in terms of community social organizations did not reveal much activity: one mosque committee, one CCB, and one cricket team. However, as measured by responses to hypothetical questions and community perceptions, there was a much higher level of social capital. For example, most of the males responded that if there were a natural disaster, they would engage in self-help and collective action to assist others. All respondents thought that the level of community trust and solidarity was very high. The response to why this was the case was "because we have the same mosque and *hujrah* and so we have more unity (*ittifaq*)."[26] Another response was that since "we are from the same tribe, it was easy to get mobilized and have consensus and other communities are impressed with our level of unity."

It is interesting how Pukhtun institutions of mosque, *hujrah*, and tribe come into play in these responses. However, while these responses are indicative, we think that we have merely touched the surface of an important research question: Does prior social capital in communities make DOs more sustainable and effective in implementing autonomous and induced collective action? It is possible that had we been able to visit the dead DOs, we would have got similar responses to the ones we got from the functioning ones.[27] We view this to be an issue requiring in-depth empirical investigation and propose a research method in the appendix.

Summary

HDF's most major accomplishment is that, notwithstanding the continued resistance to the credit component of the program in some communities, it has broken the ice and gained widespread community acceptance and goodwill in the project area. So much so, as in the best case scenario, it is being approached by communities to form DOs based on perceived benefits. It is notable that the people's hostility to and suspicion of NGOs, feelings heightened by global, national, and local events, and their "western agenda" in the project area made their task an uphill struggle. Also, it has achieved a major project objective of making self-directed and self-organized DO meetings and collective action a reality in at least the male DOs.

There is also much evidence of program learning and evolution. HDF tried several things (see chapter 9), such as joint ventures, and moved on when they did not work. The important lesson in this and in the community response to improving schools is the tension between individual incentives/motivation and collective action. Collective action is clearly possible and there were several examples of this that we have cited at the local level. However, the preconditions for this is that the benefits should be roughly evenly shared by the community rather than accruing to a particular household.

The project staff often has an idealistic mindset based on inclination or training and want to support only a collective and altruistic spirit and feel uneasy with individualistic self-motivated sentiments. This may not be called for because humans are driven by both motivations. The project challenge is to harness individual motivations that sustain an interest in the project, for both personal and collective good, though the mechanisms are different from Adam Smith's famous recognition that the market can harness private incentive for the public interest.

Apart from the evidence of autonomous collective action, the other major project success we have documented is its ability to forge linkages and partnerships with government and civil society to extend community benefits. The links with PPAF and *Khushali* (well-being) Bank stand out in this regard. Thus, while core partnerships were no longer part of the operating principle of HDF, partnerships at a broader level were very much a part of what makes the project effective.

This notion of partnership and linkages is also embodied in communities that autonomously solicited them and then mined them for community benefit. The major success in this regard was that HDF had primed communities via social mobilization such that they were able to set themselves up to benefit from the local government reform by forming and registering CCBs. That the benefits from this in the form of soliciting district government projects were limited had more to do with local patronage politics than limitations to community collective action.

Even without the core partnership in health with APPNA, HDF had the confidence as a full-fledged development organization to take over the health functions and add a curative aspect to a preventive program. Similarly, its education interventions were successful by local standards judging by the pass percentages on government external board exams and by the top positions secured by the TMF-HDF school students. Credit remained a challenge, and here HDF had innovated to try to engender sustainable livelihoods by supporting local entrepreneurship.

Although HDF has achieved much, it needs to be cautious in carefully distinguishing in its assessments of the DOs and itself by focusing on outputs (successful collective action) rather than on inputs (DO meeting and saving) and the number of DOs formed. But nothing remains the same in the development field, and signs of institutional innovation indicated that HDF had adequate flexibility to act as a learning and adapting organization. Just as we pointed to the tension between individual incentives and collective action, there is a tension between central decision making and regional office autonomy based on local knowledge. Our observations suggest that HDF will strike the right balance.

ANNEXURE 10.1

Follow-Up Field Visit to Original Female DOs

This report is based on follow-up field visits made to Fazal Killay and Kandare Jadeed villages. The three female DOs in Fazal Killay (FK) were inactive. FK I and FK II were mobilized and created in 2000 while FK III was established later in 2001. FK I and FK II DOs congregated in the homes of Sabar Jan and Guloona respectively who are sisters-in-law. These women sadly lost the household heads in the past two years, both of whom were supportive of their DO activities.

These women stated, in the presence of the female SO, that the DOs had became inactive because the SO had stopped running it. The female DOs depended on the SO to write their minutes and do the bookkeeping as none of them were literate. There had been no DO related activity in the village for the past two years and this could partly be explained by a negative history associated with the male DO in Fazal Killay.

HDF has had a very problematic relation with the local community in Fazal Killay from the project inception, going back to the attempt by the male DO president to "hijack" the DO (see chapter 6). While HDF had deliberately decided to continue its activities in the female DOs, this was understandably not a sensible strategy in the local culture of females deferring to males on most decisions.[28]

More recently, a few months prior to our field visit, an incident in Fazal Killay put a stop to all project interventions there. Two females conducting a survey on behalf of HDF got into an altercation with some young men in the village. The male conduct violated local norms of interaction between the opposite sexes, and as a result HDF stopped its interventions in the village. When questioned about whether anyone from the village reprimanded the boys, we were told that this did not happen on our street and hence on our watch and in any case "no body wants to get into these matters;" another example of conflict avoidance in Pukhtun culture.

Thus a convergence of factors resulted in the inactivity of DOs in Fazal Killay. These include a bitter history with the male DO, a change in SOs and the project's focus on new areas, death of supportive male household heads, heterogeneous nature of the settlement, conflict avoidance ingrained in the local culture, the suspicion of NGOs, and the problem of *sood* (interest).

In Kandare Jadeed, a female DO was set-up soon after the anthropologist left the project area in 2000. This village has the same makeup as the rest of the villages in the project area. It was settled by *zamidaran* (tenant farmers) from the adjoining tribal agencies such as Bajaur and Mohmand and the districts of Swat and Malakand. The Mohmands are the dominant tribal group in this village.

The initial attempts at social mobilization in the village were not successful. The project contact person at the time was not interested in following up, and the nonlocal village teacher left the village. The focal household, where the DO formation meeting and other meetings took place, belonged to the *mullah* (clerics) occupational group from Bajaur. The president of the DO, Niaz Bibi, worked to form the organization at the urging of the village women with the permission of the men of the household. The women of the village were comfortable coming to this house because it belongs to the *mullah* household. As in Fazal Killay, the DO had been inactive because the project staff stopped visiting.

However, the DO had been very active regarding the TMF school. When the male teacher departed, the family instrumental in forming the DO provided a room for the school and TMF arranged for another teacher. The female teacher designated for the school built a very good rapport with the children and community. She was transferred and replaced by another teacher who could not build a similar rapport with the students and the community. The women's DO got the original teacher back by threatening to shut down the school.

We were puzzled by and speculated as to why social mobilization among women worked so much better in Kandare Jadeed than in Fazal Killay? The family of the *mullah* household in Kandare Jadeed was not as economically well off as the households of Guloona or Sabar Jan. In addition, the Kandera Jadeed settlement is more recent compared to that of Fazal Killay. Perhaps the less well-off in this case were more interested in investing in social networks and building a sense of community. Finally, Fazal Killay is located on the main Mardan-Charssada road and is not only connected by this road to the main regional centers but this road also has an established market and has the main stop for public transport going both ways. By contrast, Kandera Jadeed's location is more isolated and this may also explain why there is a greater sense of community.

The establishment of a CHC by HDF was a new intervention. The activities of this center replaced those of APPNA who left the partnership. The only difference is that while APPNA followed-up on child health and maintained record cards for three years, HDF is doing so until the age of five.

HDF has also received a good response to their physical infrastructure interventions, such as street pavements and drainage. According to the SOs, these infrastructure projects got the community involved, especially the men, as both the projects and impacts are visible.

According to the project staff, credit recovery has been a major problem in the area, especially in Fazal Killay. Interestingly women who are on the defaulters list have taken credit before and returned it. This suggests that the issue of *sood* (interest) is not the only factor responsible for stuck-up recoveries; if that was the case then prior loans would not have been returned. The bitter history with the male DO may have something to do with the default.

Past history, the incident of an infant death (see endnote 5 in the text), the change of SOs, and the incident involving rude behavior toward project associated personnel in Fazal Killay all impacted project activities. Fewer visits were made for credit recoveries and this may have lead to the perception that HDF is not collecting loans from some DOs. During the field visit, the female DO officeholders said to the HDF staff that: "We have heard you have written off the loans of some people, and if that is the case then you should not collect installments from us as well." The project is thus under pressure to recover stuck-up loans to avoid creating precedents.

Recall that in Kandare Jadeed the household that had been active in forming the DO was from among the *mullahs* household from Bajawar. People pointed out to them the discordance of their being *mullah* folk and taking credit on interest. The female DO member response was that that their menfolk, who supported them in forming the DO, had no problem with these transactions. In fact they had also taken credit and successfully returned it.[29] As in Fazal Killay, some of the DO members, particularly the officeholders (president and secretary) in whose house the DO was formed and met were multiple recipients (some up to three loans) of credit. However, it became apparent from talking to some of the loan recipients that the credit was being utilized not as specified in project documents but according to household priorities.

ANNEXURE 10.2

Follow-Up Field Visit to Original Male DOs

The old DO was defunct, but some young men had formed a new DO in Fazal Killay.[30] This DO had 30 members, with about half of them quite active and these were the villagers we talked to in this follow-up meeting. They hold fortnightly meetings and had received training from HDF on record keeping, leadership and community management skills, and computing. The members mentioned that their motive for forming this DO was the collective good.

Since APPNA had withdrawn from this area, teachers were being trained on basic health issues which they were in turn imparting to the students. The HDF health staff also pitched in to fill the gap created by APPNA's departure; one that was being sorely felt by the community. The closest community health centre (CHC) was too far away from the village and it was difficult for the community to benefit from this facility. However, the doctor in-charge told us that they visited the villages via a mobile unit for regular examinations. Our field visit on the next day coincided with visits of the HDF health staff from the CHC to a number of villages. These were viewed as a blessing since the doctors addressed the most basic health problems and also advised the community on the principles of general health and cleanliness.

Children were performing well in school and were going on to join the formal government schools. There were six members participating in a functional PTA that in principle had the power to remove nonperforming teachers, though that has not happened in this community. In practice, the PTA recommends its decisions to the DO which implements the decision. The community wants the schools to be upgraded to the secondary level because they believed that their children were performing well in these schools.

We probed the issue of microcredit and discovered that members of the community have borrowed with interest locally. Some suggested that since they initially viewed the donors to be non-Muslim foreigners, default would have been justified.

The changing political and economic environment was notable. Ali Khan, a member of the old DO, contested the local body election but lost. The infrastructure projects resulting from HDF's partnership with PPAF had resulted in the completion of infrastructure projects in the area. We visited a couple of these schemes in Khazana Dheri and they had significantly improved the outlook of the village and were strongly supported by the community.

ANNEXURE 10.3

List of Research Questions for Field Update 2006

Institutional Issues

What is the current structure of Development Organizations (DO)?
How frequent are the DO meetings?
Any there any cluster organizations?
Did and Integrated Development Organization (IDO) get set up as planned?
What is the record of collective action (spontaneous or induced) since Dec. 2001?

What is the current exit strategy?
What is HDF doing for self-financing–project sustainability?
How is the endowment fund progressing?
Is HDF still trying to market DO products? If so, what happens to the proceeds?
How are APPNA/TMF interfacing with HDF?
Are there examples of synergy between the three programs? (HDF/APPNA/TMF—assuming they are still the partners)
Is the funding for APPNA/TMF coming via HDF or the parent organizations?
Were the original Fazal Killay and Kandare Jadeed DOs revived? In yes, how are they performing? What are the leadership dynamics? If no, were new one established?

Gender

This was to flow out of the analysis of female DOs, but we viewed it to be a crosscutting theme in each of the subjects below:

Linkages

What are relations with local government like?
(We wanted to understand the interface with devolution since that emerged after our initial fieldwork)
Document the record of linkages with the government/private sector/civil society since Dec. 2001.

Training

What kind? For whom? How frequent? Any on a commercial basis?
Are trainings linked with credit?

Health

Do Health Committees remain disbanded?
Does the Village Health Committee still report to the DO?
Is there a *sehat markaz* (health center, see chapter 7) nearby? How is it functioning?
Have women started getting promoted to the senior health assistant (SHA) positions?
Has APPNA developed a plan for backups if some one quits?
What is the sense of ownership and responsibility on the part of the community for the health initiatives?

Education

How are the schools doing overall? Is there still multigrade teaching?
What is the drop out rate by gender? Are girls stopping education after primary school? After eighth grade (after puberty)?

Is there still flexibility in timings based on the agricultural calendar?

How is the training managed? Who is providing it?

What is the nature of the student flow between TMF and government schools? By gender?

What is the community contribution for schooling?

Has teacher compensation changed? Is it tied to qualifications? To performance?

Has a secondary school been established?

How are the "School Management Funds" progressing? Is HDF still making a matching contribution? What if anything have they been used for?

Explore the nature of the memberships of the PTA. How are they functioning? How much community voice is there in running the school? Could they sack a poorly performing teacher?

What is the physical quality of the schools? One-room? Other conditions?

Can we say anything else about the quality of education?

Is APPNA still providing health education / basic hygiene classes?

What role are the teachers playing in the DOs / VDOs?

Is there a sense of ownership and responsibility on the part of the community for the schools?

Credit

Is the opposition to this on Islamic grounds still an issue?

How exactly is it working? Is peer-group pressure still being used for loan repayments?

What is the record of repayments like?

How did HDFs attempts at joint credit for joint community "schemes" work?

Is that still being done or is credit more individualized?

Other Cultural Change Issues

Is there greater cultural acceptance of HDF?

Is there any evidence of cultural change due to the project in terms of suspicion of outsiders? Female mobility?

11

Summary and Conclusion

11.1   Introduction

This concluding chapter has three sections. The first summarizes the main findings of Part II of this book. The focus is on the lesson that Human Development Foundation (HDF) as a social experiment provides for harnessing and guiding social capital. In the second section, we review its ability to establish a national presence. In the third section, we make an overall assessment of HDF and its success in harnessing and guiding social capital.

11.2   Summary

HDF is a rural support program that was established by Human Development Foundation North America (HDFNA) based on the Aga Khan Rural Support Program (AKRSP) model of participatory rural development initiated in the northern areas of Pakistan. Central to this approach is the harnessing of social capital and formalizing it in village development organizations (DOs) and then guiding them to engage in successful collective action to alleviate poverty and enhance community well-being.

In addition, these organizations create individual opportunities for self-betterment. Regular saving, microcredit based on peer pressure, and village infrastructure projects via collective action were central to this program. Once the village organizations are established, they are exposed to multisector packages based on need, opportunity, and the maturity and absorption capacity of the grassroots organizations. The success of this program induced its widespread replication throughout the country: the Rural Support Program

Network (RSPN) now has 10 members that, as of March 31, 2006, collectively operated in 93 of Pakistan's 137 districts, formed 73,908 community organizations (COs), and had a total membership of close to 1.5 million (see chapter 3).

HDF adopted the AKRSP model but innovated by forging a partnership of some field organizations for service delivery and of others for research. Thus, the initial name of the organization was Human Development Partnership (HDP).[1] The idea of the partnership was in principle sound, and instead of the DO having to build multiple expertise very rapidly in key components of human development, such as in health and education, it could partner with other organizations with the requisite delivery expertise at the grassroots level. Also, HDF could move into an area that had the prior presence of one of these partners and this would facilitate social mobilization to harness social capital as community trust would already have been earned.

Hence HDF was first established in Mardan, where the Association of Pakistani Physicians North America (APPNA) founded APPNA *Sehat* (health) that engaged in preventive health interventions. The partnership had a rough adjustment period because APPNA resented the leadership of the newcomer HDF. As Tameer-i-Millat Foundation (TMF) did not have prior basic education interventions in this area, much more cooperation was initially in evidence between it and the HDF (see chapters 5, 9, and 10).

Another conceptual underpinning for the partnership was the notion of synergy that might be realized so that the whole is larger than the sum of the parts. As indicated above, there was a teething period, but examples of synergy did start to emerge (see chapters 9 and 10). Thus the goodwill that APPNA had earned in the community from about a dozen years of work started becoming available to HDF for its social mobilization efforts. TMF provided a platform to APPNA for using school children to spread hygiene and for preventive health care practice. TMF teachers became activists and key components of the DOs that HDF was constructing for harnessing social capital. By 2006, HDF was operating on its own, and while forging partnerships with government and other civic society organizations was very much a part of its mode of operation, the original conception of formal partnerships had been abandoned.

Another HDF institutional innovation in the design stage included forging a close link of microcredit with training and livelihood based on demand assessment and this too was modified. The operational definition of a community as those going to the same mosque remained. As the project evolved, so did other institutional innovations as documented in chapters 9 and 10. These included a school management fund, building excess capacity into the education and health program, and innovating with alternative microcredit financial modes that may be more culturally and religiously acceptable to Muslim communities.

Among the main lessons that emerged from our review of the HDF attempt at harnessing social capital is that it is not possible to do this effectively without fully understanding the culture the project is operating in. The culture, in this case the Pukhtun culture (see chapter 4), can pose major challenges to the social mobilization process that goes into formalizing social capital through the construction of community organizations.

However, in one case, our concern proved wrong and the project proved correct in persisting with a tried and tested policy. Thus, we had indicated that combative Pukhtun culture, with the high premium it logically placed on conflict avoidance, did not seem well suited to the peer pressure of microcredit in which needs are openly expressed and peer pressure used for recoveries. However, this model does appear to be taking root in cases where it has got community acceptance. The communities have to provide a collective guarantee that is implicit in the joint resolution for individual credit and until existing loans are repaid, fresh applications are not entertained by the project. This has resulted in the community taking collective responsibility for determining who got the loans and for ensuring repayment.

However, not all communities have accepted the microcredit model because of the religious objection to interest-based transactions, sometimes opportunistically so. In addition, the project has had to cope with an individualistic culture, a suspicion of outside interventions, a sense that help was owed to them, and severe constraints on female mobility.

Even for an established development NGO, unlike the newly founded HDF, social mobilization and the building and sustaining local organizations, which represent the formalization and embodiment of harnessed social capital, is an extremely difficult task. Nonetheless, HDF should feel satisfied that it has managed to get coordinated program interventions off the ground despite the odds. It has established DOs that are going concerns and that have demonstrated several examples of collective action and a willingness to pay collectively for services. Training and microcredit have been imparted in significant numbers and have had a positive impact on livelihood. Also, as indicated in chapters 7 and 8, the other project partners, APPNA and TMF, have made credible health and education interventions that HDF has subsequently incorporated into its own consolidated program in other regions.

Thus in villages that APPNA intervened in, the contraception prevalent rate was 44 percent compared to a national average of 17 percent, there was near universal breast feeding and knowledge of immunization and use of iodized salt. The field workers were well trained and had a good rapport with the communities who rated their services highly. TMF similarly established well-functioning schools at very low cost, and test results demonstrated that the value added in math cognitive skills in TMF schools in our sample was 44 percent greater than in a control government school one year after the schools were established; TMF-HDF students vastly outperformed government school pupils appearing in government fifth-grade board exams.

HDF introduced new initiatives in 2005. These included manager conferences in the Mardan and Shamsabad regions. Another innovation was "activists" workshops to promote mutual learning. Exposure visits were arranged for community members to view remarkable examples of autonomous collective action for enhancing community welfare by voluntary organizations or by the DOs of more mature organizations such as the National Rural Support Program (NRSP).

11.3.   HDF as a National Development NGO

As of March 2000, there were 31 DOs (16 male and 15 female) with a total of 660 members in Mardan district.[2] In April 2000, HDP opened a regional office in the Shamsabad district (Sindh province) and in August 2000, another one in Rahim Yar Khan district (Punjab). Thus, it started expanding within the first year of its existence. HDF found different partners in different regions based on demonstrated strengths of different organizations in particular activities in the different regions. Thus, in Shamsabad, it partnered with Strengthening Participatory Organizations (SPO) for education and in Rahim Yar

Khan, with Adult Basic Education Society (ABES). However, differences in priorities and operating cultures resulted in HDF deciding to retain their original partners. However, by 2005, except for the education partnership with TMF in Mardan, it was operating on its own. As of March 2002, it had

1. formed 260 DOs across the country,
2. was operating in four districts in addition to Mardan,[3]
3. had a membership of 4,431 in its DOs,
4. served about 80,000 beneficiaries,
5. catered to 1000 most vulnerable households, provided access to preventive health care to over 250,000 people,
6. built infrastructure with community help, including a dam in Zhob, Balochistan,
7. trained nearly 2,804 for income-generating activities and assisted in the establishment of 1,700 businesses.

While it subsequently entered a consolidation phase, in 2005, 420 new DOs were formed across all regions—290 on behalf of the state-run *Khushali* (well-being) Bank—to reach a total of 1,041 DOs (44 percent female and 85 percent active). Including linkages and partnerships, the beneficiary outreach for 2005 was over 1 million.

By 2002, HDF had established 102 schools with 87 parent teacher associations and a total enrollment of 2,990 students. By 2005, the total number of schools had reached 206. The academic session was increased from 3.5 to 5 years to make its primary schooling consistent with formal schooling. HDF's objective remains to cater to students who are for some reason not enrolled in government schools, mostly girls. Refresher courses on child-friendly teaching had been developed and were being regularly delivered, and HDF was conducting its own teacher training. All the students who appeared in the government's grade 5 external board exam in the various regions passed, with four in Mardan securing top positions.

The savings and credit program continued to thrive. The project's first-year (1999) savings figure of Rs. 812,210 increased over twenty-four-fold. Cumulative credit disbursed went up eightfold compared to the end of the first year of project inception (Rs. 15.4 million) and by 2005 this figure was Rs. 71.9 million. The cumulative recovery as of March 2002 was about 50 percent (Rs. 7.2 million) and by 2005 it was 89 percent. The disbursement of Rs. 1.2 million under the Special Micro Credit Incentive Package (SMCIP) to 69 entrepreneurs produced an overall recovery rate of 100 percent.

Technical and vocational trainings via linkages or otherwise continued in courses such as basic garment making, advanced garment making, poultry and livestock management, smokeless stove use, embroidery, and computing (see chapter 10); by 2005, a total of 6,929 community members (84 percent female) had received such training.

Thus, HDF has managed to establish a national presence and was beginning to attract alternative donor funding. By 2002, it had a staff size of 53 that included 43 professional staff. Based on the infrastructure project that it executed in Zhob (Balochistan), it had been approached by the *Khushali* Bank, one of the several pillars of the government's poverty reduction strategy, to execute other infrastructure projects with community involvement. The Pakistan Poverty Alleviation Fund (PPAF) and foreign donors also approached it for similar work as documented in chapter 10.

Linkages, with both the government and civil society, are a strong mechanism to leverage and extend HDF resources for community betterment. HDF is collaborating with UNDP in Rahim Yar Khan (Punjab Province) to train DO members in IPM (integrated pest management) techniques in cotton farming. The number of insecticide sprayings has been reduced from 12 to 5 and discontinued in some cases where reliance is entirely on predator pests and the locally available *neem* plant.[4] We were informed that this reduction in the use of pesticide had not decreased farm yield.

The health program is collaborating with Lahore's nationally famous King Edward Medical College, which is conducting research on pediatrics. In the process, doctors become available at the health center, and the HDF, based on their interest in the outcome of the research, has provided a statistician. Community awareness for health and education was raised by street plays and theater in the Lahore region in collaboration with the *Insaan* (human) Foundation. Similarly, HDF collaborated with the Pakistan Swedish Teachers Association for teacher-training methodologies.

HDF has continued to be strategic in project expansion to enhance outreach. Partnerships for earthquake relief have enabled it to establish a presence in the Azad Jammu and Kashmir (AJK) area just as it earlier moved into Balochistan based on public funds made available for a dam project. After the initial project outreach, the consolidation phase begins to integrate the intervention into the HDF regular systems. Here again, HDF has forged strategic partnerships with

Khushali Bank, Rawalpindi Medical College, and International Rescue Committee to facilitate future delivery.
Other linkages were established with

1. Pakistan Council of Renewable Technology for low-fuel-consumption smokeless cooking stoves to reduce the demand for firewood,
2. SPO to provide village DOs with development program management training courses,
3. NWFP Micro Finance Network to review and analyze best practice,
4. National Database and Registration Authority (NADRA) for computerized national identity cards for community members,
5. the government departments of livestock for community training in livestock/poultry management,
6. Department of Education to register students for the grade 5 external board exam and facilitate entry into grade 6 in government schools,
7. Department of Health for health education and vaccination of children
8. Irrigation Department for community infrastructure projects (CIP) in the Zhob region.[5]

Perhaps the most gratifying part of the documentation of the 2005 annual progress report is that of the 16 examples of autonomous collective action. These included DOs registering as Citizen's Community Boards (CCB) and raising the needed 20 percent to successfully lobby local government for community projects, successfully soliciting government agencies or civil society organizations for projects for improved water supply and school upgrading, or simply engaging in autonomous collective action for enhancing community well-being.

11.4 Overall Assessment

Cost-effectiveness numbers can be gleaned from the project documents. Thus, HDF claimed a cost of US$4.70 per beneficiary per year for what it delivered in the first year of operation.[6] The number based on direct beneficiaries, and the actual expenditures for 2005 was US$4.58.[7] Overall, based on the field updates (see chapters 9 and 10), particularly evidence of autonomous collective action, project expansion, and cost-effectiveness, we conclude that HDF is a success.

The field updates shows that HDF is viable as a Rural Support Program (RSP) that is well established; has effective systems in place; has survived cultural challenges, rapid expansion, and a change in leadership in a very early stage of its existence. The regional office in Mardan and the head office operated effectively and demonstrated that they had imbibed the efficient RSP management culture.

While HDF no longer has core partners, it very effectively and strategically forges linkages and partnerships to extend its outreach. A similar concept of linkage enables communities at the grassroots level to leverage their resources to enhance their welfare. Social mobilization readied community organizations to effectively interface with the government's devolution of power plan though local-level politics limited the extent of resources they could draw on for community development projects.

Success seemed premised more on good management than on the deep harnessing and formalization of social capital in the form of sustainable local organizations that embody local trust, networks, and associations. HDF has been very successful in establishing linkages of the DOs with government and nongovernment organizations as a way of being able to deliver a larger package of services. However, the focus had been more on effective and efficient service delivery rather than on participatory development and the successful harnessing of social capital.

There are several reasons for HDF's success in service delivery. First, the RSP model is now well established in Pakistan, based on about three decades of experience. There are therefore networks and support systems that new organizations can draw on. In addition, there is the cross-learning promoted by turnover in the vast job market that has been created across the country. Career tracks and promotions are clearly evident and this component of the development sector is a large job market in and of itself. The disadvantage is a high turnover that HDF has had to contend with because it has been on the lower end of the salary scale.

AKRSP and other RSPs provide "models" for HDF and other development NGOs to take staff to experience visits. The NRSP training unit provides training for trainers in social mobilization and other necessary management skills. Thus, organizations such as HDF can internalize these skills and rapidly start their own training programs by using core staff and resource persons available locally and nationally.

The RSPs have also moved beyond a critical mass, and so there are cadres of staff at all levels that can be drawn on to staff new organizations. It is not surprising that the first country representative of HDF had prior experience in the AKRSP. The turnover is high, particularly for women staff, but such programs have attractive salary packages and career tracks relative to the rest of the job market to retain enough staff for learning to set in and for programs to be efficiently executed. The incentives and management rules are much more akin to the private sector than to the public sector, and, while protections are in place, inefficient staff can still be fired without confronting the myriad complicated rules, regulations, and appeal procedures that are common in any government-controlled institution.

Success still needs the energy and dynamism of sound leadership and the backing of steady and committed donors. HDF has managed to get both. Ghani Marwat, the first project manager in Mardan and then country representative, had plenty of hands-on experience, courage, as well as a willingness to innovate and to commit as much energy and hard work as was needed. His replacement, Azhar Saleem, is pragmatic and has sound development instincts. HDFNA had a strong social commitment to the social capital harnessing/participatory development model and enough fund-raising ability to steadily back the project. Moreover, the frontline leadership in the persons of Dr. Shahnaz Khan, Dr. Khalid Riaz, Dr. Naseem Ashraf, and Dr. Musaddiq Malik had the understanding, charisma, and credibility to inspire local effort.

Economic Development and Cultural Change is a prominent economics journal in the development field. The title is thought provoking and in many ways rings true. Cultural change is a byproduct of economic development and this is what the experience of the rural support programs such as HDF show in Pakistan. However, the journal title implies no causality and very rightly so. Our research shows that culture can be a constraint on the programming space of development NGOs and that negotiating and working with the culture, while gradually nudging the cultural change, is an important precondition for the success of such programs. Beyond that, the organizational and operating culture of such support organizations represents a cultural change as they work for the cause of development and there are spillover effects beyond these organizations.

Our research also showed that the process of social mobilization to harness social capital and to formalize and embody it in sustainable grassroots organizations is extremely challenging. We achieved a descriptive account of the process and concluded, based on the strength of the social mobilization, that other aspects of this rural development initiative may have been more important in attaining project success than the harnessing of social capital. Yet our conclusions, while based on a rigorous and detailed case study, are still only an impressionistic account of the process. In the final part of this book that we turn to now, we propose a method of acquiring more in-depth social knowledge regarding the impact of harnessing social capital on the sustainability and effectiveness of grassroots community organizations.

Part III

Harnessing Social Capital: Manual for the Field Researcher

Planning a Field Study to Assess the Role of Harnessing Social Capital for Rural Development

Field researchers have many details to worry about. The objective of this chapter is to walk a researcher through the various aspects of a field research study. The proposed study is on the impact of harnessed and guided social capital, formalized into village or community organizations (COs), on induced collective action that reduces poverty and enhances community or village well-being. As explained in chapter 3, this research study was designed but not executed and, therefore, the various aspects of the study were fully fleshed out. There have been minor revisions so that, in conjunction with this chapter, the study design constitutes a research manual.

The most difficult part of the research is to define the research questions in a way that can be made operational, but that is only the beginning. The research questions have to be formalized into research objectives that can be incorporated into terms of reference for the study. A research design, and a plan to execute it, needs to be developed to address the objectives. Based on the research objectives and research design, field instruments have to be developed and pretested. This presupposes that the researcher has already worked out an analysis plan that is incorporated into the field instruments. The field team then needs to be extensively trained and a field strategy and work plan evolved. Field studies are often solicited because it is difficult to secure the large amount of funds required to execute a carefully designed field study. However, the researcher must be prepared to negotiate the terms of reference and, being prepared to write them, can help the iterative negotiating process.

12.1   Research Questions

Fine (2001, p. 140) rightly points out that "it is impossible for the researcher not to bring analytical preconceptions to the sample survey [research study], and also to its interpretation." For example, the World Bank Web site dedicated to research on social capital has posted several related questionnaires on measuring social capital for social analysis, and analytical preconceptions are built into the questionnaires.[1] Fine also highlights the importance of being aware of "the historical specificities" of individual villages. Based on the case study in Part II, we would add to this advice the importance of being aware of cultural specificities of the research locality.

We assume that the researcher is engaged in research on the process of harnessing social capital that uses the social mobilization model of the Aga Khan Rural Support Program (AKRSP, see chapter 3). First, the central research question would need to be identified. Invariably there are other related issues of interest, but it is important to build the research design to address the main research question.

Suppose the development organization (DO) would like to know what accounts for the success of their interventions. As a social researcher, one would need to start the research process with some hypothesis in mind. This may be refuted once the research gets underway and one needs to be completely open to that possibility, but it would be advisable to go to the field with some open-ended instruments for preliminary pretesting based on the knowledge derived from the existing relevant literature and understanding of the historical and cultural context of the area in question.

Based on the research we engaged in for this book, we would hypothesize that how much social capital a village starts with (defined as the strength of their mutual trust, norms for dispute resolution, reciprocal interactions, networks, and spontaneous traditions of collective action) would be central to explaining the success of a development NGOs attempts at harnessing social capital and formalizing it in the form of sustainable COs that could be guided to engage in collective action. Failure would be assumed to have occurred when the CO withered away without any collective action. Thus no community physical or social infrastructure was constructed and poverty was not reduced. Conversely, if the COs were sustained and such infrastructure was created and the benefits derived by the most marginalized in the village, despite unequal power structures, then we would view the collective action to be a success and so also, if demonstrated by nonrejection of our hypothesis, this method of harnessing social capital.

However, as Krishna and Uphoff (2001, 2002) have argued (see chapter 1), there are competing hypotheses that might explain the success of collective action. Thus, one has to test the relevance of the concept of harnessing social capital with competing alternatives. Even so, it is possible that none of these hypotheses is of much relevance.

So, the seemingly straightforward research question we have identified above leads to several possible research studies and hence several possible research designs. First, an empirical study could be designed of the kind conducted by Krishna and Uphoff (2001, 2002) and Krishna (2001). Here collective action would be the dependent variable to be explained by a whole range of independent variables including social capital.[2]

However, this does not address the issue of whether it is the social capital harnessed in the form of community DOs and guided to engage in collective action or whether it is simply the social capital that makes a difference. Thus the research design would have to be broadened to address this issue. Finally, the development NGO may also be concerned with the sustainability of the community DOs built to harness the social capital, and, if so, the research design would need to be broader still. For the sake of illustration, we assume a two-part research question (1) How sustainable were the COs created to harness and guide social capital and (2) How successful was the collective action induced by harnessed social capital in a competing hypothesis framework.

12.2   Research Goals

Most research studies require a statement of the research goals that are then included in the terms of reference of the study. For illustration, we have spelled out the research goals based on the research questions identified above:[3]

1. The process and dynamics of CO formation within the village;
2. The extent of participation by the poor, the extent of exclusion, and why that is the case;
3. The nature of empowerment of the poor that results from CO participation;
4. The benefits of CO activities for the poor nonmembers;

5. What is likely to facilitate more participation by the poor;
6. The determinants, including social capital, of
    i. a CO's survival;
    ii. a CO's success or failure ascertained from the presence of the lack of induced collective action;
    iii. autonomous collective action in the control villages (explained below).

12.3   Research Design and Research Plan

All research studies must start with a sampling frame and fortunately, in this case, it may not be too difficult to secure. The relevant sampling frame would include all the COs constructed by the development NGO in question. Suppose the development NGO was founded in 1986. This would mean a list dating back 20 years from 2006.[4]

Depending on the size of the organization in question, this could be a very large list. One could rule out the last five years because if sustainability of COs is part of the research question, they need to have been around for at least five years. This still leaves 15 possible years, and a large development NGO could easily have constructed over 2000 COs a year and probably more in the later years than in the earlier ones. However, one could also rule out the first five years because it takes a while for the learning to take place, for systems to be put in place, and for development NGOs to standardize their methods (see chapter 9 for early organizational learning). Also, while all information collected for social science research is subject to a great deal of distortion, the further back in time one requires the information for and the more demanding the recall in communities with no written records, the greater the inaccuracy.

Thus, in this particular case, randomly selecting a year between 1990 and 2000 would be a good bet. If funds are not a major constraint (unusual) or if the interventions are not very large, more than one year could be randomly selected. Even so, after the selection, it would be important to discuss the selected year(s) with senior management to make sure that the year was routine and not unusual in terms of funding or say an unusual focus on a natural disaster. Once the year(s) is (are) selected, the sample size of COs, as the unit of analysis, is determined depending on the funds available.[5] Region is often a useful strata for the random selection as is gender if there are separate female and male COs.

The analysis plan is always embodied in the research design as it is in the research instruments. For the first part of the research question, the CO would be the unit of analysis for identifying the determinants of the sustainability of the COs. The central research question based on section 12.1 would be whether community social capital is important in explaining the survival of the CO or were there other variables more important in accounting for this.

But, as discussed above, sustainability of COs is only a means to an end. Assuming that COs are sustained, the next part of the research question is whether they have engendered collective action that reduces poverty and enhances village well-being. Even here, the research is not straightforward. The hypothesis is that harnessing social capital and formalizing and embodying it in COs make the difference. However, it is possible that other villages with the same level of social capital but no CO to formalize this are equally, if not more, successful in engaging in spontaneous collective action without any guidance. To test this, the research design would need to include control villages that are similar in socioeconomic and other conditions, villages that are close but not too close to experience project "contamination effects."[6] This is one of many places where the research practitioner needs to be familiar with the area being studied and to be able to use intuition and engage in a judgment call.

One other possible complication is the size of the village and the impact of the CO on nonmembers. Large villages have more than one CO and the stratified random selection might draw more than one CO for one village into the sample. Defining community (catchment for the CO) is one difficult challenge as is defining the extended community that could conceivably benefit from the collective action of the CO. Extended community can be defined as the sum of all households from all clearly identified neighborhoods or settlements that can, but choose not to be, members in a randomly selected CO.

To summarize, this research design plans to capture variation of the impact of harnessed social capital and other variables on induced and autonomous collective action from the following three sources: First, from a comparison of CO and non-CO households; second, from the variation across COs; and third, from the variation across control and noncontrol villages. In each case, different pertinent information would need to be collected using instruments most likely to provide the best information. Thus, information regarding benefits may be more accurately available in the privacy of a household while information on collective action may require honing via collective memory and hence a focus group discussion may be more appropriate.

In designing the research instruments, the key variables for measurement, given the research question identified above, would include a measure of social capital and a measure of effectiveness of collective action. The latter could be on an absolute scale measured against "objective criteria" or it could be comparative. For example, the development NGO's success in executing a water supply scheme with community participation could be compared with the success of the government sector in delivering the same civic amenity.[7]

12.4   Research Instruments

Relying on structured or semistructured questionnaires can be problematic. Most social scientists would rightly argue that the researchers probably prompted the desired response. Social analysis in rural settings is extremely difficult. This is because of the very complex nature of rural society and politics. Also, the dynamics of group meetings are difficult to understand, and prompting certainly contaminates this process.

We propose a preliminary pretest where the social researcher is prepared to discover that nothing that is referenced in the vast and growing social capital literature reviewed in chapter 2 is necessarily of any relevance to the categories villagers think and respond in. Thus, prior to the construction of the instruments, during the preliminary pretest, the fieldworkers should start a discussion on why the COs did not survive or why collective action did not work, but on no account should they make any reference to any of the categories such as trust, norms, or networks that are normally associated with social capital. If the communities bring up these categories as relevant, and if they did play a part in the success of collective action, then we could not refute the possible importance of the concept of harnessed social capital. However, if these categories were simply ignored and other issues such as power and appropriation was what the discussion revolved around, and if this happened in most of the preliminary pretest villages, the social significance of harnessed social capital would be called into question right at the inception of the study.

Thus, in a nutshell, the idea is to let the villagers speak in focus group discussions in the hope that some social truth may be discovered or at least categories that are not relevant to their way of thinking are sifted out. One could argue that even if the villagers made no mention of anything that resembled social capital, it would not necessarily prove that harnessed social capital was not relevant for the survival of COs. Perhaps so, but this leaves the social scientist open to the charge of assuming knowledge not acquired from the social setting in question. At worst, this is a very arrogant position to adopt and at best it is an uncomfortable one.

The instruments should be designed after the preliminary pretest.[8] Suppose the categories referred to as social capital do have resonance in the field in a particular context, even so to attempt to measure social capital and to quantitatively explore if this accounts for project success is still a major challenge. As mentioned in chapter 1, we are skeptical of measurement and quantitative exercises in this area of social knowledge but, aware of the difficulties and pitfalls of social research, feel that it is necessary to use available tools and methods of social investigation to attempt to enhance social knowledge. We propose the following field instruments based on the research questions and research objectives defined above:

A community profile questionnaire at the household level (appendix 12.1) for both the CO and non-CO households and for the control group households to identify the "stock" of social capital in the community.[9] This community profile would also contain questions to explore village prosperity, village accessibility, political heterogeneity, power distribution, and leadership. These variables have a bearing on autonomous or induced collective action. Much of the required information on village resources (extent or access), access to services, inclusion, participation, and empowerment would be available only at the household level. Information on other household characteristics such as ethnicity, political alignment, caste/clan, socioeconomic/income/ wealth status, and perceptions pertaining to village social capital (cognitive— see definitions in chapter 1), social activist, and the leadership would also need to be collected.

The questionnaire (appendix 12.2) is designed for collecting information on collective action such as that resulting through the development NGO and the created CO and also those independent of these two organizations. Apart from collective action induced by the development NGO, various kinds of collective action via various other channels could also arise in the sample villages: by leveraging collective savings, approaching local government, approaching other donors, and working with other COs as a cluster organization or otherwise. Autonomous collective action could also occur in the control villages by means of various channels and this questionnaire is designed for gathering such information.

All the information collected using the three questionnaires could provide the information necessary to explore and test the hypothesis of whether harnessed and guided social capital accounts for the success of collective action. These questionnaires could also be used to explore the alternative hypotheses that might account for the success or failure of collective action, other than the stock of social capital or harnessed social capital. As stated earlier, these include the contribution of good leadership or a social activist, intensity of need, social homogeneity or heterogeneity, quality of government or development NGO extension staff support, impact of the relative and absolute power of community notables, modernization or the lack thereof, community literacy, and other factors. This information will also make it possible to address the study objectives in a comparative context by addressing the following questions:

1. Are public goods created by the development NGO (compared to the public sector) better targeted to the poor?
2. Are they better managed?
3. Is the quality of service delivered better?
4. What is the nature of participation?
5. Has this participation led to the empowerment of the marginalized groups?
6. Has it led to less exclusion?
7. Are services captured by the elites?
8. Are the benefits more equitably distributed?

We propose tools for measuring comparative effectiveness in the next subsection, which readers can skip without loss of continuity.

12.5   Measuring Success for a Comparative Study

If the role of harnessed social capital is to be studied in accounting for the success of social sector interventions in rural water supply and primary education relative to other interventions in the public sector, then instruments would need to be designed to evaluate the effectiveness of the relevant water supply schemes and schools. In addition, for evaluating the effectiveness of primary schools, tests, say in math and comprehension skills, would need to be administered to all students of a chosen grade of the development NGO and government schools (see chapter 8).[10]

For both the water supply schemes and schools, one could build on existing concepts such as unit costs to define an "effectiveness ratio" (ER) as a summary measure of success.[11] Information collected from the questionnaire would need to be utilized to quantify ER for water supply and primary education. These ratios would need to be defined somewhat differently in the two sectors and hence need some elaboration. For the water supply schemes, ER could be defined as follows:

$$ERw = PS*QI / UC$$

Where PS is the percentage of poor served (stated objective of both development NGOs and the government for social sector interventions) by the scheme, QI is a quality index (in terms of delivery and maintenance), and UC is the unit cost. Thus the higher the quality, the larger the number of poor served, and the lower the unit cost of the scheme, the greater is the effectiveness of the scheme.

For education, ER could be defined as follows:

$$ER_E = PS*TS/UC$$

Where TS are average test scores for comprehension and math, say in the fifth grade, and the other variables are as defined above.

The ER for education is likely to be more controversial and requires some discussion.

First, while it would be possible to develop an observational measure of quality as in the case of the water supply schemes, we think that the bottom line is the test scores.

Second, it is argued that the richer and brighter students might systematically be sent to the NGO schools rather than the government schools and that, if this is the case, maybe a measure of innate ability and parental input rather than the contribution of the school are the reasons for the NGO school pupils' better performance. As we use average scores in the ER_E index, we think that it is reasonable to assume that there is a normal distribution of student innate ability in both the government and NGO schools and that the individual differences would wash out in the averaging. Also, our past research showed that there is little systematic parental input in rural schooling and no difference in this regard between government and NGO schools.[12]

Third, it is argued that the contribution of the school to the student's performance is the difference between what they knew when they entered the school relative to their performance in grade five. Once again, we assume that on average students enter grade one in government and NGO schools with the same level of knowledge. While this may not be true for the individual student, the individual differences once again wash out in the averaging. Thus the measure of ER_e proposed above is viewed as robust for comparative analysis.

12.6   Other Field Survey Issues

Once funding is secured for the study, the budget and the term of reference approved, much of the focus needs to be on designing the instruments and pretesting them again several times. This pretesting is the most important part of the training of the field team. The other aspect of the training is discussing the ethics of information collection, familiarizing the field team with the objectives of the study and the instruments and engaging the team members in mock sessions. The field team is often the most valuable resource in honing and changing and rechanging the instruments until they seem satisfactory. The field team leader needs to know whether and when to prompt, what to do about nonresponse and about coding the "other" category.

When interviewing for the field team, it is important to retain several alternatives because the final team needs to bond well together. Some very bright candidates may simply not be comfortable with and able to chat with respondents. However, it needs to be very clear up front that the whole training process is also a selection process from which they can learn much and for which they are paid. It is important therefore to budget adequately for the training process.

While there is considerable pressure at this stage to get the study underway from all stakeholders (donors, NGO, field team), the researcher(s) need to resist going into the field until completely confident that the instruments reflect the study objectives, that the required social information is likely to be procured, and that the field research team is fully comfortable with the instruments. It is important to hire the necessary expertise at this early stage to train the field team and provide input into developing a solid field strategy.

Much of the investment for a field research study has to be up front because once the fieldwork gets underway, there is little midstream correction possible. At that point, it is important to ensure as much consistency in the collection of information across the units of observation as possible. That is why the survey plan needs to ensure an optimum amount of time in the field. One that is not too long to result in survey fatigue and a change in the nature of information collected, but also long enough to ensure enough time at each site for the task to be comfortably completed.

Most research studies utilize both qualitative (focus group discussion reports and documented interviews with key informants) and quantitative information. These alternative sources of information not only provide a crosscheck on the information collected but also reinforce each other and enrich the overall data sets because it is often more useful to collect different social information in different ways. One very valuable source of qualitative information is the collective field report that the team members write after ending the fieldwork at each site.[13] Laptop computers have greatly facilitated this process. The format for the field report should be based on the study objectives. Drawing on this format, the field report should summarize the site findings, with a particular focus on insights not otherwise captured by the field instruments.

Keeping in mind the study objectives and the issues raised here, we have included a sample of a survey design, field strategy, terms of reference, and budget checklist as appendices 12.4 to 12.7. Each social science research study is unique and probably the commonality is the humbling experience that results from the enormous difficulty in conceptualizing and executing the study. This is because it demonstrates that no matter how carefully it is done with however much attention to detail, one may still remain far from social truth. The hope is that enough replication of findings results in empirical regularities that social scientists finally view as part of a valuable body of empirical knowledge.

SRNO

Questionnaire for community organizations (CO), extended community, and control village households

SRNO

SECTION A

AREA

A1. Field Unit (FU)[i]   _⊥_

A2. Name of village   _⊥_

A3. Household No.   _⊥_

A4. Name of CO   _⊥_

A5. Type of CO [M/F/Mix]   _⊥_

A6. Head of household: Male ....
Female ....

A7. Is respondent head of the household: Yes [Go to A9].............
No ....

A8. Respondent's sex   Male ....
Female ....

INTERVIEW

A9. Date   _⊥_ : _⊥_ : _⊥_

A10. Name of interviewer

A11. Interviewer's signature

[Please note that there could be more than one male or female CO per village. Please make sure that the reference throughout is to the CO randomly selected]

Respondent: CO member head of household (preferably)

Sr #	Name of household member	Gender Male 1 Female 2	Age in completed years	Marital status*	Relation to head**	Literate Yes 1, No 2 If No→8	Education level completed	Profession***
	1	2	3	4	5	6	7	8
1.								
2.								
3.								
4.								
5.								
6.								
7.								
8.								
9.								
10.								
11.								
12.								
13.								
14.								
15.								
16.								
17.								
18.								
19.								
20.								

* M. status codes: married-01, unmarried-02, widow/widower-03, divorced/separated-04

** Relation codes: wife-01, husband-02, daughter-03, son-04, grand parents-05, brother/sister-06, mother/father-07, niece /nephew-08, other relatives-09, daughter/son in law-10, sister/brother in law 11, grand son/daughter 12

*** Profession codes: manual labor-01, farming-02, business-04, govt. job-05, private sector job-06, services-07, housewife-08, student-09, jobless-10, handicraft-11, not in labor force-12

Note: Use additional sheet, if number of household members is more than 20

Note: If non-CO member or control group household, Go to Q. 34

Q1	Is CO functional (has regular meetings/ savings/activities/ projects)?	Yes [Go to Q. 3] ....1 No..2

Q2	If no, why is that the case	Low community trust 01
		Low community solidarity 02
		People not willing to participate in
		   anything here 03
		Influentials get all the benefit 04
		Poor excluded 05
		We did not need it 06
		To may castes/subcastes in this community 07
		Too many political differences in this
		   community 08
		Rich and poor can not work together here 09
		The work the CO was designed for
		   is completed 10
		Others [specify] 77

Q3	Are you the president or manager of the CO?	Yes (Go to Q. 13) ....1 No 2
Q4	If no, rate (1 – 5) the quality of the social activist (president)?	(Worst - 1) 2 3 4 (Best - 5)
Q5	If no, rate (1 – 5) the quality of the social activist (manager)?	(Worst - 1) 2 3 4 (Best - 5)
Q6	Are you or anyone from your household a member of CO?	Yes ....1 No [Go to Q. 7] 2
Q7	If yes, do you think that CO is a true representative of your interest?	Yes ....1 No 2
Q8	If no, why is that the case?	Nothing for us in the membership ....01 We (would) never get loans anyway ....02 We have no time for the meetings ....03 We are not welcome ....04 We do no trust the leadership ....05 We never take part in any community activity 06

	CO members belonged to a different caste/subcaste 07
	CO members are/were of a different ethnic group 08
	CO never delivered any real benefit 09
	Others (specify) 77

Q9 If no on Q6, have you ever been the member of the CO?

Yes (Go to Q. 13) 1
No 2

Q10 If yes [on Q9 but no on Q6], why did you leave the CO?

Nothing for us in the membership 01
We (would) never get loans anyway 02
We have no time for the meetings 03
We are not welcome 04
We do no trust the leadership 05
We never take part in any community activity 06
CO members belonged to a different caste/ subcaste 07
CO members are/were of a different ethnic group 08
CO never delivered any real benefit 09
Other (specify) 77

Q11 Is there any thing the NGO can do to get your household to be a member?

Yes 1
No (Go to Q. 13) 2

Q12 If yes, specify what?

Q13 Are you aware of and have you benefited from any of the following NGO project/service?

Projects/Activities/Services [Relevant ones Circled, FU record]	Awareness		Benefited	
	Yes	No	Yes	No
01-Boys school	1	2	1	2
02-Girls school	1	2	1	2
03-Mixed school	1	2	1	2
04-Drinking water supply scheme	1	2	1	2
05-Sewerage	1	2	1	2
06-Drainage	1	2	1	2
07-Irrigation scheme (lining water course/de-siltation)	1	2	1	2
08-Communications/roads	1	2	1	2
09-NRM (Natural Resource Management) projects	1	2	1	2
10-Agricultural machinery	1	2	1	2
11-Bio Gas	1	2	1	2
12-Environment project	1	2	1	2
13-Establishing sloping agricultural land models	1	2	1	2
14-Feul efficient stoves	1	2	1	2

15-Improvement of pasture lands	1	2	1	2
16-Vegetation/check damming	1	2	1	2
17-Forest sector development	1	2	1	2
18-Solar concentrator	1	2	1	2
19-Solar powered light emitting diodes	1	2	1	2
20-Solar pumps	1	2	1	2
21-School nutrition project	1	2	1	2
22-Feeding in school	1	2	1	2
23-Literacy program	1	2	1	2
24-Health camps/immunization	1	2	1	2
25-Family planning services	1	2	1	2
26-Credit	1	2	1	2
27-Primary health	1	2	1	2
28-Sanitation	1	2	1	2
77-Others [specify]	1	2	1	2

Q14 Are you aware of and have you benefited from any of the following NGO training provided as a recipient or beneficiary?

Trainings [Relevant ones Circled, from FU record]	Awareness		Recipient		Benefited	
	Yes	No	Yes	No	Yes	No
01-Traditional Birth Attendant	1	2	1	2	1	2
02-First aid	1	2	1	2	1	2
03-Health and hygiene	1	2	1	2	1	2
04-Sanitation	1	2	1	2	1	2
05-Lady health workers	1	2	1	2	1	2
06-Health workers	1	2	1	2	1	2
07-Homeopathic health scouts	1	2	1	2	1	2
08-Family planning workers	1	2	1	2	1	2
09-Epidemic prevention advice	1	2	1	2	1	2
10-Flood rescue advice	1	2	1	2	1	2
11-Screening camps for cataract	1	2	1	2	1	2
12-Eye care advice at home or school	1	2	1	2	1	2
13-Clean kitchen training	1	2	1	2	1	2
14-Masons training	1	2	1	2	1	2
15-Hand pump training	1	2	1	2	1	2
16-Advice on maternal health	1	2	1	2	1	2
17-Advice on gynecological and obstetrical care	1	2	1	2	1	2

18-Advice on blood pressure, TB and malaria	1	2	1	2	1	2
19-Surf (detergent) and soap making	1	2	1	2	1	2
20-Tailoring	1	2	1	2	1	2
21-Jam making	1	2	1	2	1	2
22-Tie and dye	1	2	1	2	1	2
23-Weilding	1	2	1	2	1	2
24-Vasaline making	1	2	1	2	1	2
77-Others [specify]	1	2	1	2	1	2

Schooling (Ignore if no school identified)

Q15 How many household children of primary school going age are not attending the school? *(Check from household roaster)* (If zero go to Q. 17)

Number of school going age (5–11 years) children not attending school

Q16 Why are not they attending the school?

School fee too high 01
Non-fee costs too high 02
Children not encouraged to attend due to *beraderi* (caste)/sub caste by school authorities 03
Children not encouraged to attend for other reason by school authorities...........................04
Children not treated well by other children due to Cast/sub-caste....................... 05
School no longer active 06
Need children to help with home chores and other work 07
Others (specify) 77

Water (Ignore if no water project identified)

Q17 Do you get water from the project water supply?

Yes (Go to Q.14) 1
No 2

Q18 If No, explain why not

Tariff/bill too high 01
Water only available to a particular *beraderi*/sub caste 02
Water only available for the more prosperous 03
Live on high land and water not accessible here 04
Do not need the water because have access to another source 05
Denied access by owner of land where facility placed 06
Others (specify) 77

Credit ((Ignore if no credit identified)

| Q19 | Have you applied for a loan via CO? | Yes (Go to Q.16) ....1 |
| | | No ....2 |

Q20	If No, why was that the case?	We are/were considered too poor 01
		We do/did not have enough backing of the CO leaders 02
		We are/were not the right *beraderi/* subcaste 03
		We are/were not the right political party 04
		Do/did not understand loan procedure 05
		Lack of awareness of the concept of credit [Interviewer should note] 06
		Do not believe in interest transactions 07
		Other (specify) 77

Q21	If you have never taken a loan, what might induce you to accept one?	Loans to get out of debt 1
		Loans to meet emergency needs 2
		Loans to meet cultural (marriage/ birth/death) needs 3
		Loans to fund education/health expenses 4
		Others [specify] 7

| Q22 | If yes, how many times have you received a loan? | No. of times_____ |

Q23	If yes, what did you use the loan for?	a. Agriculture 1
		b. Livestock 2
		c. Enterprise 3
		d. Emergency 4
		e. Consumption 5
		f. To pay off debt 6
		g. Others [specify] 7

| Q24 | If a–c, did an increase in household income result from the activity? | Yes ....1 |
| | | No ....2 |

Q25	Who received the loan in the household?	Man 1
		Woman 2
		Household 3

Q26	How did you repay the NGO?	Borrowed from family 1
		Borrowed from friends 2
		Borrowed from money lenders 3
		Used income from enterprise/activity 4
		Loan taken from others 5
		Others [Specify] 7

| Q27 | Has household ever defaulted on a loan? | Yes ....1 |
| | | No [Go to Q.23] ....2 |

| Q28 | If yes, did you get another loan anyway? | Yes [Go to Q. 31] ....1 |
| | | No ....2 |

Q29	If yes, why did you default?	Change in economic circumstances 1
		Sudden death if earner in household 2
		Burden of cultural norms/customs (marriage/death/birth) 3
		Health related issues 4
		Others [specify] 7

Q30	What were the consequences?	Loan guarantors applied pressure 1
		Members stopped talking to us 2
		Nothing happened 3
		Others (specify) 7

| Q31 | Have you a member of your household engaged in a collective activity (with the CO) | Yes ....1 |
| | | No (Go to Q. 33) ....2 |

| Q32 | If yes, did your household benefit from this activity? | Yes ....1 |
| | | No ....2 |

Q33	If no on Q 31, why is that the case?	There has been no collective activity 1
		We do not trust the leadership 2
		We are not welcomed 3
		The leaders appropriate all the benefits 4
		Others [specify] 7

Q33	Do you feel that that belonging to the CO has resulted in your having the power to change the course of your life? For all household members	Totally powerless 1
		Almost powerless 2
		Somewhat powerless 3
		Mostly powerful 4
		Very powerful 5

| Q34 | Have you or a member of your household engaged in a collective activity | Yes ....1 |
| | | No (Go to Q. 36) ....2 |

| Q35 | If yes, did your household benefit from this activity? | Yes ....1 |
| | | No ....2 |

Q36	If no on Q 34, why is that the case?	There has been no collective activity 1
		We do not trust the leadership 2
		We are not welcomed 3
		The leaders appropriate all the benefits 4
		Others [specify] 7

Q37	Is there a village education committee (VEC) present?	Yes ....1 No [Go to Q. 41] 2
Q38	If yes, are you a member?	Yes ....1 No 2
Q39	Do you think it is doing effective work in improving village education?	Yes ....1 No 2
Q40	If no, why is that the case?	Committee members views ignored ....1 Committee members do not have relevant expertise ....2 Others [specify] 7
Q41	Is there a village water and sanitation committee (VWSC) present?	If yes, repeat Q. 38–40
Q45	Is there a village health committee (VHC) in the village?	If yes, repeat Q. 38–40
Q49	Ethnic group	Punjabi ....1 Pusthun ....2 Potohari ....3 Hindko ....4 Afghan ....5 Other (specify) 7
Q50	Amount of land owned by household.	a. Total owned land: _____ Kanals b. Arable land: _____ Kanals
Q51	Do you own the house you live in?	Yes ....1 No 2
Q52	Describe the house	*Kaccha*[ii] ....1 *Kaccha/Pakka* ....2 *Pakka* 3
Q53	Number of rooms per *chulah*[iii]	No. of rooms: _____
Q54	Do you have any of the followings?	Electricity ....1 Telephone ....2 Natural Gas 3
Q55	Do you have any of the followings?	AC ....01 Fridge ....02 Washing machine ....03 Cooking range 04

Cooking stove 05
VCR 06
TV 07
Air Cooler 08
Radio 11
Cycle 12
Car (probe for own use and circle if yes) 16

Q56 Does any member of   Yes 1
the household get   No 2
zakat?[iv]

Q57 Which political party   Pakistan Peoples Party (PPP) 1
do you support?   Pakistan Muslim League (PML) 2
Mutihida Majlis Amal (MMA) 3
None 4
Others (specify) 7

Q58 What is your caste?

Q59 What is your
sub-caste?

Q60 If a community project   Yes 1
does not directly   No 2
benefit you but has
benefits for many
others in the
village/community,
would you contribute
in (cash/labor and
kind) to the project in
any way?

Q61 Please state whether   *Strongly*   *Agree*   *Disagree*   *Strongly disagree*
in general you agree   *Agree*
or disagree with the
following statements:
(Prompt)

Q62 Most people in this   1   2   3   4
village/community
are basically honest and
can be trusted.

Q63 If we have a problem, there   1   2   3   4
is always someone to help us.

Q64 In your opinion, is this   Peaceful 1
village/neighborhood   Conflictive 2
generally peaceful or   Mixed 3
conflictive?

Q65   Are any of the following problems serious in this community? (Prompt)

Details	Yes	No
Burglaries/Robberies	1	2
Assaults	1	2
Gangs	1	2
Vandalism	1	2
Violent disputes	1	2
Rape	1	2
Domestic violence	1	2
Drug abuse	1	2
Other problems (specify)	1	2

Q66   If yes, on any has there been an   Yes 1
adequate response to resolve the   No 2
problem by the community collectively?

Q67   If a natural disaster were to   Government 01
adversely impact the village,   Mutual assistance/collective
who do you think would help?   response....................................02
                                         NGO 03
                                         Every one would help
                                            themselves 04
                                         Village influentials 05
                                         Neighbors help each other 06
                                         The dominant caste would
                                            help all 07
                                         The dominant political
                                            faction would help all 08
                                         No one 09
                                         Others [specify] 77

Q68   If two people/households in the   No one 01
village were involved in a dispute,   Local dispute resolution
who would resolve it?   mechanism 02
                                         Local government 03
                                         Police/courts 04
                                         CO 05
                                         NGO 06
                                         Neighbours 07
                                         Beraderi 08
                                         Influentials 09
                                         Village elders 10
                                         Community 11
                                         Others [specify] 77

Q69   Overall, how would you rate   Very low 1
mutual trust in this community?   Low 2
                                         Average 3
                                         High 4
                                         Very high 5

Q70 Overall, how would you rate solidarity in this community?	Very low ....1 Low ....2 Average ....3 High ....4 Very high 5
Q71 Who are the main leaders in this community? (Probe formal and informal leadership)	Large landlords ....1 Trusted village elders ....2 *Numberdar*[v] ....3 Councilor/*Nazim*/*Naib Nazam*[vi] ....4 None ....5 Other (specify) 7
Q72 If Councilor/*Nazim*/*Naib Nazam*, are they also the big landlords?	Yes ....1 No 2
Q73 If trusted village elders, are they also the big landlords?	Yes ....1 No 2
Q74 How are decisions made within this community?	By village leaders ....1 By village leaders taking into account community views ....2 By consensus ....3 By trusted village elders ....4 Others (specify) 7
Q75 How would you rate the decisions made by the leadership?	Very effective ....1 Somewhat effective ....2 Not effective at all 3

Interviewer's signature: _____

Notes

1. This is a reference to the Field Unit or the equivalent of the development NGO that maintains village and CO information. Some of this information may be needed before the field survey, and the questionnaires appropriately marked before the interviews/focus group discussions. Refer for example to Qs. 13–14.
2. *Kaccha* refers to mud and *pakka* to bricks/concrete.
3. A cooking unit.
4. Refer to chapter 6, en. 3.
5. Rural government functionary.
6. *Nazim* is the mayor or governor at the various local government tiers. *Naib* stands for deputy.

Appendix 12.2

FGD questions on collective action for CO members

SRNO ⊥⊥⊥

SECTION A

AREA

A1. Field Unit	⊥
A2. Name of village	⊥
A3. Name of CO	⊥
A4. Type of CO [M / F / Mix]	⊥

INTERVIEW

A5. Date	⊥ : ⊥ : ⊥
A6. Name of interviewer	
A7. Interviewer's signature	

How do you define this village?

[Map, geographical boundaries, place names, and the following reference points; start with this community map as a warm-up exercise]

Where is/are the   The mosque?
                                Primary school?
                                Secondary school?
                                Sources of water?
                                Waste and garbage disposal sites?

Q1   Village topology   Plain 1
                                Hilly 2
                                Mixed 3

Q2   Total land in village

Q3   Total arable land in
      village

Q4   Number of
      beraderis

Q5   Number of
      sub castes

Q6   Village literacy
      [From field unit (FU)]

      Does the CO meet regularly   Yes 1
      as required?   No [Go to Q. 8] 2

Q7   Should the frequency with   Greater 1
      which the CO meets be   Less..2
      greater, less, or remain   The same...3
      the same?

Q8   What kind of   Community management
      trainings   skills training 01
      have the CO   Leadership management
      social activists   skills training 02
      received and   Natural resources management
      how often?   training 03
      [From FU]   Financial management training 04
                                   Subject specialist workshops 05
                                   Enterprise development training 06
                                   Social sector training 07
                                   Occupational training 08
                                   Activist workshop 09
                                   Exposure visits 10
                                   Functioning of CO 11
                                   Others [specify] 77

Q9	What has been the most important decision made in the past year?	No decision [Go to Q. 14] ....0 Decision :_____		

Q10   Thinking about this decision, did any of the following take place?

Details	Yes	No
a. Prior dissemination of in-formation	1	2
b. Consultation with grassroots	1	2
c. Widespread debate, opposing opinions, and frank discussion	1	2
d. Dissemination of results	1	2

Q11	Has the CO leadership ever changed?	Yes ....1 No 2

Q12	If yes, why was the leadership changed?	Disability/illness of social activist ....01 Death of social activist ....02 Bad behavior of social activist ....03 Caste/sub caste differences ....04 Political differences ....05 Social activist working for himself ....06 Community not satisfied with social activist ....07 NGO not satisfied with social activist ....08 Others [specify] 77

Q13	If yes, through what process did the change come about?	Election ....1 Nomination by influentials Community selected it ....3 Others [specify] 7

Q14	Is there a mechanism to replace ineffective CO officer holders?	Yes ....1 No [Go to Q. 16] ....2 Not applicable 3

Q15	If yes, are you satisfied with this mechanism?	Yes ....1 No 2

Q16	Do you think there are enough people in the community to assume leadership if necessary?	Yes ....1 No 2

Q17   Are the leaders   Yes 1
       mostly from a   No 2
       few influential
       families?

Q18   Is the CO willing   Yes 1
       and able to deal   No 2
       with membership
       related problems
       such as
       non-attendance at
       meetings or rude
       behavior?

Q19   Has the CO settled   Yes 1
       disputes among CO   No 2
       members or among
       CO members and
       non-members?

Q20   Has the CO   Yes 1
       collectively   No [Go to Q. 22] 2
       resolved (a)
       problem (s)
       confronted
       by the community?

Q21   If yes, please describe?

Q22   Has the president/   Yes 1
       manager (social   No 2
       activist) settled
       disputes among
       CO members
       or among CO
       members and
       non-members?

Q23   Has the president/   Yes 1
       manager (social   No 2
       activist) collectively
       resolved (a)
       problem (s)
       confronted by
       the community?

Q24   If yes, please describe?

Q25   Was the village   Approached the NGO 1
       approached to   NGO approached us [Go to Q. 27] 2
       form a CO or
       did you approach
       the NGO?

Q26	If 1 (approached NGO), what instigated this?	Influentials looking for benefits 1
		We learned of the good work being done by the NGO from another village 2
		We had a great need for the services/activities the NGO engaged in 3
		Others [specify] 7
Q27	Does the CO have clearly defined processes for identifying common needs and priorities of its members?	Yes 1
		No [Go to Q. 29] 2
Q28	If yes, what criterion was used for identifying such a need?	Priority is given to demand by influentials 1
		Priority is given to the needs of the poor 2
		Priority is based on common needs 3
		Others [specify] 7
Q29	Has the CO used its savings for internal lending?	Yes 1
		No (Go to Q. 33) 2
Q30	If yes, what was the interest rate?	Interest rate_____%
Q31	What was the nature of lending?	Cash 1
		Kind 2
Q32	Was the lending restricted to CO members only?	Yes 1
		No 2
Q33	For serious cases of default on NGO loans do guidelines or rules exist to expel the transgressor?	Yes 1
		No (Go to Q. 36) 2
Q34	If yes, what are these?	Social boycott 1
		Fine 2
		Expulsion 3
		Others 7

Q35   In the last three   Yes 1
years, have there   No [skip if] 2
been any resolutions
by the membership
to the NGO for a
project/activity/
service other than
micro credit?

Q36   If Yes in what way   Boys school 01
has the CO/NGO   Girls school 02
addressed these   Mixed school 03
demands?   Drinking water supply scheme 04
[List project t/   Sewerage 05
activity/   Drainage 06
service]   Irrigation scheme (lining water course / desiltation) 07
                     Communications / roads 08
                     NRM (Natural Resource Management) projects 09
                     Agricultural machinery 10
                     Bio Gas 11
                     Environment Project 12
                     Establishing sloping agricultural land models 13
                     Fuel efficient stoves 14
                     Improvement of pasture lands 15
                     Vegetation / check damming 16
                     Forest sector development 17
                     Solar concentrator 18
                     Solar powered light emitting diodes 19
                     Solar pumps 20
                     School nutrition project 21
                     Feeding in school 22
                     Literacy program 23
                     Health camps / immunization 24
                     Family planning services 25
                     Primary health 26
                     Toilets 27
                     Others [specify] 77

Q37   What was the intensity of   a. _____
the need for project/   b. _____
activity/service; rate (1 – 5)?   c. _____
                                   d. _____

Q38   Objective assessment of   a. _____
performance, rate (1 – 5)   b. _____
[Via FU record or in consultation c. _____
with the Field Engineer/Staff]   d. _____

Q39   CO assessment of   a. _____
performance (1–5)?   b. _____
                               c. _____
                               d. _____

Q40   Best one if ranked 4   _____
or 5 by CO?
[Otherwise go to Q. 42]

Q41   State why you   High community trust 01
think it was   High community solidarity 02
effective,   High level of participation in this community 03
if ranked   Benefits evenly shared in this community 04
4 or 5   Community need for service great and all worked
by CO?   Together 06
                         We are all similar and of the same *beraderi* /
                         sub caste and work well together 07
                         Few political differences in this community so we
                         work well together 08
                         Rich and poor work well together in this community ..09
                         We have excellent leadership that inspired us 10
                         We have an excellent social activist that effectively
                         mobilized us 11
                         NGO has a good reputation and there is a high
                         level of trust in this organization 12
                         Other (specify) 77

Q42   If none ranked   Low community trust 01
4 or 5 by CO,   Low community solidarity 02
why do you think   People not willing to participate in anything here 03
this was the case?   Influential get all the benefit 04
                         Poor excluded 05
                         We did not need service 06
                         Too may *baredaris* (castes) / sub castes in
                         this community 07
                         Too many political differences in this community 08
                         Rich and poor can not work together here 09
                         Poor leadership 10
                         Ineffective social activist who was unable to
                         mobilize the community 11
                         People do not trust NGOs in this community 12
                         Other (specify) 77

Q43   Do you have a   Yes 1
plan in place for   No [Go to Q. 33] 2
maintenance if
required?

Q44   If yes, what is the   Delegated (a) person(s) for maintenance on a
       maintenance plan?   voluntary basis 1
                                  Hired someone collectively to do the maintenance 2
                                  Others [specify] 7

Q45   Do you have a   Yes 1
       plan in   No [Go to Q. 49] 2
       place for
       replacement
       if required?

Q46   If yes, what is the   We will approach NGO / someone else for a new
       replacement plan?   project 1
                                  We will replace it ourselves collectively using our
                                    savings 2
                                  We have been putting money aside for this 3
                                  Others [specify] 7

Q47   What was the   Rs._____
       total cost of the
       project?

Q48   What was the   Cash Rs. _____
       contribution of   Kind Rs. _____
       the community?   Labor Rs. _____

       Other collective
       action mechanisms

Q49   Has the CO ever   Repeat Qs. 24–48 if yes
       used collective
       savings for any
       project / activity /
       service?
       [Check CO record
       for the relevant
       information]

       Have you lobbied   Repeat Qs. 24–48 if yes
       to get any service
       from the government
       on your own
       without the
       NGO assistance?

Q80   Have you lobbied   Repeat Qs. 24–48 if yes
       for government
       project / activity /
       service via CO / NGO?

Q98   Have you   Repeat Qs. 24–48 if yes
      approached
      any other NGOs
      for any services
      on your own?

Q114 Have you   Repeat Qs. 24–48 if yes
      approached
      to any other NGOs
      for any services
      through CO / NGO?

Q128 Has the CO   Repeat Qs. 24–48 if yes
      engaged in any
      joint activity
      with another CO /
      organization cluster
      in this or in another
      village?

Q143 Is there a village   Yes 1
      education   No [Go to Q. 147] 2
      committee
      (VEC) for an NGO
      managed school?

Q144 If yes, are any of   Yes 1
      you members?   No 2

Q145 If yes on Q144 do   Yes [Go to Q. 147] 1
      you think it is   No 2
      doing effective
      work in improving
      village education?

Q146 If no, why is   The views of the committee members not sought 1
      that the   Committee members views ignored 2
      case?   Committee members do not have relevant expertise 3
                         Others [specify] 7
      Other committees

Q147 Is there a village   Adapt and repeat Q144–146 if yes
      water and
      sanitation
      committee
      (VWSC) for
      the NGO
      managed
      project?

Q151   Is there a village   Adapt and repeat Q144–146 if yes
        health committee   (Similarly explore other committees)
        (VHC) for the
        NGO managed
        project?

Q155   Do you feel   Totally powerless 1
        that that   Almost powerless 2
        belonging to   Somewhat powerless 3
        the CO has   Mostly powerful 4
        resulted in your   Very powerful 5
        having the power
        to change the
        course of your life?

Q156   SUGGESTIONS
        What would you   _____
        suggest for making   _____
        the CO more   _____
        effective?   _____

Interviewer's signature: _____

SRNO

FGD questions on collective action for non-CO members and control village communities

---

$\underset{\text{SRNO}}{\llcorner\perp\perp\perp}$

SECTION A

AREA

A1. Field Unit (FU) $\perp$

A2. Name of community $\perp$

A3. Name of CO $\perp$

A4. Type of CO [M / F / Mix] $\perp$

A5. Number of *mohallas* / *dhokes* / *mohras*[1]
in the revenue community $\perp$

A6. Number of *mohallas* / *dhokes* / *dohras*
in the extended community $\perp$

A5. Distance from district headquarter
_____ km

A6. Distance from *tehsil*[2] headquarter
_____ km

INTERVIEW

A9. Date $\perp$: $\perp$: $\perp$

A10. Name of interviewer

A11. Interviewer's signature

How do you define this community?

[Map, geographical boundaries, place names, and the following reference points; start with this community map as a warm-up exercise]

Where is / are the: The mosque?
                                       Primary school?
                                       Secondary school?
                                       Sources of water?
                                       Waste and garbage disposal sites?

Q1	Community topology	Plain 1
		Hilly 2
		Mixed 3

Q2   Total land in community

Q3   Total arable land in community

Q4   Number of castes

Q5   Number of subcastes

Q6   Community literacy [rough estimate]

Q7   How may political parties in the village competed for local government elections?   _____

Q8	Has community (without CO/ NGO) engaged in any kind of collective action?	Yes 1
		No 2
		If yes, repeat questions as in Appendix 12.2

Q9	Has the local government / government been approached for any project (s) by the community on its own initiative?	Yes 1
		No [Go to Q. 13] 2
		If yes, repeat questions as in Appendix 12.2

| Q10 | If yes, did you register as a Citizen Community Board (CCB) to do so? | Yes ....1 |
| | | No ....2 |

Q11 If yes, were you   Yes 1
     successful in the   No [Go to Q. 13] 2
     lobbying for the
     project?

Q12 If Yes, state why   Our contact with MNA/MPA[3] 1
     you think the   Community notable's contact with the MNA/MPA 2
     lobbying was   It was our turn 3
     successful.   Others [specify] 7

Q13 If No, state why   Government officials ignore us 1
     you think lobbying   MNAs/MPAs break promises 2
     was not successful?   Government does not have money 3
                               Too many competitors 4
                               Our efforts were not effective 5
                               Others [specify] 7

                               If yes, repeat questions as in Appendix 11.2

Q14 Is there any   Yes 1
     other group or   No [Go to]... 2
     organization in
     this community
     (other than the
     CO mobilized
     by the NGO)?

Q15 If Yes, then list?   Community development association 01
                               Cooperative 02
                               Parent-teacher association 03
                               Health committee 04
                               Youth group 05
                               Sports group 06
                               Cultural group 07
                               Civic group 08
                               Welfare organization 09
                               None [Go to Q23] 10
                               Others [specify] 77

Q16 Which group or   _____
     organization
     above has played
     the most active
     role in helping
     improve the
     well being of
     the community
     members?
     [If any list, or end questions]

| Q17 | Is this group or organization still active? | Yes ....1 |
| | | No ....2 |

Q18	How did this group or organization get started?	Government initiated it 1
		NGO initiative 2
		Grassroots initiative 3
		Religious organization initiative 4
		Group within community set it up 5
		The whole community was involved in some way 6
		Others [specify] 7

Q19	Has this group or organization received any ongoing support from any source? [Don't prompt]	Local government 01
		National government 02
		Politicians 03
		Religious organizations 04
		NGO 05
		Prosperous influential 06
		A group within the community 07
		The community as a whole 08
		Don't know 99
		Others [specify] 77

Q20	How is / was the leadership determined	Election 1
		Appointment by community leaders 2
		Group consensus 3
		Others [specify] 7

| Q21 | Do you think that the leadership is effective? | Yes ....1 |
| | | No ....0 |

Q22	How were decisions made within these groups or organizations?	By leaders 1
		By leaders taking into account member views...............2
		By consensus 3
		Others [specify] 7

| Q23 | Has there been any other collective action via any mechanism? | If Yes, Use Qs. 24–48 from Appendix 12.2. |

BY OBSERVATION

Q24 What is the main route that inhabitants use to reach this community? [If no metal road, go to Q27]

Metal road 1
Shingle road 2
Dirt road 3
Mixed metal and dirt 4

Pagdandi[4] 5
Others [specify] 7

Q25 If metal road, what is the quality? [Observe and circle]

(Worst - 1)   2   3   4   (Best - 5)

Q26 If no metal road up to community, how far is the nearest metal road?

_____ km

Q27 Does this community have:

Garbage dumping 1
Standing water or stagnant pools 2
Waste in public places 3
Tree-cutting or forest burns 4
Commons not well maintained 5
Others [specify] 7

Q28 Overall, the current cleanliness condition of the community is:

Very good 1
Good 2
Average 3
Poor 4
Very poor 5

Interviewer's signature: _____

Notes

1. Neighborhood and subneighborhood.
2. Administrative tier below the district level.
3. Member National and Provincial Assembly.
4. Dirt road.

Appendix 12.4

Field strategy

1. Field team leader or survey team member, as delegated, will ensure collection of all relevant information at the field unit of development NGO as needed. Will have field team oriented and explore availability of guesthouses to serve as field base in the relevant areas.
2. Field team leader or survey team member as delegated will ensure collection of all relevant information at the selected community organization as needed.
3. Introduction to community by relevant social organizer or field unit staff of development organization. Transect walk and doing relevant mapping exercises as warm up and identifying extended community.
4. The field unit staff continues their own work leaving the field team with the community.
5. Conduct two simultaneous Focus Group Discussions (FGDs) with CO members and non-members.
6. Field team leader and male survey team member conduct interviews with community organization members and other households as planned.
7. Items 5–6 conducted by female team members for female COs.
8. Procedure repeated for the control villages.

Appendix 12.5

Terms of reference

Field team members

1. Will conduct household interviews and Focus Group Discussions (FGD) for women / mixed community organizations as determined by the field team leader.
2. Will maintain a diary of relevant observations and based on those and household surveys provide written inputs for field report for each site as determined by the field team leader.
3. Provide brief community profile to be appended to the field-report.
4. Any other research related task as determined by the field team leader.

Field team leader

1. Execute field study as conceptualized and summarized in the research objectives.
2. Provide one field report per site in the provided format reflecting the research objectives.
3. Provide one data set per site plus the aggregate date set to the principal investigator as mutually agreed upon.
4. Assist the principal investigator in data analysis for the research report as research collaborator/co-author.
5. Assume responsibility for the quality control and ensure high quality field reports and quantitative data.
6. Help train field team in field research methods.
7. Determine the itinerary for the field research and maintain close liaison with the donor office in this regard so that the research can be facilitated.
8. Provide inputs for the research design and determine the field research strategy.
9. Any other field report related task as determined by the principal investigator.

Survey consultant (1)

1. Help with the identification and selection of the field team.
2. Help with training of the field team in field research methods.
3. Provide inputs for the field research strategy and research design.
4. Any other field research related task as determined by the principal investigator.

Survey consultant (2)

1. Observe the field team member interviewing skills and provide inputs for improvements.
2. Train field team in FGD methods.
3. Provide inputs for field team assessments.
4. Assess, in consultation with the field team leader, when the field-team is ready for the survey.
5. Any other field team training task as determined by the field team leader.

Principal investigator

1. Conceptualize the research, research instruments, and research design.
2. Finalize research objectives in summary form.
3. Provide conceptual inputs for the field research strategy.
4. Train field team in understanding the study objectives.
5. Provide a first and revised draft of the research report.

Appendix 12.6

Survey design

NGO X has been in operation since 1993 and by May 2004 had mobilized 14,551 male CO interventions, 6,692 female interventions, and 954 mixed interventions across 18 regions. Given our limited budget, we purposely selected region Y as one of these 18 regions. This had about a fifth of all NGO X interventions (19.4 percent), by far the largest. It also had the logistic advantages of convenient access to the regional office. We were easily able to recruit and train a field-team with language skills usable across the region. In addition, this region provided a diverse topology of hilly, mixed, and flat terrain so that the impact of location on induced and autonomous collective action could also be analyzed.

We purposively selected NGO X interventions in the year 2000–2001 (July 1, 2000 to June 30 2004) in region Y as our universe. The Management Information Systems (MIS) department of the regional office provided the relevant list of COs to us. Choosing this year had the advantage that by this year NGO X's operations were fully established after the change in leadership in 1995–96 and so the diverse nature of NGO X projects, activities, services, trainings provided on its own or via linkages with the Government and other agencies could be explored over a four-year period.

NGO X had 555 interventions (COs or community organizations) cited for 2000–2001. We used type (male, female, mixed) and field unit as strata and ensured equal probability of selection across them for the COs which were the unit of analysis. We selected 50 sites via stratified random sampling that represented 9 percent of all region Y interventions in 2000–2001.

To ascertain the success of NGO X interventions in engendering collective action, 20 percent of the sample of COs was randomly selected to have an associated control village. This was the closest village to the NGO X CO village in the sample in which NGO X was not operational and we randomly selected approximately the same size of extended community to study autonomous collective action.[1]

We anticipated that the sample would also include NGO X interventions that did not succeed and there would be much to learn from that when comparing successful with unsuccessful interventions across the region in terms of induced and autonomous collective action while using social capital, harnessed via a CO or otherwise, as a key determinant. We intended to explore inclusion and exclusion of the nondestitute poor and CO benefits on non-members by using the concept of an extended community.

Note

1. Refer to chapter 11 for the definition of extended community.

Appendix 12.7

Proposed budget check-list

a. *Salaries and fees*
  i. *Data analysis and report writing*
     Principle investigator

  ii. *Data processing*
      Data processor
      Supervision and cleaning

  iii. **Fieldwork**
       Principal investigator: Questionnaire development, fieldwork training, and pre-test
       Field-team leader and interviewer
       3 field researchers (two female and one male) (for 78 days)
       Field-team training and pre-test
       Subtotal

b. *Fieldwork Expenses*
   Air fare
   Vehicle rent
   Boarding & lodging
   (78 days)
   Sub-Total

c. *Stationary and communications*
   Questionnaire printing/photocopy (lump sum)
   Telephone and Internet charges (lump sum)
   Sub-Total

Grand Total

Notes

Preface

1. A more important cause may be gender bias within and outside the household. Since, among the poor, the women are the most deprived, the HDFNA Pakistan Project has a particular focus on women's health and empowerment.
2. Banuri and Najam (1998).
3. For a description of the AKRSP and other such organizations refer to chapter 3.
4. The acronym APPNA is literally "our" in Urdu, the national language of Pakistan, and so APPNA *Sehat* translates into "our health." In the rest of the book, we will refer to the organization as APPNA.
5. The HDC was established by Mahmoob-ul-Haq in Islamabad after having successfully contributed to the development of the Human Development Indicators (HDI) that form a key element in various forms in the UNDP's annual *Human Development Reports*. HDC was renamed the Mahboob-ul-Haque Human Development Centre after the founder's death. SDPI was founded in 1992 as a public interest think tank.
6. The genesis of research done by local communities for local communities in various contexts is well formulated in the writings of Chambers (1997).
7. A key aspect of the communications strategy was producing a project video and this task was subsequently commissioned to a professional.
8. Pukhtuns are the ethnic group in the project area.
9. We speculated that development NGOs are wary of independent evaluations, even those of sympathetic researchers, since a negative review could impact donor funding.

I   Conceptual Issues: Harnessing and Guiding Social Capital

1. We have drawn on Khan (2006) for the first two sections of this chapter.
2. Field (2003, p. 9) noted that in addition to the traditional disciples, others scholars including feminists, educationists, and specialists in social and urban policy and planning contribute to applications including development, poverty, health, technological innovation, social inclusion, crime, and the investigation of civil society organizations and political systems.
3. Following Sen (2000), we assume a broad view of development as one of ensuring entitlements (including assets, livelihoods, and claims to public service) and building capabilities to deliver on freedoms (including freedom from starvation,

hunger, malnourishment, the lack of food or clothing, and restraints on travel, civic participation, and basic human rights). The implied social justice extends to current as well as future generations and hence to environmental security. Societies can aspire to the attainment of these objectives through a mix of state, market, and civil society initiatives and we discuss the role of the state and civil society further on in this chapter.

4. Refer to Haddad and Maluccio (2003, p. 2) for a tabulation of various definitions.

5. Narayan (2002, p. 58) also defines it to include the interaction of formal and informal organizations. Refer to Torsvik (2000) for a discussion of trust and different mechanisms (enlightened self-interest and "prosocial" motivations) producing trust and their separate implications for development.

6. Refer to Fafchamps and Minten (2002).

7. Refer to Meinzen-Dick, DiGregorio, and McCarthy on collective action.

8. The benefits of such collective action do not represent a zero-sum game where by the gains are at the expense of another group's welfare.

9. Collective action can be put to negative uses and examples in the literature of perverse social capital include drug cartels, the mafia, the Ku Klux Klan and Al Qaeda. Refer to Rubio (1997) and Streeten (2002, p. 44).

10. Refer to Isham, Kelly, and Ramaswamy, eds. (2002, p. 7).

11. One could argue that these still enter the utility functions but one need not head in that direction given discomfort with utility functions.

12. Rydin and Holman (2004) add to this the concept of "bracing" social capital. Other related conceptualizations include Burt (1992) on structural holes in networks and Granovetter (1974) on dense and weak ties in networks.

13. Grootaert and van Bastelaer, eds. (2002, p. 4) refer to information and collective action as the channels via which social capital has a positive impact on development.

14. Social cohesion is a useful term used by Reid and Salmen (2002).

15. Littering was very common and in the United States in the earlier 1960s. A mass communications strategy using public schools and the media, and fines, contained this problem very rapidly. Singapore used a much more draconian command and control approach for resolving this problem.

16. Following Grant (2001, p. 978), we view community as a group in a geographically defined area with everyday or frequent in person contact that shares similar interests and values, a sense of belonging together, and face common challenges.

17. For a critique, refer to Sabatini (2006). Portes and Mooney (2003, p. 308) argue that the conceptual stretch from sociology to other disciplines meant the transition from individual and household level social capital to a stock residing in a wider entity such as a nation state and this has not been well theorized.

18. For examples, in a different context, of the synergy between the state and civil society producing a virtuous circle in social capital construction in Kerala, India, refer to Heller (1996, p. 1056). Also relevant is Fox (1996) writing in a political context about social capital construction in rural Mexico.

19. Refer to the critique in section 1.3.

20. This is evident in particular in the review by Rossing and Assaf (1999).

21. Heller (1996) views it as the constructive role the state government played in the class coordination of militant labor and skittish capital in Kerala, and also the role of the state in providing redistributive goods.

22. Refer to Collier (1998, p. 15) on complementarities and substitutability of government and civil society social capital. Also refer to Wallis, Killerby, and Dollery (2004, p. 243) and Rothstein (2003) for a discussion of this issue.

23. Bebbington and Carroll (2000), Sorenson (2000) and Gugerty and Kremer (2000) are examples of such thinking. Ostrom (1997, pp. 161–162) discusses this concept of building and sustaining social capital.

24. For an extensive annotated bibliography of the literature up to the 1990s refer to Feldman and Assaf (1999).

25. The reference is to the 1990s and the first decade of the twenty-first century. Refer to Field (2003, pp. 11–43) for an account of the contribution of these scholars, and the critical reception to their theories, in the context of classical social theorists. Many scholars trace the origin of this concept to philosophers or scholars earlier in the twentieth century or before. For example, in the edited work cited above, Paterson traces the roots of the concept to eighteenth-century Scottish thinking and Wallis, Killerby and Dollery (2004, p. 240) trace the first use back to L.J. Hanifan in 1916. MacGillivray and Walker (2000, pp. 198–199) include Jane Jacobs and Paul Ekins as additional early contributors. Pantoja (2000, p. 1) cites Goran Hyden (1997) who traced the concept to the nineteenth century. Rossing and Assaf (1999, p. 2) cite Lyda Judson (1920) and Jane Jacobs (1960) as early pioneers. Pretty and Smith (2004, p. 633) cite Tönnies (1887) and Jane Jacobs and Loury (1977) is frequently cited as having introduced the concept into the social sciences. Refer also to Sabatini (2006) for a review of the first use of social capital and the origins of the concept and to Woolcock (1998) for a review of its intellectual history.

26. Refer to Fine (2000) for a more sympathetic view.

27. Boix and Posner (1998) address this puzzle and argue that part of the answer is the relatively greater equality in the North that enabled greater cooperation whereas feudal lords in the South jealously guarded their power and quashed the emergence of cooperative activity.

28. Narayan and Pritchett (1999) make this argument. While most scholars characterize the flow as benefits derived from positive collective action, Robison and Flora (2003) characterize the flow as socioemotional goods.

29. Refer to Lin (2001), one of the early contributors to the field, for a sociologist's conceptualization.

30. This is a summarized account of a detailed and complex exposition.

31. Also refer to Sabatini (2006) for a critical perspective on the empirics of social capital and economic development.

32. In so doing, they concede that at least in some, if not in all cultural settings, an important component of what drives human behavior is excluded from economic models since individual decisions can be part of larger community decisions.

33. Interestingly, this neoclassical formulation comes close to that of the Marxist scholar Bourdieu who referred to the use of social contacts for maintaining a class position. Neoclassical economists such as Grootaert (nd.) and Narayan and Pritchett (1997) do empirically test for whether social capital is vested in individuals or the village, as a broader entity, in terms of its expenditure effects. Thus the former concludes that the effects at the village level are more pronounced while the latter finds they are more pronounced at the individual level while conceding a small sample size as a possible reason for the weak association at the village level.

34. Refer to Baron, Field, and Schuller (2000, pp. 26–31) for a discussion of measurement challenges, although scholars have nonetheless attempted measurement. Refer to Narayan and Pritchett (1999) for measurement in a low-income country context and MacGillivay and Walker (2000) for measurement in a high-income country context and also van Deth (2003). Refer to Grootaert and van Bastelaer, eds. (2002) for an account of the various ways in which it is measured depending on whether the empirical study in question is at a micro, meso, or macro level. Haddad and Maluccio (2003) distinguish between measurement based on associational activity (membership in clubs and voluntary associations) and those based on the underlying mechanism of trust, norms, rules, and transactions cost and combine these for their empirical work. Most of the numerous quantitative studies cited in chapter 2 all find ways of measuring social capital with reference to the conceptualizations in section 1.2. The World Bank has facilitated this process of measurement with the publication of Grootaert and van Bastelaer, eds. (2002). The annexure to their volume contains instruments for social capital measurement for practitioners that have been field tested in various countries and these are also posted on the World Bank Web site. Also refer to part III of this book that demonstrates how these tools can be adapted to particular cultural and social conditions.
35. Dasgupta (1999). Also refer to Mancinelli and Mazzanti (2004).
36. Refer to Astone et al. (1999) for a discussion of issues of alienability, fungibility, and depreciation of social capital from a broader social theory of exchange perspective. They also discuss from this perspective how social capital comes into being in the first place, an issue they view as under-researched. Also refer to Sobel (2002) on economic concepts pertaining to social capital and to Robison, Schmid, and Siles (2002) who deconstruct the properties of capital and reason that social capital meets the criteria including transformation capacity, durability, flexibility, substitutability, decay, reliability, ability to create other capital forms and investment (disinvestments) opportunities.
37. The extension rather than depreciation with use is an important distinction between social and physical capital. Networks and reciprocal relations based on trust thrive when in use. The goodwill spreads by word of mouth, and others are brought into the network. This is also true of the "created" social capital such as the peer- group saving societies initiated by the Grameen Bank. Success bred success and the social intervention flourished and spread within Bangladesh and outside. The social demand for other multifunctional COs also increases when they are perceived as doing good work and community trust is secured. Thus, "supply can create its own demand" in the mesoeconomy as suggested by the classical French political economist Jean-Baptiste Say (1767–1837) for the macroeconomy. Ostrom (1997, pp. 162–163) compares social and physical capital and points out that since social capital is premised on a shared cognitive understanding, it is not as fungible and the conversion to liquid capital is limited. Again, it is not visible or tangible like physical capital and harder to construct since doing so requires an understanding of local cultures.
38. Grootaert and van Bastelaer (2002, p. 5).
39. However, there is irony in this critique given the challenge to neoclassical economics regarding the difficulties in measuring physical capital. Refer to Cohen and Harcourt (2003) for an update on this controversy.

40. Also refer to Molyneux (2002).
41. Marx's reference is to physical capital. For reflections on Fine's and other critiques refer to Bebbington (2002, 2004).
42. The references here are to Glaeser, Laibson, and Sacerdote (2000) and Stiglitz (1998).
43. Most, if not all, of the research is cross-sectional whereas the development of social capital and its impact on various key variables occurs over time. Some researcher use initial conditions but this only partially addresses this criticism. Refer also to Quibria (2003, pp. 31–34). While econometric problems can be overcome with sophisticated techniques, it is more difficult to address the critique of trying to capture historical processes with cross-sectional analysis. Krishna and Uphoff (2001, pp. 115–121) cite references that dispute the centrality of history in the formation of social capital and provide evidence to the contrary in the formation of village social capital. Brune et al. (2005) demonstrate that social capital can be constructed with leadership and management training and Mosley and Verschoor (2004) use experimental methods to demonstrate the possibility of building trust, a key component of social capital, based on factors other than social history.
44. Refer to Fox (1997) for a critical treatment of the Bank's handling of social capital in the Mexican context.
45. Grootaert and Bastelaer (2002, p. 5) and Dika and Singh (2002, p. 44) mention the "activation" of social capital in passing. We take the view that the activeness of social capital is a question of degree, but that it needs to be active for it to be harnessed and guided. Falk and Kilpatrick (2000) theorize that some aspects of social capital could be harnessed. Their interest is in processes that might produce social capital via networks in rural communities. Based on ethnomethodological principles, conversation analysis is used to demonstrate this for a rural Australian community.
46. Thus we adopt an instrumental view of social capital. We are aware that this instrumental approach has been criticized by among others, those who view social capital as an end in and of itself [Fine (2000, p. 87)]. However, the latter approach has been subjected to the criticism of circularity whereby social capital is both a "means" and an "ends." On this issue of circularity refer to Portes and Mooney (2003) and Baron, Field, and Schuller (2000, pp. 29–30).
47. Grant (2001, p. 989) makes this point. Dowla (2006) makes a persuasive case that the Grameen Bank creates bonding, bridging, and linking social capital and that this process is premised on enhancing trust, norms and networks. We do not dispute this, but would also add an additional hypothesis to test that the more successful groups are likely to be the ones that start with a higher level of bonding social capital and this is what Grameen harnesses and banks on.
48. Such organizations could switch their role from delivery to oversight to ensure quality delivery.
49. Banuri and Amalric (1992) have referred to the unwillingness or inability of the poor to engage in collective action as "deresponsibilization" resulting from the dependency of the poor created due to the presence of an interventionist state. More relevant here, they document the crowding out, or impeding of, social capital formation or collective action due to the presence of dominant state or market institutions such as the village headman or middle-man.

One problem is that while the dependency has been created, the delivery is either not forthcoming or is inadequate and of poor quality.

50. For a review of this concept and its application in the Pakistani development scene refer to Khan (1999, chapter 1).

51. Refer to Khan (1999, chapter 1) for the distinction between induced collective action, via this form of building social capital, and spontaneous collective action via grassroots organizations or institutions created by the poor to resolve common problems.

52. This is a reference to a results-based matrix (RBM) now commonly used for assessment and evaluation by aid and development agencies such as CIDA (Canadian International Development Agency). This approach also avoids the circularity problem referred to in fn. 46.

53. In this regard, the example of Six-S cited by Sorenson comes closest to the association of the development NGO and created VOs that is the subject of this book, although Six-S builds on traditional social organization while we investigate newly created organizations.

54. The private sector will underinvest in an activity when all those who benefit cannot easily be charged for that benefit.

55. Sorenson (2000, p. 14) points out that that the existence of social capital, such as farmers associations, in a village facilitates extension service, as they are more receptive and more willing to share information.

56. This issue is taken up in chapter 3.

57. In particular refer to Harriss and de Renzio (1997, p. 920).

2 Empirical Applications of Social Capital to Growth, Poverty Alleviation, and Rural Development

1. Refer to Fine's criticisms of regression analysis in chapter 1. In addition, reviewing three highly cited empirical studies, Durlauf (2002) points out that these studies "suffer from various identification problems" and suggests ways of addressing this shortcoming. A more extensive discussion of empirical short-comings of econometric studies is contained in Durlauf and Fafchamps (2004).

2. Refer also to the readings reviewed by Quibria (2003, p. 31). The findings from cross-country studies are subject to the criticism of assuming structural similarity across very diverse countries.

3. They also disaggregated social capital and found that the number of member-ships, internal diversity and participation in decision making as the key aspects of social capital that are significant and positively associated with higher per capita household expenditure and also that returns to social capital were higher for the poor. The paper ended with some sensible caveats includ-ing the need for historical, institutional and cultural analysis to understand how social capital comes about in the first place and the need for caution in policy intervention because an understanding of what kinds of social capital at what levels make a noteworthy difference is limited.

4. Galasso and Ravillion (2001).

5. Also refer to Francis et al. (1998) for the association of social capital and schooling.

6. Refer to Curran (2002) for a discussion of methodological issues including the impact of social capital on migration and the subsequent impact on coastal ecosystems.

7. Also refer to Pretty and Ward (2001).

8. An interesting observation was that based on the coercion experienced by the villagers in the Ujama Village Project, villagers were actually wary of induced collective action.

9. The authors point out that the federations waxed and waned but survived and, as is generally true, individuals played a key role in the process.

10. Bebbington (1997) mentioned the critical role of demand in enabling such organizations to market their produce and the role of the state in this context and Carroll and Bebbington (2000) pointed out that the created social capital can be misdirected.

11. The impact of other variables, including land inequality, on social capital was also explored and the quadratic of the Gini coefficient for land holding was found to have a significant and negative sign, that is, beyond some threshold level, the size of landholdings adversely influenced village social capital.

12. This process is likely to have marginalized the poorest doing day labor.

13. The literature on microcredit or microfinance is now vast and the issues more complex than initially portrayed. Refer to Yunus (2002, 2003) and Dowla (2006) for a more recent account.

14. For a review of the application of this model in the Philippines refer to Quinones Jr. and Seibel (2000). Using cultural homogeneity and geography as proxies for social connectedness, Kaplan (2005) shows how the latter results in more positive outcomes in group lending in Peru.

15. Also refer to Amin, Rai and Topa (1999), Khandkar, Khilily, and Khan (1994), and Pitt, Khandkhar, and Cartwright (2003).

16. Also refer to Mayoux (2001) in this regard.

3   Harnessing and Guiding Social Capital in Pakistan

1. Many thanks to Shandana Khan, the Executive Director of the Rural Support Program Network, for valuable comments, particularly on the relationship of the government and Rural Support Programs. We have drawn on Khan (2006) for the first two sections of this chapter.

2. For other ways in which the state can contribute to the "construction" of social capital refer to Evans (1996).

3. NRSP accounts for about half the outreach of all constituent members of RSPN.

4. Depending of the size and social dynamics of the village, there could be more than one VO in a village.

5. The eighteenth AKRSP Annual Report (2000) was dedicated to this theme of partnerships. This report has been drawn on to provide information about AKRSP on this theme.

6. World Bank (2002) concludes that the AKRSP has been very effective in working with the government at the local level, although there has been some envy (due to higher pay scales) and jealously (due to successes) mixed with admiration of the project on the part of local government officials. In the Federal Capital, the concerned officials at the highest level have been appreciative and supportive.

7. Refer to Bebbington and Perreault (2003) and Sirivardana (2004), as documented in chapter 2, for examples of such supraorganizations or Federations in Ecuador and Sri Lanka respectively.

8. World Bank (1990) verified that income in the AKRSP program area doubled in the first ten years of the project.

9. One $ was the equivalent to about Rs. 58 in 2004.

10. Smillie and Hailey (2001, pp. 107–109) have documented this process.

11. The next few paragraphs draw on this report [World Bank (2002)]. The sample of VOs selected was purposive in consultation with project staff and not random and this needs to be taken into account in interpreting the numbers.

12. Refer to pp. 8–9 for the various qualifications pertaining to the difficulties of attribution.

13. Externalities in this context would be the benefits derived beyond the community that has engaged in building the social or physical infrastructure that then functions as a public good.

14. Being a member of the VO did not necessarily result in statistically significant higher earnings and so free riding occurs as is expected with collective action.

15. The two notable areas of weakness are the poor performance of women's VOs and the continued donor dependence. As AKRSP continues to reinvent itself, the latter is an issue it is trying to deal with.

16. World Bank (2002).

17. This brief account is based on Ebrahim (2003). The Aga Khan Rural Support Programs for India and Pakistan respectively will be referred to as AKRSP (I) and AKRSP (P) in this subsection.

18. AKRSP (I) formally uses PRA (participatory rural appraisal) that it has adapted and systematized for its dialogue and social mobilization process.

19. As in the case of AKRSP (P), the VOs form clusters or federations in particular areas. Unlike the homogenous communities in Northern Pakistan, differentiation by caste and class made it difficult to mobilize the whole village in some areas (Junagadh) compared to other more homogeneous areas (Bharuch) and VOs have evolved into different forms, more function specific, in the different areas.

20. Again, the credit for this goes to Akhtar Hameed Khan and Shoaib Sultan Khan, who persuaded their colleagues in government in senior positions by example or dialogue that this was an approach worth pursuing. A strategic partnership with donors, who liked what they saw, accelerated the process.

21. Dastgeer (2001) and internal RSPN documents.

22. Shoaib Sultan Khan referred to the RSPN as a coordinating body of 10 independent "owners" or organizations where key personnel periodically get together and exchange information.

23. An average household size of 8 means an outreach to 11.5 million people.

24. Union councils are the lowest administrative tier in the local government system.

25. In summarizing economic impact, Rasmussen et al. cite studies that suggest that membership in a CO resulted in 7.5 percent higher household income and lower poverty levels. Also, 68 percent ate better, 50 percent cited health improvements, and 85 percent mentioned a sustainable increase in income resulting from access to credit.

26. Founded in 1972 with the independence of the country, the BRAC Web site (June 2006) reports that is now a multifaceted organization with over 37,410

full-time staff, 2,439 project staff, 53,205 teachers, and it has a presence in over 65,000 villages, in all the 64 districts of Bangladesh.

27. This was stated in a private conversation to one of the authors of this study in July 2003. For a fascinating study of these social activists from an anthropological perspective refer to Bielke (2004). Bielke's focus is on the role of leadership in social transformation and this study highlights the role of tradition, staying power of local elites, and village social dynamics in the process of leadership change.

28. Thanks are due to Dr. Rashid Bajwa, the Chief Executive Officer of NRSP, for comments and Zafar Ahmad of RSPN for making documentation available for this section. Baluch (2002), Cool and Eastman (1998), Uddin (2004), M.H. Khan (nd.), NRSP (2004a), NRSP (2004b), and Rassmusen et al. (2004) have been drawn on.

29. The professional staff size in early 2005 was 1,454.

30. Refer to Cool and Eastman (1998) for an account of this linkage.

31. To free up the time and energies of the social activists and the CO for other activities, NRSP has developed and is experimenting with a social appraisal tool that works like a credit check and is implemented by the credit officer at the field unit level. The initial results showed a big jump in disbursements and recovery rates.

32. This leveraging enables it to run programs worth Rs. 2 billion with a Rs. 500 million endowment fund.

33. In the first phase, 90 projects were satisfactorily completed that benefited 34, 463 households. Refer to Baluch (2002) for an account of this partnership.

34. These public-private partnerships that entail the RSPs acting as contractors in lieu of the conventional tendering process, has been engaged in by the other RSPs also. Refer to Uddin (2004) and section 3.6 for details.

35. While political governments have assumed a supportive or hostile position based on whether they initiated the project or later tried to control it (section 3.5), the military government (1999–) has been extremely supportive. Given the "a political" approach of the RSPs, this is not surprising.

36. Government of Pakistan, National Reconstruction Bureau, (2000, pp. 18–21).

37. Ibid. (2001, pp. 51–59). For a review of the design flaws refer to Khan (2001).

38. Government of Pakistan (2000) and RSPN (2002).

39. Twenty-five percent of a districts' development budget is allocated to CCBs.

40. A unique aspect of the NRSP schooling contract was the contribution of Rs. 6 million from a firm in the corporate sector with an interest in improving the area's schooling. RSPN (2005, pp. 7–8) lists 46 RSP partnerships with district governments between May 2004 and March 2005 in the health, education, infrastructure, and capacity building areas and selectively documents some of them to identify the mode of operation, project design and implementation.

41. Refer to Khan and Zafar (1999).

42. Refer to Portes and Mooney (2003, p. 326) for a case study of similar attempts by the El Salvadorian community in the United States in initiating community development projects in their home country. The lack of an institutional structure like the HDFNA accounted for one possible reason for the limited sustainability of such initiatives.

43. Refer to the preface for details.

4   Cultural Context

1. The other three are Balochistan, Punjab and Sindh. In additions, there are Federally and Provincially administered tribal areas and the Federally administered disputed territory of Azad Jammu and Kashmir (AJK). The project area is very close to Mardan city, the capital of Mardan district. Refer to a map of the country and province, with Mardan district identified, in Annexure 4.1. The project area is canal irrigated and farming is the main occupation of the villages targeted for project interventions. Sugarcane, rice, wheat, maize, tobacco and sugar beet are the main crops grown in this area.

2. Pathan is generally the term used in the English language. Urdu, the national language of Pakistan, uses all three terms.

3. This was the dialect in use at the field site and thus we use these terms in this book.

4. The Shi'a is the other major sect, estimated to be about 15 percent of all Muslims.

5. The Great Game is a term that has been used to describe the rivalry and strategic conflict between the British and the Czarist empires. While the British Empire was consolidating its holdings in the Indian subcontinent, the expanding Russian Empire was closing in on the Khanates of central Asia. The British felt threatened by this forward expansion of Russia toward the Indian subcontinent, which was the jewel in the British crown. This resulted in a subtle game of espionage between the Russians and the British for political control of the northwest of the Indian subcontinent. The classic Great Game dates from about 1813 to 1907, but the tensions have been carried forward in various forms to this day. For more details on the Great Game refer to Hopkirk (1992), Meyer and Brysac (1999) and Brobst (2005).

6. The current Musharraf administration in Pakistan is trying to fence the border and to monitor the movement of populations across it as part of its anti-Taliban campaign. In keeping with the position of past Afghan administrations, the current Karzai administration in Afghanistan also disputes the Durand line and hence has opposed this move by Pakistan.

7. These links are social capital as represented by Bourdieu in another context (refer to chapter 1), but they are not the direct focus of this book.

8. A *mullah* (cleric) mediates petty problems.

9. According to local legend, a man inadvertently sought and was mistakenly granted refuge from the relatives of an individual he had murdered. He had protection while in the house he had been granted hospitality in.

10. There has been extensive research on the settlement of the canal colonies in the Punjab Province but not on the parallel settlement in the NWFP. Refer to Ali (1988), Pasha (1998), and Van de Dungen (1972).

11. That is why the community has not attained homogeneity and permanence, as evident from APPNA surveys. New settlers still keep moving in while some households move out to settle in other areas. Apart from agriculture, the inhabitants of the area also explore other avenues of revenue generation and these are also a source of mobility. A considerable number of men from the area have sought work in the southern port city of Karachi, the largest city in the country, or in the Middle East. For more information on the Mohmands of the project area refer to Hussain (2000).

12. Refer to Khan (1999) and Khan, Khan, and Akhtar (2007, chapter 3).
13. Attitudes change and in the course of time women in the project area were marketing within and beyond the village (refer to chapter 11).
14. The distance between the rural project area where SDPI conducted its field-work and Mardan city is about 5 miles.
15. Our focus is on the Pakistan side of the Durand line. Edwards (1996) and Anderson (1978, 1992) have researched Pukhtuns on the Afghan side of the border.

5   HDF Interventions

1. The distinction between project and program is important at the onset. Throughout this book, we refer to HDF as the "project" following HDFNA's reference to it as "The Pakistan Project." Thus the area HDF operates in is referred to as the project area and its activities are referred to as program. This can be confusing because some of the HDF activity is in the form of projects or schemes.
2. Other NGOs approached to join the partnership included the NRSP to provide the training and engage in the social mobilization, Aurat for the gender aspects of the project and the SDPI to be the research partner and provide on going input during the project inception (refer to the preface).
3. A medical doctor was associated with the field team to facilitate with the health data collection and analysis.
4. Thanks are due to Ayesha Khan for help in formulating these research issues.
5. The association of one of the founding members with Mardan could explain APPNA's initial presence in Mardan. Expansion plans, particularly premature expansion, is premised on contributors in North America desiring a presence in their area of origin.
6. DO is the HDF counterpart to VOs or COs—refer to chapter 3.
7. Details on HDF's expansion to other parts of the country are provided in chapter 10.
8. Collier (1998) rightly argues that the opportunity cost of time of the poor is lower. This is true in an absolute sense because they earn less, but not in a relative sense because the marginally utility of income foregone is likely to be much higher, notwithstanding the difficulties of intrapersonal utility comparisons. This is particularly likely to be the case since they often operate at a subsistence level and the loss of a day's work could be the loss of food for that day.
9. The term partnership is reserved by registration authorities for commercial enterprises based on the traditional concept of business partnerships. The term economic development unit was adopted subsequently for functions performed by HDF.
10. Important work in defining communities in Pakistan has been done by Gazdar, Khan and Khan (2002).
11. Subsequently, many of them returned to the school when the anger subsided.
12. BRAC is among Bangladesh's oldest and largest development NGOs. Refer to its Web site for details.
13. Khan (1987).
14. Ibid, chapter 1.
15. Refer to Yunus (2002, 2003).

16. This is taken to great lengths. In the control village, a government village health unit ostensibly employed two young girls. These girls had moved out of the village after getting married, but continued to collect their salaries as "ghost workers." The villagers avoided reporting this even though they were deprived of a service.
17. This was to encourage credit for female activity that initially was rightly perceived to be a reflection of male needs.

6 Social Mobilization

1. In the project area the DOs were referred to by the locals as *tanzeems* (organization in local parlance). DO was used by the project staff in the regional and head office, but in the field the project staff also used the term *tanzeem*.
2. Units include about 1000–1200 contiguous households each spread over one or more villages.
3. The two parts of Fazal Killay (FK) differ in endowments. Many people from FK east are working abroad and, due to remittances, it is relatively more prosperous than FK west. By contrast, FK west is endowed with a homogenous population, whereas FK east has a more heterogeneous population including Bajauris, Swatis, Momands, and Malakian. These factors can came into play during the social mobilization and DO formation and sustainability phases.
4. *Zakat* represents charitable contributions for Muslims. In Pakistan, this has been made operational as an annual deduction (2.5 percent) on saving accounts of most belonging to the *Sunni* sect (followers of the Hanafi jurisprudence can claim exemption). Individuals are also free however to withdraw funds from their accounts prior to the first of *Ramzan* (the month of fasting), the preannounced date of collection. The banks pass on the amount collected to the state for onward distribution via *zakat* committees.
5. Virtually all cultivation in the project area is done by tenants who have taken possession of the land. However, though there is relative equality in this regard, even among tenants some cultivate more land and in this sense assume the position of village notables with more power and assumption of economic, social and political authority relative to other households. The landlords continue to attempt to reclaim there lands in legal battles and in 2006 matters once again got heated temporarily with tenants displaying firearms (see chapter 4).

7 Health

1. Apart from HDFNA that contributed about a third of total funds until 2000, the other substantial donors include Trust for Voluntary Organizations (TVO), which contributed 27.6 percent, and Canadian International Development Agency (CIDA), which contributed 21.3 percent.
2. The information in this section has been drawn from a project document *APPNAIYET*, 1989–2000, and the presentation of the Chairman of the President's Task Force on the Social Sectors to the National Reconstruction Bureau, November 22, 2001.
3. Urdu is Pakistan's official language, though the provincial languages are different and there are over 50 languages and dialects spoken within its geographic boundaries.

4. In Mardan, no coverage is provided for weekends and holidays. However, there are Public Call Offices (PCOs), some private telephones and privately owned transport vehicles in the villages. Therefore, some means of communication are available in case of need and emergencies. All villages have some supply of electricity.
5. All statistics cited pertain to this time duration.
6. UNDP (2000, p. 188). Note that the national statistics include both urban and rural estimates. Since access to health facilities in urban areas is much better, the APPNA achievements would be even more impressive if compared only to other rural areas.
7. Ibid.
8. Government of Pakistan, (2004, p. 135).
9. As is always the case in such sample surveys, there was nonresponse on some questions and this has been duly noted in the analysis.
10. UNDP (2000, p. 225).
11. Ibid, p. 192.
12. Ibid.
13. During field-visits, mothers reported some recollection of ORS public advertisements on TV.

8   Education

1. Drawn from a TMF document.
2. Refer to Khan et al. (2005).
3. Some children even below the entry age of five sat in the class without being registered.
4. The bigger village is Charcha Kali and HDF named the school after it, but the school was located in Kandare Jadeed, a small extension of Charcha Kali (refer to chapter 6).

9   Field Update 2001

1. Thanks are due to Sara Hamid for covering the female aspects of the project update and for writing a competent report based on the fieldwork.
2. The RPM's response to this was that he would go to the United States himself if HDFNA could so easily arrange it.
3. They were cancelled only if other important meetings were to be attended by the project staff or in case of a wedding or a funeral.
4. The Statistical Supplement of *Economic Survey* 2000–2001 (p. 155) reported the daily wage of unskilled labor to be Rs. 80 in Peshawar, which means they could earn more than TMF teachers with a BA if they worked 24 days in a month. However, it is a buyer's market and teachers with a BA and Certificate of Teaching (CT) are in plentiful supply. Recall that the results reported in appendix 8.2 did not indicate that higher teacher qualifications necessarily led to a greater value added in student cognitive skills.
5. This Islamic mode of financing is referred to as *mudaraba*, and there is consensus that this is permissible.
6. For details and an analysis refer to Khan (2001). Also refer to chapter 10 for how devolution in time interfaced with HDF at the field level.

10   Field Update 2006

1. Mr. Mohammad Ishaq, who was a SO during our fieldwork in 1999, had left the organization for three years and then earned the position of the RPM three weeks prior to our field visit. Since we had established a close link with him during our initial fieldwork, this greatly helped our follow-up fieldwork in the regional office (the disadvantage was his recent appointment as RPM). Also, a summary of our first report was well received by the new chief executive officer, Lt. Col. (Rtd.) Azhar Saleem, and he pulled out all the stops and this also greatly facilitated our work in the region with all personnel, sites, and documents freely accessible. We also got access to all the documents we requested from the head office and had a long interview with the CEO and were pleasantly surprised at how sharp his development instincts were, given our false preconceptions in this case of the limited versatility of military training and experience. We would like to acknowledge both these individuals and also Mount Holyoke College for the research grant that made this follow-up research possible.

2. Of the 403 DOs formed, 157 had not succeeded. Given hostility to the project, the dead DOs were difficult to visit and we excluded those and others that had not been in operation for at least one year and were left with 164 DOs as the sampling population. Using gender and funding by the PPAF (discussed later in the chapter) as strata, we randomly selected 14 DOs, eight male and 6 female, with equal probability of selection using the list of DOs provided by the regional office as a sampling frame. The DOs in the sample were widely dispersed in the project area. Unfortunately, we were unable to contact the resource person for one of the eight male DOs.

3. Units have about 1000 to 1200 households; 25 to 30 villages and were established based on the project baseline surveys at project inception. HDF is currently contemplating redefining units to conform territorially to the union councils that are the lowest tier of local government.

4. A list of follow-up questions, based on chapters 5–8 and the fieldwork done for chapter 9, are included as Annexure 10.3.

5. Naturally registers were not available for the dead or inactive DOs. HDF explained that 41 DOs had become inactive because opposing factions formed in local government elections. The faction that lost, manipulated and directed the anger at HDF (which is nonpartisan and apolitical by registration charter) and burnt a CHC due to the death of a new-born and withdrew from paying back loans and warned the project to stay away. HDF viewed this departure as a convenient pretext for having gotten out of paying back loans. Interestingly, the female project staff continued to visit to collect credit installments due, but used public rather than HDF transportation.

6. These meetings for men could be viewed as a variation on regular congregations at the *hujrah* to discuss a wide range of issues. Such meetings for women are a novelty since, prior to the HDF intervention, there was no such congregation in a public space. As earlier indicated and evident again from this survey, female DOs are much more dependent on the presence of an SO. As before, the SO does the record keeping if the office holders are not literate or if a male DO member related to the female office holders does not maintain the register.

7. This negative perception was directed not only at credit, which was quite clearly referred to as un-Islamic (*kufr*). Nonetheless, four out of the six female DOs engaged in the credit program.

8. Two won *nazim* (roughly a mayor) seats, one a *naib* (deputy) *nazim* seat, and ten councilor seats. HDF is by registration "apolitical." However, the social organization probably carries over to the political realm in a nonpartisan fashion. While organizations such as HDF could rightly take some credit in that the social mobilization prepares the ground for political participation, they are prone to taking too much credit and risk denying the agency of the social activist. These are the very activists that development NGOs critically depend on, and they may also find in political participation another avenue for their impulse for leadership and community contribution.

9. The manipulation could occur on both sides. The community was quite aware of how the project was judging its performance and knew of its chips in this "tug-of-war" with the project that in turn attempted to induce "discipline" according to its criteria and tailored incentives accordingly.

10. AKRSP refers to it as Productive Physical Infrastructure (PPI—refer to chapter 3).

11. This also applies to credit-allocation targets. The head office sets the limits on credit pools and the surplus including the "interest," referred to as mark-up, reverts to the head office.

12. This is an Islamic mode of financing such that all parties invest and share proportionately in the profit or loss of an investment. Refer to Khan (1987, chapter 2).

13. This shows the persistence of historic subcontinental practice since Islam in principle shuns the caste-system.

14. Trainings on CCB formation had been arranged and contracted out by the National Reconstruction Bureau (NRB), the agency in charge of devolution, and hence were readily available.

15. PPAF insists on a composite package including credit (on which it takes a markup) and the infrastructure projects are a sweetener. HDF managed to disassociate the two, as a special concession, and only secures funding for infrastructure projects.

16. The formalization of this procedure is in stark contrast to the practice during project initiation (refer to chapter 6).

17. Our survey of DOs indicated successful linkages with the Rural Water Supply and Sanitation Project (RWSSP) funded by the Department for International Development (DFID), United Kingdom. One of these DOs was within the catchment of the National Commission for Human Development (NCHD) and it had availed of its education related interventions.

18. This is only the case in Mardan where the appellation TMF-HDF school is used, but HDF manages the entire education program, including the teacher training, on its own in the other units in the rest of the country.

19. While these continued to be much lower than equivalent government sector salaries, scales for teacher qualifications had been established as Rs. 1,500 for a matriculate (Matric or Secondary), Rs. 1,800 for an FA (Fellow of Arts or Higher Secondary) and Rs. 2,000 for a Bachelors or Masters. A teacher coming from outside the village is given some travel allowance. Since these salaries were below the minimum wage rate, HDF viewed the difference as the

community contribution, given that this is designed to be a participatory project. As indicated earlier, the community views the contribution of the room as an individual rather than a community contribution.

20. Teachers get two annual trainings and some refresher courses regularly, the most recent on activity-based learning.

21. The fee varied from Rs. 5 to Rs. 20. The teachers were fully aware of the financial position of all the households and, in case of free-riding by the parents, the teacher would take the issue up at the PTA meetings. There was no immediate plan for the school management funds, and they represent an insurance in case of exit by the HDF.

22. Three of the seven male DOs had availed the credit facility at some point, one of which had discontinued due to public criticism.

23. Our follow-up survey revealed that there was a disproportionate amount of credit going to the DO office holders, both male and female. This points once again to the tension between private gain and collective well being in social activist motivation.

24. UNDP (2005), particularly chapters 1 & 2.

25. Six of the seven male DOs we visited for the field update consisted of homogenous kin groups from the same (Mohmand) tribe. The one exception included members from other tribes (Yusufzai and Banuri) but all were from the same neighborhood. Similarly five of the six female DOs were composed of the same kin group (Mohmands). The commonality in the sixth was that their children attended the same TMF school and they belonged to the same *mullah* (cleric) neighborhood.

26. HDFs defining community by mosque catchment seems to be vindicated.

27. As indicated in endnote 4, we were advised to stay away from these communities due to possible hostility to the project.

28. This probably also played into the suspicion and the conspiracy theory held among conservative communities that NGOs are furthering the "western agenda" of misleading women into changing their role.

29. Their current loan was in default because a family member had been arrested and they had used the money to bail him out of jail.

30. There was no male DO active in Kandare Jadeed.

11   Summary and Conclusion

1. It was subsequently registered as HDF for legal reasons as advised by the registration authority.

2. Information about HDF is based on quarterly project documents, a report presented by the Chairman of the President's Task Force on Human Development to the National Reconstruction Bureau, November 22, 2001, interviews with the HDF country representative and staff, and internal project documents including the 2005 Annual Progress Report.

3. These included Shamsabad, Rahim Yar Khan, Zhob and Karachi, in the squatter settlement in Malir.

4. This is a local plant with antipest and other medicinal properties.

5. In addition, there were several other region specific linkages forged in 2005. For example, in the Karachi *Kachi Abadi* (squatter settlements), linkages were established with Rotary International for school supplies, Shafi Qureshi

Foundation and The Citizen Foundation for education, Thardeep Rural Development Program (TRDP) for training in embroidery, carpet weaving, and *zari* work, and with a civil society organization for exploring drug addition in the project area. Linkages in health include those with Islamic Relief (UK) to set up an eye camp and refer children with refraction errors for free treatment to Al-Shifa Eye Trust, Sheikh Zaid Medical College / Hospital to set up a medical camp for treatment of diseases such as malaria and typhoid, and Network (advocacy NGO for consumer protection) for a publication that disseminates information on health issues.

6. These calculations were based on dividing the actual expenditures by the actual beneficiaries.

7. This is an overstatement because HDF now reaches approximately an additional 800,000 people via linkages and partnerships that does not draw on its resources. Both numbers were deflated using the general prices index with 2000–2001 as base. Refer to Government of Pakistan, 2006, Economic Adviser's Wing, Finance Division, *Economic Survey*, Statistical Annexure p. 65.

12   Planning a Field Study to Assess the Role of Harnessing Social Capital for Rural Development

1. www.worldbank.org/spoverty. This site leads to readings, recent research, and tools for measurement of social capital.

2. Refer to Durlauf and Fafchamps (2004) and Fine (2001) on the dangers of quantitative empirical work.

3. Naturally there could be more than one research question. However, a narrow focus is often critical to the successful execution and documentation of a field study.

4. In our case, the list had to be compiled from the records of the regional offices of the rural development NGO, fortunately computerized. Refer to appendix 11.6.

5. A five to 10 percent sample size may be reasonable, based on acceptable standard errors on key variables.

6. While the area is selected by RSPs based on poverty, the particular village is selected for project interventions based on the contacts forged by chance by the social organizer in the field. Thus, this research design represents a randomized experiment.

7. We stated in chapters 3 that we view development NGOs as government partners and at times contractors but not as displacers of government provision of services for human development. First, the capacity for such displacement simply is not present in most cases and even if it were, we do not consider this to be desirable, given that most states have a constitutional responsibility for such provision. However, development NGOs can evolve effective models of service delivery that the state sector could eventually adopt.

8. The lead researcher of this study earlier designed a study on the impact of devolution of power to the grassroots level on law and order and the dispensation of justice. Fully designed structured and semistructured instruments were taken to the field for the pretest only to discover the total irrelevance of the research design. Villagers in general were simply not willing to openly discuss the issues on the questionnaires. By going back to the drawing board, with the input from the field research team and team leader, we develop a much more round about

research design that entailed slowly winning the confidence of the community and moving through the village in a "snowball" method after collecting relevant prior information. For details refer to chapter 7 in Khan, Khan, and Akhtar (2007).

9. This and the other questionnaires started with the World Bank social capital research instruments and then radically altered them to suit our research objectives and local specificities. Other examples of adaptations are the studies by Krishna and Uphoff (2001, 2002).

10. Sample questionnaires for measuring the effectiveness of rural water supply schemes and schools (including tests) can be made available by the authors on request.

11. We propose this as complementary to the full analysis of the questionnaires on the effectiveness of the school and water supply schemes.

12. Refer to chapter 5 in Khan (2005).

13. Collective field reports must be completed before the fieldwork for the next site begins since the information of the sites can start to merge and become fuzzy if more than one field report is written at the same time.

References

Preface

Banuri, T., and A. Najam, 1998, "Project Pakistan: A Report Prepared for the Human Development Foundation of North America," Sustainable Development Policy Institute, Islamabad.

Chambers, R., 1997, *Whose Reality Counts? Putting the Last First* (London: Intermediate Technology Publications).

I Conceptual Issues: Harnessing and Guiding Social Capital

Arrow, K., 1999, "Observations on Social Capital," in ed. P. Dasgupta and I. Serageldin, *Social Capital: A Multifaceted Perspective* (Washington DC: World Bank).

Ashman, D., L.D. Brown, and E. Zwick, 1998, "The Strength of Strong and Weak Ties: Building Social Capital for the Formation and Governance of Civil Society Resource Organizations," *Nonprofit Management and Leadership*, Vol. 9, No. 2.

Astone, N.M., C.A. Nathanson, R. Schoen, and Y.L. Kim, 1999, "Family Demography, Social Theory, and Investment in Social Capital," *Population and Development Review*, Vol. 25, No. 1.

Banuri, T., and F. Amalric, 1992, "Population, Environment and De-responsibilization: Case Studies from the Rural Areas of Pakistan," SDPI Monograph Series No. 7, Islamabad.

Baron, S., J. Field, and T. Schuller, eds., 2000, *Social Capital: Critical Perspectives* (Oxford: Oxford University Press).

Bebbington, A., 2002, "Sharp Knives and Blunt Instruments: Social Capital in Development Studies," *Antipode*, Vol. 34, No. 4.

———, 2004, "Social Capital and Development Studies 1: Critique, Debate, Progress?" *Progress in Development Studies*, Vol. 4, No. 4.

Bebbington, A., and T.F. Carroll, 2000, "Induced Social Capital and Federations of the Rural Poor," Social Capital Initiative, Working Paper No. 19, World Bank, Washington DC.

Boix, C., and D.N. Posner, 1998, "Social Capital: Explaining its Origins and Effects on Government Performance," *British Journal of Political Science*, Vol. 28, No. 4.

Brune, N., T. Bossert, D. Bowser, F. Solis, and V.R.D. Herrara, 2005, "Building Social Capital through Human Capital Development Programs in Rural Nicaragua: An Evaluation of MSH Management and Leadership Programs in Wasala and Pantasma," Final Report, Harvard School of Public Health and Management Sciences for Health (MSH).

Burt, R.S., 1992, *Structural Holes: The Social Structure in Competition* (Cambridge: Harvard University Press).

Cleaver, F., 2005, "The Inequality of Social Capital and the Reproduction of Chronic Poverty," *World Development*, Vol. 33, No. 6.

Cohen, A.J., and G.C. Harcourt, 2003, "Retrospectives: Whatever Happened to the Cambridge Capital Theory Controversy," *The Journal of Economic Perspectives*, Vol. 17, No. 1.

Coleman, S.J., 1989, "Social Capital in the Creation of Human Capital," *American Journal of Sociology*, Vol. 94 (supplement), pp. s.95–s120.

Collier, P., 1998, "Social Capital and Poverty," Social Capital Initiative, Working Paper No. 4, World Bank, Washington DC.

———, 2002, "Social Capital and Poverty: A Microeconomic Perspective," in ed. C. Grootaert and T. van Bastelaer, *The Role of Social Capital in Development: An Empirical Assessment* (Cambridge: Cambridge University Press).

Dasgupta, P., 1999, "Overview: Economic Progress and the Idea of Social Capital," in ed. P. Dasgupta and I. Serageldin, *Social Capital: A Multifaceted Perspective* (Washington DC: World Bank).

Dika, S.L., and K. Singh, 2002, "Applications of Social Capital in Educational Literature: A Critical Synthesis," *Review of Educational Research*, Vol. 72, No. 1.

Dowla, A., 2006, "In Credit We Trust: Building Social Capital by Grameen Bank in Bangladesh," *The Journal of Socio-Economics*, Vol. 35, No. 1.

Durlauf, S.N., and M. Fafchamps, 2004, "Social Capital," National Bureau of Economic Research Working Paper No. 10485.

Fafchamps, M., and B. Minten, 2002, "Returns to Social Network Capital among Traders," *Oxford Economic Papers*, Vol. 54, No. 2.

Falk, I., and S. Kilpatrick, 2000, "What is Social Capital? A Study of Interaction in a Rural Community," *Sociologia Ruralis*, Vol. 40, No. 1.

Feldman, T.R., and S. Assaf, 1999, "Social Capital: Conceptual Framework and Empirical Evidence—An Annotated Bibliography" Social Capital Initiative, Working Paper No. 5, World Bank, Washington DC.

Field, J., 2003, *Social Capital: Key Ideas* (London: Routledge).

Fine, B., 1999, "The Development State is Dead—Long Live Social Capital?" *Development and Change*, Vol. 30, No. 1.

———, 2001, "The Social Capital of the World Bank," in ed. B. Fine, C. Lapavistsas, and J. Pincus, *Development Policy in the Twenty-first Century: Beyond the Post-Washington Consensus* (London: Routledge).

Fine, B., and F. Green, 2000, "Economics, Social Capital, and the Colonization of the Social Sciences," in ed. S. Baron, J. Field, and T. Schuller, *Social Capital: Critical Perspectives* (Oxford: Oxford University Press).

Fox, J., 1996, "How Does Civil Society Thicken? The Political Construction of Social Capital in Rural Mexico," *World Development*, Vol. 24, No. 6.

———, 1997, "The World Bank and Social Capital: Contesting the Concept in Practice?" *Journal of International Development*, Vol. 9, No. 7.

Fukuyama, F., 2001, "Social Capital, Civil Society and Development," *Third World Quarterly*, Vol. 22, No. 1.

Glaeser, E.L., D. Laibson, and B. Sacerdote, 2002, "The Economic Approach to Social Capital," *Economic Journal*, Vol. 112 (November), pp. F437–58.

Granovetter, M.S., 1974, *Getting a Job: A Study of Contacts and Careers* (Chicago: University of Chicago Press).

Grant, E., 2001, "Social Capital and Community Strategies: Neighborhood Developments in Guatemala City," *Development and Change*, Vol. 32, No. 5.

Grootaert, C., nd., "Social Capital, Household Welfare and Poverty in Indonesia," Local Level Institutions Study, Social and Development Department, The World Bank, Revised draft.

———, 1998, "Social Capital: The Missing Link?" Social Capital Initiative, Working Paper No. 3, World Bank, Washington DC.

Grootaert, C., and T. van Bastelaer, eds., 2002. "Quantitative Analysis of Social Capital," in ed. C. Grootaert and T. van Bastelaer, *Understanding and Measuring Social Capital: A Multidisciplinary Tool for Practitioners* (Washington DC: World Bank).

———, 2002, *Understanding and Measuring Social Capital: A Multidisciplinary Tool for Practitioners* (Washington DC: World Bank).

Gugerty, M.K., and M. Kremer, 2000, "Does Development Assistance Help Build Social Capital?" Social Capital Initiative, Working Paper No. 20, World Bank, Washington DC.

Haddad, L., and J.A. Maluccio, 2003, "Trust, Membership in Groups, and Household Welfare: Evidence from KwaZulu-Natal, South Africa," *Economic Development and Cultural Change*, Vol. 51, No. 3.

Harriss, J., and P. de Renzio, 1997, "Missing Link or Analytically Missing? The Concept of Social Capital," *Journal of International Development*, Vol. 9, No. 7.

Heller, P., 1996, "Social Capital as a Product of Class Mobilization and State Intervention: Industrial Workers in Kerala, India," *World Development*, Vol. 24, No. 6.

Isham J., T. Kelly, and S. Ramaswamy, eds., 2002, *Social Capital and Economic Development: Well-Being in Developing Countries* (Cheltenham, UK: Edward Elgar).

Khan, S.R., 1999, *Government, Communities and Non-Government Organizations in Social Sector Delivery: Collective Action in Rural Drinking Water Supply* (Aldershot: Ashgate).

———, 2006, "Learning from Some South Asian 'Successes': Tapping Social Capital," *South Asia Economic Journal*, Vol. 7, No. 2.

Krishna, A., and N. Uphoff, 2001, "Assessing Social Factors in Sustainable Land-Use Management: Social Capital and Common Land Development in Rajasthan, India," in ed. N. Heerink, H. van Keulen, and M. Kuiper, *Economic Policy and Sustainable Land Use: Recent Advances in Quantitative Analysis for Developing Countries* (Heidelberg and New York: Physica).

———, 2002, "Mapping and Measuring Social Capital Through Assessment of Collective Action to Conserve and Develop Watersheds in Rajasthan, India," in ed. C. Grootaert and T. van Bastelaer, *The Role of Social Capital in Development: An Empirical Assessment* (Cambridge: Cambridge University Press).

Lin, N., 2001, *Social Capital: A Theory of Social Structure and Action* (Cambridge: Cambridge University Press).

Loury, G., 1977, "A Dynamic Theory of Racial Income Differences," in ed. P.A. Wallis and A.M. LaMond, *Women, Minorities and Employment Discrimination* (Washington DC: Heath).

Lyon, F., 2000, "Trust, Networks, and Norms: The Creation of Social Capital in Agricultural Economies in Ghana," *World Development*, Vol. 28, No. 4.

MacGillivray, A., and P. Walker, 2000, "Local Social Capital: Making it Work on the Ground," in ed. S. Baron, J. Field, and T. Schuller, *Social Capital: Critical Perspectives* (Oxford: Oxford University Press).

Mancinelli, S., and M. Mazzanti, 2004, "Agents Cooperation and Network Sustainability: A Note on a Microeconomic Approach to Social Capital," *Economia Politica*, Vol. 21, No. 2.

Mayer, M., and K.N. Rankin, 2002, "Social Capital and (Community) Development: A North/South Perspective," *Antipode*, Vol. 34, No. 4.

Meinzen-Dick, R., M. DiGregorio, and N. McCarthy, 2004, "Methods for Studying Collective Action in Rural Development," *Agricultural Systems*, Vol. 82, No. 3.

Molyneux, M., 2002, "Gender and the Silences of Social Capital: Lessons from Latin America," *Development and Change*, Vol. 33, No. 2.

Mosley, P., and A. Verschoor, 2004, "The Development of Trust and Social Capital in Rural Uganda: An Experimental Approach," paper presented at The Royal Economic Society Conference http://www.swan.ac.uk/economics/res2004/program/papers/MosleyVerschoor.pdf.

Narayan, D., 2002, "Bonds and Bridges: Social Capital and Poverty," in ed. J. Isham, T. Kelly, and S. Ramaswamy, *Social Capital and Economic Development: Well-Being in Developing Countries* (Cheltenham, UK: Edward Elgar).

Narayan, D., and L. Pritchett, 1999, "Cents and Sociability: Household Income and Social Capital in Rural Tanzania," *Economic Development and Cultural Change*, Vol. 47, No. 4.

Ostrom, E., 1997, "Investing in Capital, Institutions, and Incentives," in ed. C. Clague, *Institutions and Development: Growth and Governance in Less-Developed and Post-Socialist Countries* (Baltimore: Johns Hopkins University Press).

Pantoja, E., 2000, "Examining the Concept of Social Capital and its Relevance for Community Based Development: The Case of Coal Mining Areas in Orissa, India," Social Capital Initiative, Working Paper No. 18, World Bank, Washington DC.

Portes, A., and M. Mooney, 2003, "Social Capital and Community Development," in ed. Guillén, M.F., R. Collins, P. England, and M. Meyer, *The New Sociology: Developments in an Emerging Field* (New York: Russell Sage Foundation).

Pretty, J., and D. Smith, 2004, "Social Capital and Biodiversity," *Conservation Biology*, Vol. 18, No. 3.

Putnam, R.D., 1993, *Making Democracy Work: Civic Traditions in Modern Italy* (New Jersey: Princeton University Press).

Quibria, M.G., 2003, "The Puzzle of Social Capital: A Critical Review," *Asian Development Review*, Vol. 20, No. 2.

Rankin, K.N., 2002, "Social Capital, Microfinance, and the Politics of Development," *Feminist Economics*, Vol. 8, No. 1.

Reid, C., and L. Salmen, 2002, "Qualitative Analysis of Social Capital: The Case of Agricultural Extension in Mali," in ed. C. Grootaert and T. van Bastelaer,

Understanding and Measuring Social Capital: A Multidisciplinary Tool for Practitioners (Washington DC: World Bank).

Robison, L.J., and J.L. Flora, 2003, "The Social Capital Paradigm: Bridging Across Disciplines," *American Journal of Agricultural Economics*, Vol. 85, No. 5.

Robison, L.J, A.A. Schmid, and M.E. Siles, 2002, "Is Social Capital Really Capital?" *Review of Social Economy*, Vol. 60, No. 1.

Rossing, T., and S. Assaf, 1999, "Social Capital: Conceptual Framework and Empirical Evidence," Social Capital Initiative, Working Paper No. 5, World Bank, Washington DC.

Rothstein, B., 2003, "Social Capital, Economic Growth and Quality of Government: The Causal Mechanism," *Political Economy*, Vol. 8, No. 1.

Rubio, M., 1997, "Perverse Social Capital—Some Evidence from Columbia," *Journal of Economic Issues*, Vol. 31, No. 3.

Rydin, Y., and N. Holman, 2004, "Re-evaluating the Contribution of Social Capital in Achieving Sustainable Development," *Local Environment*, Vol. 9, No. 2.

Sabatini, F., 2006, "The Empirics of Social Capital and Economic Development: A Critical Perspective," http://mpra.ub.uni-muenchen.de/2366/01/MPRA_paper_2366.pdf

Sen, A.K., 2000, "What is Development About?" in ed. G.M. Meier and J.E. Stiglitz, *Frontiers of Development Economics: The Future in Perspective* (New York: Oxford University Press), pp. 506–513.

Silvey, R., and R. Elmhirst, 2003, "Engendering Social Capital: Women Workers and Rural-Urban Networks in Indonesia's Crisis," *World Development*, Vol. 31, No. 5.

Sobel, J., 2002, "Can We Trust Social Capital?" *Journal of Economic Literature*, Vol. 40, No. 1.

Solow, R.M., 1999, "Notes on Social Capital and Economic Performance," in ed. P. Dasgupta and I. Serageldin, *Social Capital: A Multifaceted Perspective* (Washington DC: World Bank).

Sorensen, C., 2000, "Social Capital and Rural Development: A Discussion of Issues," Social Capital Initiative, Working Paper No. 10, World Bank, Washington DC.

Stiglitz, J., 1998, "Towards a New paradigm for Economic Development: Strategies, Policies, and Process," Prebish Lecture, UNCTAD, Geneva.

Streeten, P., 2002, "Reflections on Social and Anti-Social Capital," in ed. J. Isham, T. Kelly, and S. Ramaswamy, *Social Capital and Economic Development: Well-Being in Developing Countries* (Cheltenham, UK: Edward Elgar).

Torsvik, G., 2000, "Social Capital and Economic Development: A Plea for Mechanisms," *Rationality and Society*, Vol. 12, No. 4.

Uphoff, N., and C.M. Wijayaratna, 2000, "Demonstrated Benefits from Social Capital: The Productivity of Farmer Organizations in Gal Oya, Sri Lanka," *World Development*, Vol. 28, No. 11.

van Deth, J.W., 2003, "Measuring Social Capital: Orthodoxies and Continuing Controversies," *International Journal of Social Research Methodology*, Vol. 6, No. 1.

Wallis, J., P. Killerby, and B. Dollery, 2004, "Social Economics and Social Capital," *International Journal of Social Economics*, Vol. 31, Nos. 3–4.

Woolcock, M., 1998, "Social Capital and Economic Development: Towards a Theoretical Synthesis and Policy Framework" *Theory and Society*, Vol. 27, No. 2.

———, 2002, "Social Capital in Theory and Practice: Where Do We Stand?" in ed. J. Isham, T. Kelly, and S. Ramaswamy, *Social Capital and Economic Development: Well-Being in Developing Countries* (Cheltenham, UK: Edward Elgar).

2   Empirical Applications of Social Capital to Growth, Poverty Alleviation, and Rural Development

Adger, W.N., 2003, "Social Capital, Collective Action, and Adaptation to Climate Change," *Economic Geography*, Vol. 79, No. 4.

Aguilera, M.B., and D.S. Massey, 2003, "Social Capital and the Wages of Mexican Migrants: New Hypotheses and Tests," *Social Forces*, Vol. 82, No. 2.

Amin, S.A., S. Rai, and G. Topa, 1999, "Does Micro-credit Reach the Poor and Vulnerable? Evidence from Bangladesh," Center for International Development Working Paper No. 28.

Baron, S., J. Field, and T. Schuller, eds., 2000, *Social Capital: Critical Perspectives* (Oxford: Oxford University Press).

Beall, J., 1997, "Social Capital in Waste—a Solid Investment?" *Journal of International Development*, Vol. 9, No. 7.

Bebbington, A., 1997, "Social Capital and Rural Intensification: Local Organizations and Islands of Sustainability in Rural Andes," *The Geographical Journal*, Vol. 163, No. 2.

Bebbington, A.J., and T. Perreault, 2003, "Social Capital, Development, and Access to Resources in Highland Ecuador," *Economic Geography*, Vol. 75, No. 4.

Brune, N., T. Bossert, D. Bowser, F. Solis, and V.R.D. Herrara, 2005, "Building Social Capital through Human Capital Development Programs in Rural Nicaragua: An Evaluation of MSH Management and Leadership Programs in Wasala and Pantasma," Final Report, Harvard School of Public Health and Management Sciences for Health (MSH).

Carroll, T.F., and Bebbington, A.J., 2000, "Peasant Federations and Rural Development Policies in the Andes," *Policy Sciences*, Vol. 33, Nos. 3–4.

Carter, M.R., and J.A. Maluccio, 2003, "Social Capital and Coping with Economic Shocks: An Analysis of Stunting of South African Children," *World Development*, Vol. 31, No. 7.

Colletta, N.J., and M.L. Cullen, 2002, "Social Capital and Social Cohesion: Case Studies from Cambodia and Rwanda," in ed. C. Grootaert and T. van Bastelaer, *The Role of Social Capital in Development: An Empirical Assessment* (Cambridge: Cambridge University Press).

Cramb, R., 2005, "Social Capital and Soil Conservation: Evidence from the Philippines," *The Australian Journal of Agricultural and Resource Economics*, Vol. 49, No. 2.

Curran, S.R., 2002, "Migration, Social Capital, and the Environment: Considering Migration Selectivity and Networks in Relation to Coastal Ecosystems," *Population and Environment: Methods of Analysis, Population and Development Review*, Vol. 28.

Daniere, A., L.M. Takahashi, and A. NaRanong, 2002a, "Social Capital and Environment Management: Culture, Perceptions and Action among Slum Dwellers in Bangkok," in ed. J. Isham, T. Kelly, and S. Ramaswamy, *Social*

Capital and Economic Development: Well-Being in Developing Countries (Cheltenham, UK: Edward Elgar).

———, 2002b, "Social Capital, Networks, and Community Environments in Bangkok, Thailand," *Growth and Change*, Vol. 33, No. 4.

de Hann, Nicoline, 2001, "Of Goats and Groups: A Study of Social Capital in Development Projects," *Agriculture and Human Values* (Spring), Vol. 18, No. 1.

Dowla, A., 2006, "In Credit We Trust: Building Social Capital by Grameen Bank in Bangladesh," *The Journal of Socio-Economics*, Vol. 35, No. 1.

Durlauf, S.N., 2002, "On the Empirics of Social Capital," *Economic Journal*, Vol. 112, (November), pp. F459–79.

Durlauf, S.N., and M. Fafchamps, 2004, "Social Capital," National Bureau of Economic Research Working Paper No. 10485.

Francis, P.A. et al., 1998, "Hard Lesson: Primary School, Community, and Social Capital in Nigeria," World Bank Technical Paper No. 420, Africa Region Series, Washington DC.

Galasso, E., and M. Ravillion, 2001, "Decentralized Targeting of an Anti-Poverty Program," Policy Research Working Paper No. 2316, World Bank, Washington DC.

Gebremedhin, B., J. Pender and G. Tesfay, 2004, "Collective Action for Grazing Land Management in Crop-Livestock Mixed Systems in the Highlands of Northern Ethiopia," *Agricultural Systems*, Vol. 82, No. 3.

Goetz, A., and R. Sengupta, R., 1996, "'Who Takes the Credit?' Gender, Power, and Control over Loan Use in Rural Credit Programs in Bangladesh," *World Development*, Vol. 24, No. 1.

Gomez, R., and E. Santor, 2001, "Membership Has its Privileges: The Effect of Social Capital and Neighborhood Characteristics on the Earnings of Microfinance Borrowers," *Canadian Journal of Economics*, Vol. 34, No. 4.

Grant, E., 2001, "Social Capital and Community Strategies: Neighborhood Developments in Guatemala City," *Development and Change*, Vol. 32, No. 5.

Gray-Molina, G., W. Jiménez, E.P. de Rada, and E. Yáñez, 2001, "Poverty and Assets in Bolivia: What Role Does Social Capital Play," in ed. O. Attanasio and M. Székely, *Portrait of the Poor: An Assets-Based Approach* (Washington DC: Inter-American Development Bank).

Grootaert, C., nd., "Social Capital, Household Welfare and Poverty in Indonesia," Local Level Institutions Study, Social and Development Department, The World Bank, Revised draft.

Grootaert, C., and D. Narayan, 2004, "Local Institutions, Poverty and Household Welfare in Bolivia," *World Development*, Vol. 32, No. 7.

Grootaert, C., and T. van Bastelaer, eds., 2002, *The Role of Social Capital in Development: An Empirical Assessment* (Cambridge: Cambridge University Press).

Grootaert, C., G. Oh, and A, Swamy, 2002, "Social Capital, Education, and Credit Markets: Empirical Evidence from Burkino Faso," in ed. J. Isham, T. Kelly, and S. Ramaswamy, *Social Capital and Economic Development: Well-Being in Developing Countries* (Cheltenham, UK: Edward Elgar).

Gugerty, M.K., and M. Kremer, 2000, "Does Development Assistance Help Build Social Capital?" Social Capital Initiative, Working Paper No. 20, World Bank, Washington DC.

Haddad, L., and J.A. Maluccio, 2003, "Trust, Membership in Groups, and Household Welfare: Evidence from KwaZulu-Natal, South Africa," *Economic Development and Cultural Change*, Vol. 51, No. 3.

Healy, K., 2002, "Building Networks of Social Capital for Grassroots Development among Indigenous Communities in Bolivia and Mexico," in ed. J. Isham, T. Kelly, and S. Ramaswamy, *Social Capital and Economic Development: Well-Being in Developing Countries* (Cheltenham, UK: Edward Elgar).

Isham, J., 2002, "The Effect of Social Capital on Fertilizer Adoption: Evidence from Rural Tanzania," *Journal of African Economies*, Vol. 11, No. 1.

Kähkönen, S., 2002, "Does Social Capital Matter in the Delivery of Water and Sanitation?" in ed. J. Isham, T. Kelly, and S. Ramaswamy, *Social Capital and Economic Development: Well-Being in Developing Countries* (Cheltenham, UK: Edward Elgar).

Katz, E.G., 2000, "Social Capital and Natural Capital: A Comparative Analysis of Land Tenure and Natural Resource Management in Guatemala," *Land Economics*, Vol. 76, No. 1.

Khandkar, S., B. Khilily and Z. Khan, 1994, "The Grameen Bank: What Do We Know?" World Bank, Washington DC.

Knack, S., 2002, "Social Capital, Growth, and Poverty: A Survey of Cross-Country Evidence," in ed. C. Grootaert and T. van Bastelaer, *The Role of Social Capital in Development: An Empirical Assessment* (Cambridge: Cambridge University Press).

Knack, S., and P. Keefer, 1997, "Does Social Capital Have an Economic Payoff? A Cross-Country Investigation," *The Quarterly Journal of Economics*, Vol. 112, No. 4.

Krishna, A., 2001, "Moving from the Stock of Social Capital to the Flow of Benefits: The Role of Agency," *World Development*, Vol. 29, No. 6.

Krishna, A., and N. Uphoff, 2001, "Assessing Social Factors in Sustainable Land-Use Management: Social Capital and Common Land Development in Rajasthan, India," in ed. N. Heerink, H. van Keulen, and M. Kuiper, *Economic Policy and Sustainable Land Use: Recent Advances in Quantitative Analysis for Developing Countries* (Heidelberg and New York: Physica).

———, 2002, "Mapping and Measuring Social Capital Through Assessment of Collective Action to Conserve and Develop Watersheds in Rajastan, India," in ed. C. Grootaert and T. van Bastelaer, *The Role of Social Capital in Development: An Empirical Assessment* (Cambridge: Cambridge University Press).

Lyon, F., 2000, "Trust, Networks, and Norms: The Creation of Social Capital in Agricultural Economies in Ghana," *World Development*, Vol. 28, No. 4.

Mayoux, L., 2001, "Tackling the Down Side: Social Capital, Women's Empowerment and Microfinance in Cameroon," *Development and Change*, Vol. 32, No. 3.

Ma, Zhongdong, 2002, "Social Capital Mobilization and Income Returns to Entrepreneurship: The Case of Return Migration in Rural China," *Environment and Planning*, Vol. 34, No. 10.

McIlwaine, C., and C.O.N. Moser, 2001, "Violence and Social Capital in Urban Poor Communities: Perspectives from Columbia and Guatemala," *Journal of International Development*, Vol. 13, No. 7.

Molinas, J.R., 1998, "The Impact of Inequality, Gender, External Assistance, and Social Capital on Local Level Cooperation," *World Development*, Vol. 26, No. 3.

Mondal, A.H., 2000, "Social Capital Formation: The Role of NGO Rural Development Programs in Bangladesh," *Policy Sciences*, Vol. 33, Nos. 3–4.

Morris, M., 1998, "Social Capital and Poverty in India," IDS Working Paper No. 61, Sussex, Brighton.

Mubangizi, B.C., 2003, "Drawing on Social Capital for Community Economic Development: Insights from a South African Rural Community," *Community Development Journal*, Vol. 38, No. 2.

Narayan, D., 2002, "Bonds and Bridges: Social Capital and Poverty," in ed. J. Isham, T. Kelly, and S. Ramaswamy, *Social Capital and Economic Development: Well-Being in Developing Countries* (Cheltenham, UK: Edward Elgar).

Narayan, D., and L. Pritchett, 1999, "Cents and Sociability: Household Income and Social Capital in Rural Tanzania," *Economic Development and Cultural Change*, Vol. 47, No. 4.

Ostrom, E., 1997, "Investing in Capital, Institutions, and Incentives," in ed. C. Clague, *Institutions and Development: Growth and Governance in Less-Developed and Post-Socialist Countries* (Baltimore: Johns Hopkins University Press).

Pargal, S., D.O. Gilligan, and M. Haq, 2002, "Does Social Capital Increase Participation in Voluntary Solid Waste Management? Evidence from Dhaka, Bangladesh," in ed. C. Grootaert and T. van Bastelaer, *The Role of Social Capital in Development: An Empirical Assessment* (Cambridge: Cambridge University Press).

Parmar, A., 2003, "Micro-Credit, Empowerment, and Agency: Re-evaluating the Discourse," *Canadian Journal of Development Studies*, Vol. 24, No. 3.

Pitt, M.M., S.R. Khandker, and J. Cartwright, 2003, "Does Micro-Credit Empower Women? Evidence from Bangladesh," World Bank Policy Research Working Paper No. 2998, Washington DC.

Pretty, J., and D. Smith, 2004, "Social Capital and Biodiversity," *Conservation Biology*, Vol. 18, No. 3.

Pretty, J., and H. Ward, 2001, "Social Capital and the Environment," *World Development*, Vol. 29, No. 2.

Quibria, M.G., 2003, "The Puzzle of Social Capital: A Critical Review," *Asian Development Review*, Vol. 20, No. 2.

Quinones Jr., B.R., and H. D. Seibel, 2000, "Social Capital in Micro-Finance: Case Studies in the Philippines," *Policy Sciences*, Vol. 33, Nos. 3/4.

Reid, C., and L. Salmen, 2002, "Qualitative Analysis of Social Capital: The Case of Agricultural Extension in Mali," in ed. C. Grootaert and T. van Bastelaer, *Understanding and Measuring Social Capital: A Multidisciplinary Tool for Practitioners* (Washington DC: World Bank).

Richards, P., K. Bah, and V. James, 2004, "Social Capital and Survival Prospects for Community-Driven Development in Post-Conflict Sierra Leone," Community-Driven Development, Conflict Prevention and Reconstruction Paper Series No. 12, World Bank, Washington DC.

Rodriguez, L.C., and U. Pascual, 2004, "Land Clearance and Social Capital in Mountain Agro-Ecosystems: The Case of Opuntia Scrubland in Ayacucho, Peru," *Ecological Economics*, Vol. 49, No. 2.

Sirivardana, S., 2004, "Innovative Practice amidst Positive Potential for Paradigm Shift: The Case of Sri Lanka," in ed. Wignaraja and S. Sirivardana, Pro-Poor Growth and Governance in South Asia: Decentralization and Participatory

Development (New Delhi, India/Thousand Oaks, CA/London: Sage), pp. 241–259.

Smale, M., and V. Ruttun, 1997, "Social Capital and Technical Change," in ed. C. Clague, *Institutions and Development: Growth and Governance in Less-Developed and Post-Socialist Countries* (Baltimore: Johns Hopkins University Press)

Temple, J., 1998, "Initial Conditions, Social Capital and Growth in Africa," *Journal of African Economies*, Vol. 7, No. 3.

Uquillas, J.E., and M.V. Nieuwkoop, 2003, "Social Capital as a Factor in Indigenous Peoples Development in Ecuador, Indigenous Peoples Development Series, Latin America and Caribbean Region," Sustainable Development Working Paper No. 15, World Bank Washington DC.

Westermann, O., J. Ashby, and J. Pretty, 2005, "Gender and Social Capital: The Importance of Gender differences for the Maturity and Effectiveness of Natural Resource Management Groups," *World Development*, Vol. 33, No. 11.

Whiteley, P.F., 2000, "Economic Growth and Social Capital," *Political Studies*, Vol. 48, No. 3.

Winters, P., B. Davis, and L. Corral, 2002, "Assets, Activities and Income Generation in Rural Mexico: Factoring in Social and Public Capital," *Agricultural Economics*, Vol. 27, No. 2.

World Bank, 2000, "Panama Poverty Assessment: Priorities and Strategies for Poverty Reduction," Washington DC.

Yunus, M., 2002, "Poverty Alleviation: Is Economics Any Help? Lessons from the Grameen Bank Experience," in ed. P. Athukorala, *The Economic Development of South Asia* (Northampton, MA: Edward Elgar).

———, 2003, *Banker to the Poor: Micro-lending and the Battle against World Poverty* (New York: Public Affairs/Perseus Book Group).

Zaman, H., 2004, "The Scaling Up of Microfinance in Bangladesh: Determinants, Impacts, Lessons," World Bank Policy Research Working Paper No. 3398, Washington DC.

3 Harnessing and Guiding Social Capital in Pakistan

Aga Khan Rural Support Programme, 2000, "Towards a Shared Vision: Partnerships for Development," Annual Report 2000, Gilgit, Pakistan.

Baluch, M.S., 2002, "Implementation of Khushal Pakistan Program through NRSP," NRSP, Islamabad.

Bebbington, A.J., and T. Perreault, 2003, "Social Capital, Development, and Access to Resources in Highland Ecuador," *Economic Geography*, Vol. 75, No. 4.

Bielke, K.V., 2004, "Leadership and Transformation—in Pakistan's Northern Areas," Master Thesis, Institute of Anthropology, University of Copenhagen.

Cool, J., and P. Eastman, 1998, "Interim Evaluation: National Rural Support Program," UNDP, Pakistan, Islamabad.

Dastgeer, A., 2001, "The Rural Support Program Network," Islamabad.

Ebrahim, A., 2003, *NGOs and Organizational Change: Discourse, Reporting and Learning* (Cambridge: Cambridge University Press).

Evans, P., 1996, "Government Action, Social Capital and Development: Reviewing the Evidence on Synergy," *World Development*, Vol. 24, No. 6.

Government of Pakistan, 2000, "Devolution of Power and Responsibility: Establishing the Foundation of Genuine Democracy—Local Government Proposed Plan," National Reconstruction Bureau, Islamabad.

———, 2001, "The SBNP Local Government (Model) Ordinance 2001," National Reconstruction Bureau, Islamabad.

Khan, M.H., nd., "The Rural Support Programs in Pakistan: Methods of Cost Assessment and Impact" (Islamabad: Rural Support Program Network).

Khan, S.R., 2001, "Promoting Democratic Governance: the Case of Pakistan," *European Journal of Development Research*, Vol. 13, No. 2.

———, 2006, "Learning from Some South Asian 'Successes': Tapping Social Capital," *South Asia Economic Journal*, Vol. 7, No. 2.

Khan, S.R., and F. Zafar, 1999, "Capacity Building and Training of School Management Committees," SDPI Monograph Series No. 10, Islamabad.

National Rural Support Program (NRSP), 2004a, "Update: Social Sector Services: As of January 2004," Islamabad.

———, 2004b, "The National Rural Support Program's Participation in Large Scale Land and Natural Resource Based Projects," Monitoring Evaluation and Research Section, Islamabad.

Portes, A., and M. Mooney, 2003, "Social Capital and Community Development," in ed. Guillén, M.F., R. Collins, P. England, and M. Meyer, *The New Sociology: Developments in an Emerging Field* (New York: Russell Sage Foundation).

Rasmussen, S.F., M.M. Piracha, R. Bajwa, A. Malik, and A. Mansoor, 2004, "The World Bank and People's Republic of China—A Global Exchange for Scaling Up Success. Reducing Poverty, Sustaining Growth: What Works, What Doesn't and Why? Pakistan Case: Scaling Up RSPs, Shanghai," May 25–27.

Rural Support Program Network (RSPN), "The RSPs of Pakistan: Exploring Options for Working with Social Government," Proceedings of a Conference, November 2001–June 2002, Islamabad.

Rural Support Program Network (RSPN), 2005, "A Documentation of RSPs' Experiences with Public and Private Partnerships, Islamabad, Pakistan."

Sirivardana, S., 2004, "Innovative Practice Amidst Positive Potential for Paradigm Shift: The Case of Sri Lanka," in ed. Wignaraja and S. Sirivardana, *Pro-Poor Growth and Governance in South Asia: Decentralization and Participatory Development* (New Delhi, India/Thousand Oaks, CA/London: Sage), pp. 241–259.

Smillie, I., and J. Hailey, 2001, *Managing for Change: Leadership, Strategy and Management in Asian NGOs* (London: Earthscan).

Uddin, Iftikhar, 2004, "Public-Private Partnerships: Case Studies or RSPs Working with the Government," RSPN, Islamabad, draft.

World Bank, 1990, "The Aga Khan Rural Support Program in Pakistan: A Second Interim Evaluation," Washington DC.

———, 2002, "The Next Ascent: An Evaluation of the Aga Khan Rural Support Program, Pakistan," World Bank Operations Evaluation Department, Washington DC.

4 Cultural Context

Ahmed, A.S., 1976, *Millennium and Charisma Amount Pathans: A Critical Essay in Social Anthropology* (London: Routledge and Kegan Paul).

——, 1980, *Pukhtun Economy and Society: Traditional Structure and Economic Development in a Tribal Society* (London: Routledge and Kegan Paul).

——, 2004, *Resistance and Control in Pakistan* (London: Routledge and Kegan Paul).

Ali, I.A., 1988, *The Punjab under Imperialism, 1885–1947* (Delhi: Oxford University Press).

Anderson, J., 1978, "There Are No Khans Anymore: Economic Development and Social Change in Tribal Afghanistan," *The Middle East Journal*, Vol. 32, No. 2.

——, 1992, *Poetics and Politics in Ethnographic Texts: A View from the Colonial Ethnography of Afghanistan. In Writing the Social Text: Poetics and Politics in Social Science* (New York: Aldine de Gruyter).

Baha, L., 1978, "NWFP Administration under British Rule 1901–1919," Commission on Historical and Cultural Research, Islamabad.

Bannerjee, M., 2000, *The Pathan Unarmed: Opposition and Memory in the North West Frontier* (Oxford: Oxford University Press).

Barth, F., 1959, *Political Leadership among Swat Pathans* (London: University of London, Athlone Press).

——, 1970, "Ethnic Groups and Boundaries: The Social Organization of Cultural Difference," in ed. F. Barth, *Ethnic Groups and Identity* (London: George Allen & Unwin).

——, 1981, *Features of Person and Society in Swat: Collected Essays on Pathans* (London: Routledge and Kegan Paul).

Bobst, P.J., 2005, *The Future of the Great Game: Sir Olaf Caroe, India's Independence, and the Defense of Asia* (Akron, Ohio: The University of Akron Press).

Caroe, O., 1958, *The Pathans 550 B.C.–A.D. 1957* (London: Macmillan).

Edwards, D., 1996, *Heroes of the Age: Moral Fault Lines on the Afghan Frontier* (Berkeley, California University Press).

Hopkirk, P., 1992, *The Great Game: The Struggle For Empire in Central Asia* (New York: Kodansha America Inc.).

Hussain, S.I., 2000, *Some Major Pukhtoon Tribes Along the Pak-Afghan Border* (Peshawar: Area Study Center Peshawar and Hanns Seidel Foundation).

Khan, M.H., 1999, "Agricultural Development and the Changes in Land Revenue and Land Tenure Systems in Pakistan," in ed. S.R. Khan, *Pakistan's Economy: Traditional Topics and Contemporary Concerns* (Oxford: Oxford University Press).

Khan, S.R, F.S. Khan, and A.S. Akhtar, 2007, *Initiating Devolution for Service Delivery in Pakistan: Forgetting the Power Structure* (Karachi: Oxford University Press).

Lindholm, C., 1982, *Generosity and Jealousy: The Swat Pukhtun of North Pakistan* (New York: Columbia University Press).

——, 1996, *Frontier Perspectives: Essays in Comparative Anthropology* (Karachi: Oxford University Press).

Meyer K.E., and S.B. Brysac, 1999, *Tournament of Shadows: The Great Game and the Race for Empire in Asia* (Washington DC: Counterpoint).

Pasha, M., 1998, *Colonial Political Economy: Recruitment and Underdevelopment in the Punjab* (Karachi: Oxford University Press).

Spain, J.W., 1962, *The Way of Pathans* (Karachi: Oxford University Press).

Van den Dungen, P.H., 1972, *The Punjab Tradition: Influence and Authority in Nineteenth-Century India* (London: George Allen and Unwin Ltd).

5   HDF Interventions

Collier, P., 1998, "Social Capital and Poverty," Social Capital Initiative, Working Paper No. 4, World Bank, Washington DC.

Gazdar, H., A. Khan and T. Khan, 2002, "Land Tenure, Rural Livelihoods and Institutional Innovation," Collective for Social Science Research, Karachi, draft.

Khan, S.R., 1987, *Profit and Loss Sharing* (Karachi: Oxford University Press).

Yunus, M., 2002, "Poverty Alleviation: Is Economics Any Help? Lessons from the Grameen Bank Experience," in ed. P. Athukorala, *The Economic Development of South Asia* (Northampton, MA: Edward Elgar).

———, 2003, *Banker to the Poor: Micro-lending and the Battle against World Poverty* (New York: Public Affairs/Perseus Book Group).

7   Health

Government of Pakistan, 2004, Pakistan Economic Survey, Finance Division, Economic Advisor's Wing, Islamabad.

UNDP, 2000, *Human Development Report* (New York: Oxford University Press).

8   Education

Akerhielm, K., 1995, "Does Class Size Matter?" *Economics of Education Review*, Vol. 14, No. 3.

Angrist, J.D., and V. Lavy, 1999, "Using Maimonides' Rule to Estimate the Effects of Class Size on Scholastic Achievement," *Quarterly Journal of Economics*, Vol. 114, No. 2.

Card, D., and A.B. Krueger, 1992, "Does School Quality Matter? Return to Education and the Characteristics of Public Schools in the United States," *Journal of Political Economy*, Vol. 100, No. 1.

———, 1996, "Labour Market Effects of School Quality: Theory and Evidence," in ed. G. Burtless, *Does Money Matter? The Effects of School Resources on Student Achievement and Adult Success* (Washington DC: Brookings Institute Press).

Coates, D., 2003, "Education Production Functions Using Instructor Time as an Input," *Education Economics*, Vol. 11, No. 3.

Coleman, J.S., E.Q. Campbell, C.J. Hobson, F. McPartland, A.M. Mood, and F.D. Weinfeldl., 1966, "Equality of Educational Opportunity," U.S. Department of Health, Education and Welfare, Washington DC.

Dearden, L., J. Ferri, and C. Meghir, 1997, "The Effect of School Quality on Educational Attainment and Wages," IFS Working Paper No. W98/3, Institute for Fiscal Studies, London.

Ehrenberg, R.G., and D.J. Brewer, 1994, "Do School and Teacher Characteristics Matter? Evidence from High School and Beyond," *Economics of Education Review*, Vol. 13, No. 1.

———, 1995, "Did Teachers' Verbal Ability and Race Matter in the 1960s? Coleman Revisited," *Economics of Education Review*, Vol. 14, No. 10.

Feinstein, L., and J. Symons, 1999, "Attainment in Secondary School," *Oxford Economic Papers*, Vol. 51, No. 2.

Ferguson, R., 1991, "Paying for Public Education: New Evidence on How and Why Money Matters," *Harvard Journal on Legislation*, Vol. 28, No. 2.

Glewwe, P., and M. Kremer, 2005, "Schools, Teachers, and Education Outcomes in Developing Countries," in ed. E.A. Hanushek and F. Welch, *Handbook on the Economics of Education 2* (Amsterdam: Elsevier)

Hanushek, E.A., 1986, "The Economics of Schooling: Production and Efficiency in Public School," *Journal of Economic Literature*, Vol. 24, No. 3.

———, 1996, "Measuring Investment in Education," *Journal of Economic Perspectives*, Vol. 10, No. 4.

Hanushek, E.A., and J.A. Luque, 2003, "Efficiency and Equity in Schools around the World," *Economics of Education Review*, Vol. 22, No. 5.

Heckman, J., A. Layne-Farrar, and P. Todd, 1996, "Does Measured School Quality Really Matter? An Examination of the Earning-Quality Relationship," in ed. G. Burtless, *Does Money Matter? The Effects of School Resources on Student Achievement and Adult Success* (Washington DC: Brookings Institute Press).

Hedges, L.V., R.D. Laine, and R. Greenwald, 1994, "Does Money Matter? A Meta-Analysis of Studies of the Effects of Differential School Inputs on Student Outcomes," *Educational Researcher*, Vol. 23, No. 3.

Heinsen, E., and B. K. Graversen, 2005, "The Effect of School Resources on Educational Attainment: Evidence from Denmark," Bulletin of Economic Research, Vol. 57, No. 2.

Hoxby, C., 1999, "The Effects of Class Size on Student Attainment, New Evidence from Population Variation," Quarterly Journal of Economics, Vol. 115, No. 4.

Khan, S.R., Sajid Kazmi, and Zainab Latif, 2005, "A Comparative Institutional Analysis of Government, NGO and Private Rural Primary Schooling in Pakistan" *The European Journal of Development Research*, Vol. 17, No. 2.

Kremer, M., E. Miguel, and R. Thornton, 2004, "Incentives to Learn," National Bureau of Economic Research Working Paper No. 10971, Cambridge, MA.

Levin, J., 2001, "For Whom the Reductions Count: A Quintile Regression Analysis of Class Size and Peer Effects on Scholastic Achievement," *Empirical Economics*, Vol. 26, No. 1.

Monk, D., 1990, *Educational Finance: an Economic Approach*, (New York: McGraw-Hill).

Monk, D., and J. King, 1994, "Multi-level Teacher Resource Effects on Pupil Performance in Secondary Mathematics and Science: The Role of Teacher Subject Matter Preparation," in ed. R.G. Ehrenberg, *Contemporary Policy Issues: Choices and Consequences in Education* (Ithaca, NY: ILR Press).

Wilson, K., 2001, "The Determinants of Educational Attainment: Modeling and Estimating the Human Capital Model and Education Production Functions," *Southern Economic Journal*, Vol. 67, No. 3.

9   Field Update 2001

Khan, S.R., 2001, "Promoting Democratic Governance: The Case of Pakistan," *European Journal of Development Research*, Vol. 13, No. 2.

10   Field Update 2006

Khan, S.R., 1987, *Profit and Loss Sharing* (Karachi: Oxford University Press).

UNDP (United Nations Development Program), 2005, *Human Development Report 2005* (New York: Oxford University Press).

12   Planning a Field Study to Assess the Role of Harnessing Social Capital for Rural Development

Durlauf, S., and M. Fafchamps, 2004, "Social Capital," National Bureau of Economic Research Working Papers No. 10485.

Fine, B., 2001, "The Social Capital of the World Bank," in ed. B. Fine, C. Lapavistsas, and J. Pincus, *Development Policy in the Twenty-first Century: Beyond the Post-Washington Consensus* (London: Routledge).

Khan, S.R., F.S. Khan, and A. S. Akhtar, 2007, *Initiating Devolution for Service Delivery in Pakistan: Forgetting the Power Structure* (Karachi: Oxford University Press).

Khan, S.R., 2005, *Basic Education in Rural Pakistan: A Comparative Institutional Analysis of Government, Private, and NGO Schools* (Karachi: Oxford University Press).

Krishna, A., 2001, "Moving from the Stock of Social Capital to the Flow of Benefits: The Role of Agency," *World Development*, Vol. 29, No. 6.

Krishna, A., and N. Uphoff, 2001, "Assessing Social Factors in Sustainable Land-Use Management: Social Capital and Common Land Development in Rajasthan, India," in ed. N. Heerink, H. van Keulen, and M. Kuiper, *Economic Policy and Sustainable Land Use: Recent Advances in Quantitative Analysis for Developing Countries* (Heidelberg and New York: Physica).

———, 2002, "Mapping and Measuring Social Capital Through Assessment of Collective Action to Conserve and Develop Watersheds in Rajastan, India," in ed. C. Grootaert and T. van Bastelaer, *The Role of Social Capital in Development: An Empirical Assessment* (Cambridge: Cambridge University Press).

Index